D0783636

Mind, body and culture

Mind, body and culture

Anthropology and the biological interface

Geoffrey Samuel

Senior Lecturer in Sociology,
University of Newcastle, New South Wales

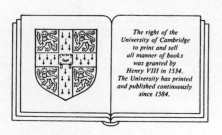

The right of the
University of Cambridge
to print and sell
all manner of books
was granted by
Henry VIII in 1534.
The University has printed
and published continuously
since 1584.

Cambridge University Press

Cambridge
New York   Port Chester
Melbourne   Sydney

Published by the Press Syndicate of the University of Cambridge
The Pitt Building, Trumpington Street, Cambridge CB2 1RP
40 West 20th Street, New York NY 10011, USA
10 Stamford Road, Oakleigh, Melbourne 3166, Australia

First published 1990

Transferred to digital printing 1999

Printed in the United Kingdom by Biddles Short Run Books

British Library cataloguing in publication data
Samuel, Geoffrey
Mind, body and culture: anthropology and the
biological interface.
1. Anthropology
I. Title
301

Library of Congress cataloguing in publication data
Samuel, Geoffrey
Mind, body and culture: anthropology and the biological
interface/Geoffrey Samuel.
    p.   cm.
ISBN 0-521-37411-1
1. Sociobiology.   2. Cognition and culture.   I. Title.
GN365.9.S25   1990
304.5 – dc20   89-15717 CIP

ISBN 0 521 37411 1

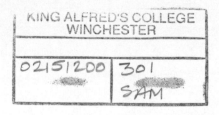

In memory of
Dr Sydney Herbert Samuel
(1912–1982)

Contents

Contents

viii

Contents

Preface

The origins of this book go back to 1981–2, when I spent nine months as a research associate at the Anthropology Department of the University of California at Berkeley. Most of it was completed in 1987 when I was at the Department of Social Anthropology at Manchester University. I doubt that I would have written it without the hospitality and the intellectual stimulation I received during these two periods of leave, and I am deeply grateful to Professor Nelson Graburn, Professor Marilyn Strathern, and to the staff of the two departments for their support and assistance. I would also like to thank the University of Newcastle, New South Wales, for making these two visits possible.

Many people have provided help, comments or encouragement during this period. Among them are Michael Allen, Jane Azevedo, Arie Brand, Hiram Caton, Matthew Ciolek, Alex Comfort, Tony Cohen, Prem Das, Derek Freeman, Ernest Gellner, Sandra Grimes, Janet Gyatso, Kai Hahlweg, Monica Hayes, Cliff Hooker, Joachim Israel, Norton Jacobi, Bruce Kapferer, Roger Keesing, Lise McKean, Per Matthiesen, Linley Paskalis, Marie Reay, Ralph Robinson, Ariel Salleh, Bob Scholte, Ilana Silber, Martin Southwold, Patricia Uberoi, Tony van Fossen and Dick Werbner. I would like to thank all of them, and any others whom I have inadvertently omitted.

Many more people have helped me with the Tibetan research which underlies the short section on Tibetan society in chapter 10. I hope to acknowledge them individually in a forthcoming full-length treatment of religion and society in Tibet.

I first encountered anthropology as a graduate student at Cambridge, and I owe particular thanks to Professor Meyer Fortes for enabling me to move from theoretical physics to social anthropology and for his subsequent support and friendship. I would also like to thank Andrew Strathern, Lucy Mair, Dell Hymes and John Kesby, and my three doctoral supervisors, Stanley Tambiah, Edmund Leach and Peter Wilson.

I owe a particular debt of gratitude to my two editors at Cambridge University Press, Susan Allen-Mills and Wendy Guise, for their support and encouragement, and to Michael Fischer and Ward Goodenough, who read the manuscript for Cambridge University Press. The book has been much improved by their generous and detailed comments.

Elvira Sprogis provided encouragement, tolerance and understanding throughout the completion of this book, as well as a careful and greatly appreciated reading of the final text.

The book is dedicated to the memory of my father. He would probably have disagreed with much of what I say in it. Its underlying purpose nevertheless owes much to his example.

1 New paradigms and modal states

The idea of scientific paradigms came to the attention of the social sciences in the late 1960s. Thomas Kuhn's suggestion was that scientific knowledge in a particular area at any one time was limited and structured by its basic theoretical framework ('paradigm') and that scientific revolutions, as in the case of those associated with Galileo and Newton in the seventeenth century, and with Einstein, Heisenberg, Schrödinger and others in the late nineteenth and twentieth centuries, involved the replacement of one 'paradigm' by another (Kuhn 1970).

Ironically, Kuhn seems to have regarded the social sciences as never having achieved their first proper paradigm (cf. Kuhn 1970: 15). However, as Nick Perry has noted, the concept of the paradigm was immediately attractive to social scientists (Perry 1977). Anthropologists and sociologists soon decided that their fields of study already had a number of fully fledged 'paradigms' (such as functionalism, conflict theory, culture-and-personality and social interactionism). A corollary was the tantalizing idea of a *new* paradigm that might resolve many of the difficulties within the social sciences and provide a needed source of revitalization.

More recently, the growth of significant new approaches in the physical sciences, such as those of David Bohm and Ilya Prigogine (e.g. Bohm 1981, Factor 1985, Hiley and Peat 1987, Prigogine 1980), in psychology (Pribram 1971, 1984) and in evolutionary theory (e.g. Maturana and Varela 1980) have encouraged suggestions that equally radical trans-formations might be possible and appropriate in the social sciences (e.g. Loye et al. 1986, Brown 1988). So far, to my knowledge, not much has materialized in the form of explicit theoretical proposals.

This book introduces what could be termed a new 'paradigm' for the general area of social and cultural anthropology. The approach suggested

1

is a radical one in many respects, and I hope that it will be found stimulating and productive in a variety of fields within and outside anthropology. However, the whole idea of a drastic 'paradigm change', of a scientific revolution on the Newtonian or Einsteinian scale, in which one whole way of looking at the world becomes replaced by something quite different, needs some careful consideration.

Such a dramatic process of conversion may have been appropriate to the relatively confined circles within which Western scientific thinking took place up to the earlier part of this century. Today, whether we like it or not, the *de facto* state of affairs in the academic world is far more pluralistic. The old idea of all branches of knowledge growing, as it were, out of the trunk of a single tree, reducible to a single basic set of understandings, is finally fading.

The main Western incarnation of this idea since the nineteenth century has been the suggestion, not quite dead even today, that the sciences are hierarchically linked. Thus biology and geology, for example, should be reducible to chemistry, and chemistry in its turn to physics, which ideally consists of a few basic laws from which everything could be deduced by strict mathematical procedures. Transformations in physics itself, and for that matter in mathematical logic (Gödel's theorem), have long since made this whole programme implausible.

As far as anthropology is concerned, the one major attempt at such reductionism in recent years has been the biological reductionism of Edward Wilson, Richard Alexander and others. It is now becoming clear that the more sophisticated practitioners of sociobiology and related approaches are finding it necessary to concede a largely autonomous area to human 'culture' in some form.[1] The quote marks around 'culture' refer to the unsatisfactory nature of the concept, and among other things this book will have some suggestions about new ways of conceptualizing 'culture' and about the whole problem of the interface between biology and anthropology.

More generally, though, the tree with its many branches is losing its credibility as an image for knowledge, to be replaced, perhaps, as Gilles Deleuze and Félix Guattari have suggested in the opening chapter of *Mille Plateaux*, by the many-centred, multiply interconnected underground network of the rhizome. An ideal of many ways of knowing, each with their uses but none with claims of ultimate hierarchical dominance, is perhaps one of the central features of the 'post-modern' situation. This point has been made in relation to anthropology by, among others, Victor Turner (1985: 177ff.) and Marilyn Strathern (1987).

This perspective seems to me also to be appropriate to how the world's body of knowledge as a whole is developing today. There will increasingly be a plurality of ways of knowing on the global scale, and none of these approaches to knowledge is going to have absolute authority or primary status.[2]

This is, in a sense, an unavoidable feature of a world where Washington, Moscow, Beijing and the other centres of once-autonomous understandings are increasingly having to learn to coexist, and where it is no longer a question of 'Western' knowledge going to the 'East' or of 'Eastern' knowledge coming to the 'West', but of a single world society learning how to live with and make use of its multiple heritage. That situation may still be an unfamiliar one for many people but it undoubtedly has its positive aspects. It underlies much of the thinking behind this book.

The new theoretical framework proposed in this book (the multimodal framework or MMF) is intended to be appropriate to, and to provide a description of, such a context of multiple ways of knowing. As a 'paradigm' for anthropology it provides a resolution for several complex theoretical issues, in particular those concerning the relationship between individual and society, and (as mentioned already) between anthropology and biology. It is intended, however, to be part of a developing group of approaches, rather than to form a central framework for a unified social science.

One of the strongest points of the MMF is its ability to make sense of concepts and modes of operating within traditional societies that have been very hard to incorporate effectively within Western modes of knowing. Here I refer in particular to procedures such as shamanism, spirit-possession, and rituals relating to 'gods' and 'spirits' in non-Western society in general. My own need to find an adequate theoretical framework for understanding such processes in Tibetan society was a primary motive for the initial development of the MMF, and I have applied the MMF to Tibet in a series of studies (Samuel 1984, 1985c, 1989).

Another central motive behind the construction of the MMF was a desire to provide a satisfactory theoretical foundation for the group of anthropological approaches generally known as 'interpretive' or 'symbolic' anthropology. I believe that this school of anthropology (one might take Clifford Geertz, Victor Turner and Claude Lévi-Strauss as exemplars) incorporates some vital and important insights into the human condition. Nevertheless, as its critics have demonstrated, there are serious problems with its underlying theoretical assumptions. Beginning in chapter 3 with the work of some of the more prominent critics of interpretive anthropology, I demonstrate how a more thoroughgoing reconceptualization of the field suggests a new type of framework within which interpretive anthropology can form part of a consistent scientific approach to anthropology. The MMF is an example of such a framework.

The MMF incorporates a number of features that I believe are suggestive of the directions in which anthropology as a whole should develop over the next couple of decades. Among these are

(i) the deliberate dissolving of individual–society, subject–object and mind–body dichotomies;
(ii) an explicitly anti-empiricist position that goes along with the pluralism mentioned above with regard to systems of knowledge;
(iii) a willingness to make use of concepts that are, in Western terms at least, not particularly 'experience-near' (cf. Geertz 1985), and
(iv) a readiness to treat established social scientific vocabulary as radically open to question.

Concerning (iii) and (iv), major 'paradigm changes' of the past have demonstrated that genuine scientific innovation involves as much un-learning of old concepts as acquisition of new ideas. This book would probably fail in its purpose if it did not make many of its readers uncomfortable at one place or another at the dismissal (or at least relativization) of some cherished idea. (If it is any consolation, the MMF still has the same effect at times on its author.)

The whole question of the 'scientific' nature of the MMF is likely to disturb some readers. A significant school of anthropologists has in recent years begun to see anthropology as a primarily humanistic and interpretive discipline rather than as a science. These scholars regard scientific formulation as inappropriate and even antithetical to the sensitive awareness of other modes of understanding the world and of their intrinsic values. As I explain in chapter 2, I have considerable sympathy with this point of view, but I have explicitly rejected it in this book. Anthropology is here conceived of as constituting a *natural science of society* (to adopt a phrase used by A. Radcliffe-Brown, see Kuper 1977: 25).

By this I mean that anthropology, like other sciences, operates in terms of one or more theoretical frameworks, each ideally consistent within itself, and each providing the basis for a description and understanding of certain aspects of the 'real world'. I use the term 'theoretical framework' rather than 'paradigm', both because 'paradigm' has come to be very loosely used in recent years, and also because the precise level of application of 'paradigm' has always been something of a difficulty (cf. Kuhn 1970:175ff.). I conceive of a 'theoretical framework' as something underlying and more basic than a specific theory. It provides a language, including not only vocabulary but a syntax and a semantics, within which theories may be framed.

One message of this book is that anthropologists and other social scientists should treat the fundamental presuppositions that constitute their theoretical frameworks as much more open to change and modification than has generally been the case. This level of theory should be seen as something that is consciously *designed* in order to be most appropriate for the task in hand. In this way anthropology can be both scientifically rigorous (where appropriate) and explicitly pluralistic. The MMF is presented both because of its intrinsic value and also as an example of the kind of theoretical framework that I believe anthropologists could now profitably begin to explore.

In the remainder of this first chapter I give an introduction to the MMF. Chapters 2 to 6 give some theoretical background to the MMF along with a more detailed exposition of the framework itself. In chapters 7 to 12 I apply the MMF to some ethnographic material and consider its consequences for anthropology and for the social and human sciences.

What is the multimodal framework?

As I have already implied, the MMF differs in a number of ways from established frameworks in the social sciences, in particular in its rejection of assumptions implicit in ordinary language such as the mind–body and individual–society dichotomies. It can therefore be a little difficult, on a first encounter, to understand just what the MMF does. There is a natural tendency to reinterpret it in familiar but inappropriate terms. Here I shall start with a relatively intuitive approach, using the idea of 'informal knowledge', and then proceed to a more systematic presentation.

If we begin with the Kuhnian conception of the scientific paradigm, then one way to regard the MMF is as resulting from a kind of *extension* of the paradigm concept to cover the area of informal and non-scientific knowledge.

By 'informal knowledge' I mean the knowledge that is implicit in our daily activities, in the collection of techniques, information and ways of behaving that we use to carry on the business of living, in what Pierre Bourdieu refers to as the *habitus* (Bourdieu 1977). Some of this knowledge may appear to us as factual knowledge: the bus routes by which we get to work, the differences between the prints left by various animals in the bush. Other parts may scarcely seem knowledge at all: the ways in which we have learnt to walk, to carry our bodies, to operate our brains and central nervous systems. All these, however, may be considered as 'knowledge', since none are given to us directly by nature, even where, as in the case of how we learn to operate our nervous system, there is probably a strong genetic component in the particular behaviour.

I have deliberately given examples that pertain to 'mind', examples that relate to 'body' and examples that might be somewhere in between, because the picture of informal knowledge that I am trying to construct for the reader is not of something contained within the mind, but of a patterning of mind and body as a totality. This, as I have already suggested, is an explicit feature of the MMF.

At the level of this kind of informal knowledge people differ a little, and perhaps more than a little, from each other. Operating successfully in the world places certain constraints on what we do, but there is undoubtedly a wide range of personal bodies of informal knowledge each of which enables an individual to survive, after a fashion, within his or her social context.

But what is the relationship between this informal knowledge and the systems of formal knowledge familiar to us, for example, through science? Presumably, in some way, the systems of formal knowledge must derive from the informal knowledge of past and present human beings. They must have 'crystallized' out of the changing flux of informal knowledge systems and attained some degree of stability and independent existence.

Such 'crystallized' systems, which include law codes, forms of bureaucratic organization, formal systems of etiquette, and the like, as well as scientific theories, are an important part of social reality, and once formed they act back upon the changing flux of informal knowledge in complex ways. Once they have been created, they have a certain stability but they are not eternal and in time dissolve back into the general flow of informal knowledge. While we have learnt to represent certain systems of formal knowledge in purely conceptual terms (e.g. as a scientific theory) they derive from more complex patternings of mind and body and retain in some form their origin in such patternings.

All this gives us a picture of social life as describable in terms of a kind of continuing flux of informal knowledge out of which systems of formal knowledge gradually crystallize and which they, in turn, act back upon. This metaphor of 'crystallization' has some limits. For one thing, a crystal is clearly delimited from the solution out of which it forms. This is not so true of systems of formal knowledge. It is unclear whether we should locate them in or outside the individuals who create, use, and are in turn structured by them. Here, as with the mind–body division, we have a dichotomy that the MMF explicitly rejects.

Another difference between real crystallization and the formation of knowledge systems is that real crystals may differ in size and structure, but they either form or do not form. The equivalent process in social life does not have this all-or-nothing character. In a sense, any intersubjective agreement between two individuals about anything represents a little bit of this process of crystallization of knowledge. Systems such as the sciences are at the other extreme, with a formal external representation in the form of writing and an existence that spans centuries of time and millions of people. All human beings partake in at least one system of this kind: language.

We can begin to see that informal knowledge has the potential to be a very central and basic category, including all aspects of social life. The MMF is, in a sense, a framework that describes human social life precisely in terms of this changing flux of informal knowledge and of the processes of crystallization and dissolution within that flow.

To get much further, we need a language with which to speak of the flux of informal knowledge and of the processes of crystallization. The key terms of the MMF provide such a language. Before considering them directly, it is worth trying to specify rather more clearly what this informal knowledge consists of and where it is located, and in particular what the rejection of the mind–body and individual–society dichotomies might imply.

Neither mind nor body

We will begin with the MMF's rejection of a mind–body dichotomy, since this is probably easier to explain than its rejection of the dichotomy between individual and social modes of explanation. The basic variables or quantities within the MMF explicitly include both mind and body processes. It is assumed that these are parallel aspects of a total system.

For example, the techniques involved in hunting wild animals, gathering wild plants, or entering a shamanic trance, are all regarded as techniques of both mind and body. They involve both specific modes of perception (involving the training of the sensory organs), and certain concepts and mental distinctions. They also involve specific internal bodily processes. These allow human beings, for example, to make subtle distinctions in the vegetation surrounding them, or to enter a trance state and generate new 'cultural' content from within it.

The learning of these techniques is regarded in the MMF as something that takes place in the totality of the mind–body system, rather than primarily 'in' the mind or 'in' the body. In other words, within the MMF, the question of whether a particular process happens at the level of 'mind' or 'body' is improperly put and does not make any sense. Much the same is true of the question of whether a particular item of behaviour is willed by the 'individual' or determined by biological or social pressures.

The MMF is not interested in claiming that what goes on within the human mind is 'really' just electrical impulses or hormonal discharges (cf. Changeux 1986). Nor does the MMF assert that what goes on in the mind

7

involves anything outside the mind–body complexes of human beings. However, the MMF also holds that those mind–body complexes cannot ultimately be analysed separately from each other and from their total physical and biological environment. An important part of that environment is made up of other human beings, which brings us to the second dichotomy that the MMF deliberately erases, the opposition between 'individual' and 'society'.

Neither individual nor social variables

The MMF rejects the present dichotomy between two kinds of explanatory language in the social sciences, one dealing in *individual* variables and one dealing in *social (group)* variables such as society or culture. In philosophical language, the MMF is neither a form of 'individualism' nor a form of 'holism' (or 'collectivism') as normally understood (e.g. O'Neill 1973, Agassi 1975).

Social scientists have generally assumed that it is necessary to operate in terms of one or another, or perhaps a combination, of these kinds of explanation, but there is no *a priori* reason why this must be so. The assumption derives merely from our past mental habits. The ordinary (commonsensical) human modes of perception and explanation in modern Western culture have long seen human social reality as constituted by the actions and intentions of individual human beings. Several generations of sociologists, anthropologists and other social scientists have established an alternative mode of explanation in terms of an autonomous realm of social variables (Durkheim's 'social facts'), and these explanations have themselves become part of popular discourse. There is no reason to accept that these two types of explanation are the only ones possible or appropriate.

Explanations in terms of both individual and social variables, separately or together, have been useful and productive. Virtually all social scientific explanation has so far employed them. Nevertheless, the attempt to develop these modes of explanation, singly or in combination, into an adequate and consistent social theory leads to a series of paradoxes that have bedevilled the social sciences for generations. The paradoxes are exemplified below in chapter 3 for the case of interpretive anthropology.

The present situation of the social sciences has some analogies to that of classical (seventeenth- to nineteenth-century) physics. Classical physics was brought into being when Newton, Descartes and others made an initial departure from the modes of thought of ordinary human perception. We might draw a rough parallel with the creation of 'society' as an autonomous realm of explanation in the work of the nineteenth-century sociologists. However, in physics it became apparent towards the end of the nineteenth

8

century that a second and a more radical break was required. This involved a move to modes of theorizing that were considerably more distant from the habits of our normal perceptions and had fewer inbuilt assumptions about the nature of things.

We can take as an example what happened to the concepts of space and time as they developed through the introduction of general relativity. An important point is that this transformation involved more than the simple replacement of one mathematical description (theory) of space and time by another more correct description. It brought with it a new attitude to the whole notion of theory, an attitude that was eventually to manifest itself in the philosophy of science in the writings of authors such as Karl Popper, Thomas Kuhn or Paul Feyerabend.

Consider Erwin Schrödinger's well-known introduction to general relativity, *Space–Time Structure*, first written in 1950 (Schrödinger 1954). Schrödinger begins by abandoning conventional notions of space and time completely and assuming merely a generalized and unstructured 'manifold', a mere assemblage of all points in space and time. He then gradually introduces elements of structure in the form of mathematical relationships (constraints) applying to the points in the manifold. His aim is to find the simplest and most limited set of assumptions that will generate observed experience, in other words, that will give something close enough to ordinary observable space and time in those areas where Newtonian assumptions work.

I emphasize the steps involved here, since I shall follow an analogous procedure below in introducing the MMF. Ordinary categories are first held in abeyance, and the area of reality in question considered in as general, free and unstructured a form as possible (the 'manifold'). A set of appropriate concepts is then tried out. These concepts can be seen as possible 'constraints' upon the freedom of the unstructured manifold. Rather than rushing to reconstitute all of the concepts through which we customarily view the world, the point is to find the minimal set of assumptions that will generate observed experience. These may or may not bear much resemblance to previously familiar concepts. Typically they are quite different. Thus 'gravity' in general relativity is no longer, except in a secondary and derivative sense, Newton's force operating between discrete 'objects' in dependence upon their mass and the distance between them. Instead it is incorporated as a kind of 'curvature' of the structure attributed to space and time.

At the risk of labouring the point somewhat, the question is not whether gravity is in fact a force between two objects or a curvature of space–time. This kind of question could only apply in an empiricist science. The question is which of the two descriptions is simpler, more appropriate and more useful, in the sense of being able to describe accurately as wide a range of phenomena as possible.

The general relativity description has to be mathematically equivalent to the Newtonian description to a high degree of accuracy within 'normal' circumstances. This must be so, because the Newtonian description is known to be accurate within those circumstances. Newtonian physics describes the orbits of the planets within the solar system, for example, to a high (though not perfect) degree of accuracy. It is only where very high velocities or very long periods of time are involved that the predictions of Newtonian physics are significantly different from those of general relativity. Similarly, the probability fields of quantum mechanics have to produce recognizable, conventional, discrete 'objects' within the realm of direct human observation, but they do not necessarily do so for phenomena at very much smaller than human dimensions or at very high temperatures.

The MMF involves this kind of move away from a conventional way of seeing the world, though at this stage in a less mathematical form. The reality that we interpret normally in terms of 'human beings', individual or collective, and their behaviour, is taken as being representable by some kind of general unstructured field or 'social manifold', within which neither 'human individuals' or 'societies' are identified. Structural variables are then introduced, which can be regarded as descriptions of, or constraints upon, the structure of the manifold. These variables are not defined in terms of 'individual' or 'social' entities. They form an autonomous realm of activity from which our conceptions of 'individuals' and 'societies' may be seen as deriving.

A strong argument in favour of such an approach is that conceptions of 'person' or 'individual' are well known to be culturally variable to a great degree (cf. Heelas and Lock 1981; Carrithers, Collins and Lukes 1985; Marsella, DeVos and Hsu 1985). If we assume a basically Western (or for that matter any specific non-Western) model of the person we are taking for granted something that is more appropriately treated as a cultural product. Any such procedure is likely to generate theories poorly adapted to deal with the diversity of concepts of person, individual and self in the real world.

Another point about this approach is that it helps to shift our focus away from the exclusive and competitive claims of individual theoretical frameworks and towards those connections that existing frameworks fail to capture. My own (somewhat neo-Kantian or neo-Madhyamika) assumption is that the 'social manifold' is considerably, if not infinitely, more complex than any representation we can make of it. At any rate our theories so far plainly allow only for limited and simplistic representations of aspects of the manifold and can be assumed to conceal as much as they reveal. The MMF directs our attention towards certain features not well represented in existing frameworks, and I believe that it represents a fruitful direction for future theoretical innovation.

The 'social manifold' and its conventional readings (Types I and II)

To proceed further, it will be useful to have some kind of image or model of what our social manifold is about, of what matters it refers to. Any image already imposes a certain conceptual structure on reality. It renders reality selectively, including some aspects and ignoring others. The intention of this very general metaphor is to assist us in retaining as many as possible of the relevant aspects of reality. It is important to avoid a premature limitation of the aspects our theories are able to consider.

Since the intention of the MMF is to provide a more inclusive and general approach than interpretive anthropology, we might begin with a suggestion by that well-known interpretive anthropologist, Clifford Geertz, for which he cites Max Weber as authority, to the effect that 'man is an animal suspended in webs of significance he himself has spun' (1973: 5). More recently, the late Bob Scholte reminded us that there are limits to 'defin[ing] men and women in terms of the webs of significance they themselves spin', since in state societies 'a select few do the actual spinning while the vast majority is simply caught' (1984: 540).

We may accept the 'webs of significance' as a reasonable image for what interpretive anthropology centrally deals with. We note that these webs are neither purely individual (once spun, they take on a life of their own) nor are they purely social (they have spinners). This suggests that it might be worth looking for some kind of conceptual space, itself neither individual nor social, within which the webs have their existence.

These processes of spinning and being caught happen in time (through history), and if we are to describe them adequately, we should give time an explicit place within our image. Rather than speaking of 'webs of significance', therefore, I suggest that we view the structures of meaning and feeling in which and through which we live as patterns formed by the currents in the course of a vast stream or river. The direction of the stream is the flow of time. Geertz's 'webs' now correspond to semi-permanent currents, or to use William Blake's term, 'vortices',[3] that have become established in the onward flow of the river. This metaphor may help us to appreciate the dynamic and processual nature of social life more clearly, as well as offering some hope of escape from the spiders in the shadows.

At any point in the river, including the present, we can draw a cross-section through the river and see a structure of 'webs' laid out on the two-dimensional surface across the flow. In fact, though, the webs have a third dimension, time, and it is this third dimension that the metaphor is intended to bring to our attention.

As individual human beings and as members of social groups, we are not simply driven along blindly by the currents. We can orient ourselves in relation to them and steer ourselves to some degree in the direction that we prefer. We presumably have some ability to affect the flow through our actions. These currents, however, are the environment within which we move. They are the field of forces within which our activity takes place and we cannot step outside of them. For the most part, too, they are much bigger and stronger than we are, at least as individuals. This is what gives the Durkheimian analysis, with its 'social facts', its strength and plausibility. We need to remember, however, that the currents cannot ultimately be separated from the individuals who both constitute them and *are constituted by them*.

We might describe the 'substance' within which this flow takes place as something like 'relatedness' or 'connectedness'. The currents within the flow are concerned with the patterning of relationships between human beings. They also describe the patterning of relationships between individual human beings and other animal and plant species, and relationships between human beings and the physical environment (natural and man-made) within which they exist. How these various kinds of relationships operate forms the subject-matter of much of anthropology, as of the other social sciences. From another point of view it can be seen as the subject-matter of human biology.

When we consider how we might begin to impose further structure on the 'relatedness' that constitutes the manifold, we can see that there are at least two approaches characteristically employed by social scientists for this purpose. We might refer to these as generating two types of *reading* of the social manifold. They correspond to the 'holistic' and 'individualistic' positions referred to above. Readings of Type I ('individualist') impose structural variables that are identified as properties of individual actors. Readings of Type II ('holist'), while generally admitting the existence of such variables, treat them as secondary to and derivative from structural variables that are identified as properties of social groups.

Type III readings of the 'social manifold': the MMF

Are other types of reading possible? If both cultural and individual factors are to be included on an equal status, with neither subordinate to the other, the relationship of priority between them has somehow to be resolved. The logical way to do this is to treat both cultural and individual factors as subordinate to and derivative from some other level of variables. This gives our third kind of reading (Type III). The MMF is an example of such a reading.

In the MMF the new variables operate within the social manifold itself. They can be thought of as providing a description of the semi-permanent currents or vortices that were mentioned above as existing within the social manifold. To use a physical metaphor, they can be imagined as eigenstates of the manifold. I refer to them as *modal states* (for short MS or MS_m, the subscript emphasizing that these are modal states of the social manifold itself), and I assume that the manifold can be described as some kind of combination of these states.

In terms of ordinary space and time, a particular set of values of the states corresponds to a particular 'density' or 'intensity' of certain types or styles of 'connectedness' at various places and times. They might correspond, for example, to greater degrees of hierarchy or autonomy, to patrilateral or matrilateral emphases in kinship systems, or to the varying extent of investment of the population at that point and time into specific kinds of technology or particular kinds of physical movement. While the states themselves are in a sense beyond space and time, viewed in space and time they have a strong dynamic or directional quality, since, as will be seen, the patterns of 'connectedness' correspond to certain kinds of human activity that may lead to relative stability or change.

The kind of quantities seen as fundamental in Type I and Type II readings are treated as derivative from these modal values. In order to generate Type I quantities, individuals and their behaviour are treated as being defined by a series of *modal states of the individual* (MS_i). Type II quantities may be reached by defining *cultural modal states* (MS_c).

Over time specific MS_c grow and fade in importance, new ones are introduced and so on. These correspond, for example, to such social phenomena as the Protestant ethic in early modern Europe, the cult of the bodhisattva Chenrezi (Avalokiteshvara) in Tibet (see chapter 10), movements in the history of ideas, art history and the like. When these matters are described in terms of the MMF, the corresponding MS_c are seen as derivative from the underlying modal states of the social manifold (MS_m), which are explicitly concerned with both individual and collective components, and are reducible to neither.

It is sometimes useful to have a term to refer specifically to the directional and dynamic nature of the MS_m through time. I refer to these directional processes within the manifold as *modal currents*.

Individual modal states (MS_i), like cultural modal states, are again explicitly derivative from the underlying modal states of the manifold

(MS_m). It follows that to the extent that the MMF implies a psychology, the quantities with which that psychology operates are seen as derivative from the MS_m, which are collective as well as individual. The same applies to, for example, human biology seen within the MMF.

Individual behaviour and the MS_i

Such a language is difficult to reconcile directly with the vocabulary of intentions, goals and actions within which we generally conceive of individual behaviour. However the *process-language* to which our ordinary terms refer may be translated into a *state-language* more directly equivalent to the MMF's modal states and currents.

Within this state-language each individual is seen as having a 'repertoire' of individual modal states (corresponding to the MS_i defined within the MMF) and as operating at any time within one or another of these states. The states may be taken as corresponding in some sense to states of the brain and central nervous system. The state at any time governs the behaviour of the individual. It also governs transitions to other states, which take place in response to the individual's ongoing stream of experience (internal and externally originated). However, it needs to be remembered that the individual modal state is only an approximation within the MMF. It would be as, or more, valid to speak of a single state referring to two individuals, or to a group.

What is at issue here includes the difficult question of 'structure' versus 'agency', to use Anthony Giddens' terms (e.g. Giddens 1984), itself a contemporary reworking of the ancient Western philosophical and theological opposition between free will and determinism. The MMF allows for both structure and agency. Structure operates in broad terms,

(1) through the relationship with the social manifold, which presents the individual at any point with a limited repertoire of individual modal states, and
(2) through the specific pattern of response to the ongoing flow of events that is associated with each modal state.

Individual agency is represented by

(3) the individual's ability to switch between available states in his or her repertoire and so respond to a situation in one of a number of ways. In doing so the individual strengthens the modal states of the manifold (MS_m) corresponding to the MS_i selected;
(4) the individual's ability to create new states in response to a new situation by rearranging the elements of the available states, and (perhaps) by introducing entirely new material, so initiating a new cultural modal state.

When we speak here of 'structure' and of 'individual agency' we are concerned not with the ultimate locus of control, since the MMF sees this as neither collective nor individual as such, but at most with the perceived or experienced locus of control. Unfortunately any mention of individuals within our language forces us to think in terms of a Type I or II reading, seeing individuals as either determining or determined. The central point of the MMF is that neither is appropriate. There is an unavoidable conflict between the MMF and the English language, which is shot through with individualistic and holistic assumptions.

This is why the whole procedure with the social manifold and the MMF was introduced, as a way to suggest to the reader the possibility of a mode of conceptualization that lies outside those modes natural to the English (and other Western) languages. Nevertheless, any discussion of the MMF already involves us in the use of conventional English language terms, unless we choose to adopt a purely mathematical formalism (as does modern physics). Few social scientists would feel at home with such an approach. Some relief might be brought about by devising further new English terms to supplement the social manifold and the modal states, along lines such as those of David Bohm's suggestions in *Wholeness and the Implicate Order* (Bohm 1981 : 28–47). This, too, hardly seems justifiable in the present introductory context. Within this book I shall proceed in more or less ordinary English, while asking the reader to remain as aware as possible of the problems involved.

Later I shall provide some argument for the particular features of the individual that are subsumed under the MS_i (and hence seen as being ultimately derivative from the modal states of the overall social manifold). Here I shall simply list them:

(1) The MS_i (modal state of the individual) has a cognitive function. It splits up or interprets the individual's stream of experience in characteristic ways, so that certain features of the external environment and of the body's internal processes are consciously perceived and others are not;

(2) Each MS_i is associated with a set of images or symbols, in part shared by individuals within a given cultural context, by which that MS_i may be referenced or evoked;

(3) Each MS_i corresponds to specific moods, motivations, feelings and emotions;

(4) Each MS_i corresponds to a particular decision structure. Within it the individual will respond in certain ways to certain events, will subjectively find certain goals attractive and others unattractive;

(5) Each MS_i corresponds to a particular subjective sense of self and a particular way in which the individual perceives of his or her relationship to other individuals and other aspects of the environment;

(6) Each MS_i corresponds to certain physiological correlates, such as posture, muscle tension, blood pressure, and the like;

(7) MS_is differ in terms of possible transitions to other MS_is. They may be more or less well connected to other states. They may also allow for more or less innovation in the creation of new states.

This brief and schematic presentation has introduced the basic concepts of the MMF. In chapters 3 to 6 the MMF will be introduced at greater length, beginning with a discussion of some relevant problems and developments in contemporary anthropology. In the subsequent chapters, 7 to 12, the MMF will be applied to a series of problem areas within anthropology, and some of its implications for the social and human sciences more generally will be considered.

First, though, in chapter 2, we will consider the proposition that was mentioned earlier in this chapter: that anthropology should be seen as a 'natural science of society'. I shall explain what I mean by this in some detail and look at some possible objections.

2 A natural science of society

In considering the suggestion that anthropology may be seen as a
natural science of society, we should remember that the natural sciences
proper are no longer what they were in their nineteenth-century heyday.
The natural sciences in this sense (positivist, empiricist, numerical) began
to break down with the radical changes within the physical sciences at the
end of the nineteenth and early twentieth centuries (special and general
relativity and quantum theory in particular). As I mentioned in chapter 1,
similar changes are now becoming apparent within other natural sciences.
These are not merely changes in 'paradigm', but, increasingly, changes in
what scientists do and in how they understand what they are doing.

It is primarily because of these changes that the natural sciences have
undergone since the days of Wilhelm Dilthey and Max Weber that it now
makes more sense to talk of a unity of method between natural and social
science than to maintain the traditional opposition between *Naturwis-
senschaften* and *Geisteswissenschaften*. To consider some of the implications of
the status of a natural science today we can turn to the academic discipline
that has attempted to understand science as an enterprise: the philosophy
of science.

The philosophy of science, as is well known, has itself undergone a major
conceptual revolution over the last thirty or so years, as a result of the need
to make philosophical sense of the implications of the transformations
within physics in particular. Thomas Kuhn, whose work has become
familiar to social scientists at least in the form of the concept of the
'paradigm', was himself a part of this attempt to construct a new and more
plausible view of the scientific enterprise. Others, such as Sir Karl Popper,
Imre Lakatos or Paul Feyerabend, to name only members of the older
generation, have played equally significant parts.

What this work has done, among other things, is to make it clear that theories in all branches of science are never value-free and that reality is rarely such as to provide unequivocal endorsement for one theory over another. Contemporary positions in the philosophy of science may differ in their degree of commitment to the theoretical possibility of what Popper called 'objective knowledge' (Popper 1973). Nevertheless, virtually all shades of realism or relativism accept that in practice our theories and models are partial and imperfect and thàt they incorporate assumptions that cannot be ultimately justified.

This much is true even of Popper's cautious and (in present-day terms) relatively conservative hypothetico-deductive model. Popper's model held that the ultimate result of the painstaking making, testing and falsifying of hypotheses would indeed constitute 'objective knowledge' of a kind. However, this achievement was implicitly relegated to the infinitely distant future. Virtually everyone who has followed Popper has taken at least as weak a position on the possibility of objective knowledge. Philosophers of science today in practice accept that science is a matter of competing theoretical frameworks, theories and approaches, each with their own degree of truth-content. They concede, in other words, a substantial degree of relativism in terms of the pragmatic coexistence of competing theories and concepts.

This issue of conceptual relativism will reappear in later chapters, in relation to the validity of knowledge systems in traditional societies. Here it concerns us primarily in that it removes a traditional distinction between the natural sciences and social sciences. It is no longer possible to see natural science as the gradual acquisition of objective knowledge, in contrast to disciplines such as anthropology, which have long been characterized by a variety of competing frameworks and theories each generally accepted as having some degree of validity and truth-content. It may still be possible to define truth-content in terms of ideas such as accurate correspondence to, or representation of, some aspect of reality, but 'truth' in such a sense can now only be part of the social functioning of scientific ideas. Nor can we any longer assume that truth content may be evaluated simply in terms of agreement with the currently accepted body of formal knowledge within the natural sciences in our own society.

We can put this in slightly different terms. Anthropologists are usually aware of a variety of possible approaches (or 'theories') that can be used to understand any given field situation, and they are unlikely to assume that one is unequivocally right and the others equally clearly wrong. Each approach will emphasize different aspects of a situation that is too complex to be encompassed by any one of them, and the selection of aspects corresponds to a more or less conscious value-choice at the base of the theory.

What is now becoming evident is that such situations are as characteristic of the natural sciences as of the social sciences. Consider, for example, the question of how one understands the activity of the mind. Does one assume, as has on the whole been conventional within neurology in recent decades, that the action of the mind can be reduced to electrical currents within the brain? Or does one argue, as in Richard Bergland's recent book, that the key events are not electrical currents but chemical flows (Bergland 1985)? Meanwhile philosophers and psychologists provide a variety of alternative theoretical languages for mental activity that cover, in a sense, 'the same' domain but that are very far from being reducible to each other or to the electrical or chemical accounts.

It is naive in the extreme to suppose that one of these theories is unequivocally right and the others wrong.[1] Any realistic picture surely has to include, in some sense, *all* these aspects, or at any rate most of them. However, it is difficult to get very far with such a problem without arriving at an exceedingly complex theory, in part because the languages used are in important respects difficult to reconcile with each other.

This does not worry neurologists, psychologists or philosophers very much, because for the most part they simply do not talk to each other. These scientists work in different academic contexts and can continue using their own partial descriptions of the situation without risk of overt conflict.[2] The equivalent problem in anthropology tends to be more immediate, since the competing approaches are being put forward among the same group of disciplinary specialists.

In making such choices we are not just choosing a theory, but selecting certain aspects of the situation as significant and dismissing other aspects as less essential. Consequently the choice between frameworks cannot be value-free. As Max Weber pointed out, the choice of a domain of enquiry cannot be separated from the value-orientation of the researcher (e.g. Brand 1987).

Weber held that once a particular choice of domain had been made it was possible to proceed in an objective and value-free manner. Being objective, in the sense of respecting the reality of the situation one studies, is a straightforward criterion of good research. However, the assumption that values can be restricted to the area of selecting a domain of enquiry is much harder to take seriously now than in Weber's day.[3] To see why this is so, we need to take a look in a little more detail at why the positivistic tradition in science has collapsed over the last fifty years.

Science after positivism

The assessment of scientific knowledge and of scientific theories as value-free corresponds to a particular view of the relationship between scientific theory and reality, generally known as 'positivism', sometimes also as 'empiricism'.[4] In this view, the scientific account of the world is seen in essence as a straightforward *description* of the world.

A metaphor frequently employed for this view of reality is the *mirror*.[5] What science says about a particular phenomenon is seen as *mirroring* or *reflecting* that phenomenon within the real world. Scientific statements are believed, in the positivistic view of reality, to be simple refinements of observation. They are straightforward generalizations from facts or data, which are held to be reliable descriptions of events in the real world.

At any particular stage in the development of science, our mirroring of reality may be incomplete and faulty but in principle it is simply a matter of refining and improving the description to give a better fit. In more developed versions of positivism, the growth of scientific knowledge is understood in terms of the gradual discovery of *laws* that are simply abstract descriptions of observed regularities, uniformities within the reflected image. These laws enable the observed facts to be summarized in statements of increasingly greater generality.

Part of the strength of this positivistic conception of knowledge is that it corresponds closely, at least as far as the observation of facts is concerned, to a strongly held common-sense view of knowledge within our own society.[6] That view has a certain emotional attraction, and we can speculate on historical, psychological or even psychoanalytic arguments for its attractiveness. As the basis for a conception of science it is inadequate in many respects.

This inadequacy first became a major issue in modern Western thought as a result of the radical transformations in physical theory at the beginning of this century, in particular the development of special and general theories of relativity and quantum mechanics. According to the positivistic view of science such transformations, which represented radical changes in how the universe was understood, were not supposed to happen. The acquisition of scientific knowledge should be smooth and progressive, a gradual accumulation of a better and better representation (mirroring) of reality.

Consequently, a new understanding of the nature of science has gradually developed. It would be wrong to suggest that there is unanimity among current approaches, even if we put to one side the increasingly tortuous and convoluted attempts to reintroduce something like positivism under a new name. However, if the mirror metaphor is a capsule description of the old epistemology, many of the new epistemologies can be viewed as having something like a 'map' metaphor at their centre (cf. Samuel 1985a, Azevedo 1986, Hooker 1987).

According to these approaches, a scientific theory can be likened to, for example, a map of a landscape. We can make a map of a landscape in any of a large number of ways. For example, we can include vegetation, contours, roads, buildings or geological structure, or some combination of them. We could choose a scale of 1:50,000 or 1:5,000,000. In each case we would arrive at a different map; some features would be ignored and others included.[7]

The critical point here is that it is in no way true to say that one of these maps is right and another wrong. In the same way different fields of human knowledge (chemistry, physics, sociology) and different theories within those fields (quantum theory, structuralist analysis) would select different aspects of the total situation. It is important to note that such a perspective does not imply that all maps are equally accurate. A road map still has to show the roads in the right places. The 'map' metaphor does, however, imply that there are two different sets of criteria for whether a map (or theory) is satisfactory. We can ask whether the map (or theory) does what it sets out to do, in other words, whether a map that shows the road and towns has them in the right places. But we can also ask whether it does what we want it to do; a geological map of Europe may be perfectly correct, but no help for finding the road to London.

Since any particular piece of territory (in the analogy, any piece of reality) has a potentially infinite number of significant features, we can never be sure of including the information relevant to all possible requests within a given map. Similarly, any scientific theory represents a selection of aspects of reality and omits other aspects. This selection corresponds to the *mapping conventions* by which it is decided that certain aspects of the territory are to be represented and others ignored. The discovery of a radically new theory can be likened to the invention of a new mapping convention, which displays interconnections that could not be properly represented on the old maps.

The map metaphor is a useful way of pointing to the changing conception of science, but we should be wary of taking it too literally. Even a map is not just a selective representation of reality. Its conventions of representation also encode theories about the nature of reality, if only at the level of equating objects that are similarly represented, and implying differences between others. A geological map, for example, implies a whole theory of stratification and a complex set of equivalences between geological formations believed to have been created at the same period.

In the case of a scientific theory, the extent to which the theory goes beyond being a selective representation of reality into being a construction of reality may be very much greater. The theory creates linkages between events and phenomena, for example in the form of assumptions about processes of causation, and it is not at all obvious in what sense these linkages exist 'in reality'. This is particularly so since our ideas about causality ultimately derive from common-sense perceptions of the world. Such perceptions may be more artefacts of how human beings have learnt to operate within their environment than genuine representations of that environment. In other words, the assumption of causality is not necessarily 'true'. All that we really know is that the assumption of causality is a more or less successful way of 'getting along in the universe'.[8]

We can cite here, for example, David Bohm's suggestion in his *Wholeness and the Implicate Order* (1981) that the 'explicate order' of our perceptions is a transformation of an 'implicate order' within which space and time in our sense simply do not exist, or Humberto Maturana's statement in *Autopoesis and Cognition* that

> perception should not be viewed as a grasping of an external reality, but rather as the specification of one, because no distinction [is] possible between perception and hallucination in the operation of the nervous system as a closed network.   (Maturana and Varela 1980:xv)

The radical implications of such positions as Bohm's and Maturana's are explored in this book only implicitly, and to a limited degree. They should, however, serve to remind us that understanding the world, in both common-sense and theoretical manners, is a complex activity and one that we know relatively little about.

In the present context, our primary concern is with the value dimensions of theory. It is important to note here that while such aspects are often more obvious in the social sciences, they are equally present in the natural sciences. The map metaphor implies that they are always present in any theory, at the level of the criteria by which we select what our map or theory is going to include. Here it can be seen why I differ from Max Weber and the neo-Kantians, and also from Jürgen Habermas and his followers, in failing to recognize any difference of nature between natural and social sciences. It seems to me that the entire modern history of the natural and social sciences points in the direction of an essential unity of nature between them.[9] At any rate, I can see no coherent boundary to be drawn.

It is this that leads me to suggest that we look for an overall theoretical framework that bridges the natural and social sciences and that avoids reducing either to the other. The MMF, briefly introduced in chapter 1, serves, among other things, as a sketch of what such a framework might look like. It is not intended as final or conclusive, but it incorporates the kind of view of science that I have been suggesting in the last few pages, as a tentative and always fallible process of construction of maps or models of reality, all of them by their very nature highly selective and value-laden.

Establishing such a framework can be seen as opening up a space within the natural sciences where anthropology, and the social sciences more generally, can construct their own theories with a much fuller comprehension of what they are doing, and without any need to apologize or regard themselves as inferior to the so-called 'hard' sciences. At the same time it has the potential to constitute a critique of the natural sciences themselves, more viable because it begins with a coherent set of assumptions about what science as a whole is.

Objections to a 'natural science of society'

It is worth considering some of the objections that may be made to the kind of picture of anthropology I am here proposing, particularly by some of those involved in the general area of symbolic or interpretive anthropology. There are two types of problems that I shall discuss in some detail here: (1) the general question of the validity (and morality) of the natural scientific approach and (2) the moral and ethical issues involved in the relationship between anthropologist and subject of research. These issues also involve questions of textuality and genre in anthropological discourse. Among anthropologists who have presented criticisms of these two types are James Boon (1982), Bob Scholte (1986) and Roger Keesing (1987). I shall deal with the two groups of problems separately, although there are some obvious interconnections.

The validity and morality of the natural science model

This first line of argument is perhaps the more radical of the two, since the whole nature of the anthropological enterprise depends upon what response is made to it. Anthropology deals with the construction of knowledge in society, yet anthropology itself is a form of knowledge constructed within a particular society. Does this 'reflexive' nature of anthropological knowledge invalidate its claims to be considered a science? Can the results of anthropology ever be validly abstracted from the social matrix in which they are produced?

One can observe the effects of this line of argument in the work of many anthropologists since the mid-1970s. Clifford Geertz constitutes a typical and eminent example. His response in recent years has been to reject the project of developing a scientific model of society entirely. In its place he proposes the less philosophically risky project of offering translations from one society to another, of giving readings of exotic texts that are always, in the nature of the enterprise, versions made *for us*. In the place of a science of society Geertz offers us a humanistic interpretation of an Other forever irreducible to Western scientific language (e.g. Geertz 1985).

One can sympathize with the dilemma faced by Geertz and others who have taken a similar line (Clifford and Marcus 1986, Marcus and Fisher 1986) but still find his answer unsatisfactory. It should be understood, first of all, that the problem here is not just a problem for anthropology, but for *all* science, social and natural. That the subject-matter of anthropology consists of the behaviour of other human beings, who have their own competing interpretation of events, only adds point to a situation that is implicit in all scientific endeavour (Samuel 1985a). The theorist is part of every theory.

This is, of course, a familiar argument against positivism in science. I have already presented a version of it earlier in this chapter. Much of the work in the philosophy of science referred to earlier is concerned with understanding the consequences of this argument for science more generally and with developing non-positivistic models of the nature of science. To the extent that the sciences are successfully developing such non-positivistic models, the objection loses much of its point.

The natural and social sciences as they are today differ greatly among themselves in the degree to which they have accepted the critique of positivism. At one end of a continuum can be found theoretical physics, where the presence of the observer, and the consequent limitations on what can be known, are built into the fundamental assumptions and equations of quantum theory. Understandably, theoretical physics has been a fruitful area for subsequent speculation on the relationship between 'consciousness' and 'reality'. David Bohm's work, referred to above, provides an example with considerable relevance to anthropology (Bohm 1981; cf. also Bohm 1976, Comfort 1981).

At the other end of the continuum are sciences that still operate, to all intents and purposes, with a positivistic methodology. Large parts of empirical sociology and experimental psychology, for example, are still in this situation, modelling themselves on a conception of science that physics was forced to abandon sixty years ago. The negative associations that have become attached to science for many anthropologists would seem to derive at least in part from reactions to this kind of naive quantification, still practised in many sociology and psychology departments.

I have no intention of arguing that anthropology should become a science of *this* kind. The scope for quantitative methods seems to me to be quite limited in anthropology, at any rate at present. Nevertheless, quantification is not a *sine qua non* of science, or at least of post-positivistic science. It is a tool that is applicable in certain circumstances. It can only be secondary to the development of the theoretical models that generate hypotheses to be examined quantitatively (or in some other manner). Reversing the process leads to bad science, as critical and radical social scientists have been pointing out for many years.

The real point of the objection to science is not quantification *per se*, but the use of any kind of systematic and consistent theoretical framework. Such frameworks ('paradigms', in Kuhn's model) are at the centre of the scientific process, whether that process is conceived of in positivistic or post-positivistic terms. It may be true that these frameworks remain for the most part fragmentary and incomplete, and that historically attempts at closure have frequently heralded the collapse of the paradigm. It is, nevertheless, also true that achieving such a consistent framework of clearly defined concepts and assumptions remains a central aim of science, whether that science be behaviourist psychology or quantum theory.

Such considerations become less pressing when a particular scientific discipline is seen, as suggested in chapter 1, as merely one of a variety of bodies of knowledge operating within the world, rather than as part of an attempt to provide the single all-encompassing and unified system. I have suggested above that the limitations of a scientific framework correspond to value judgments implicit in the construction of that framework (cf. Samuel 1985a). No framework can encompass the whole of reality, and the selection of aspects of reality on which the framework concentrates cannot be justified within the terms of the framework itself. Does this imply that scientific frameworks are useless?

If the question is phrased as baldly as this, the answer is surely that they are manifestly not useless. The technological achievements that science has made possible bear witness to this. A large part of modern industrial society is build around the employment of these scientific frameworks. Yet it is precisely this employment of Western science for instrumental purposes that has been frequently characterized as a major problem of modern Western society. It has been linked to exploitative behaviour towards human beings, other species and the natural environment itself. Leaving aside the question of the validity of science, what about its morality?

The characterization of the social role of science as exploitative and damaging undoubtedly contains some truth. It seems to me that the most useful (and most ethically desirable) response is not to attempt to avoid personal responsibility for the destructive effects of some scientific knowledge by withdrawing into a conception of anthropology as a humanistic discipline. To do this is simply to leave the business of science to others who are less scrupulous and to ensure that the awareness of and sensitivity to human meanings and experiences that anthropology at its best has achieved will not become part of the science according to which our society operates.

It seems to me preferable that anthropologists step out of the hermeneutic circle and take the risk of formulating their knowledge in the form of a systematic and testable framework of ideas. Doing so involves an acceptance that those formulations will always be arbitrary and incomplete, and that they may become the basis of action in the real world in ways their makers cannot foresee, with all the moral consequences that derive from that unpredictability.[10] It does, nevertheless, allow for a real possibility that what anthropologists have learnt can become part of the collective knowledge according to which society directs itself. If anthropologists feel it to be desirable that scientists recognize the arbitrary and incomplete nature of what they are doing, they are more likely to be heard by entering into a genuine dialogue with scientific modes of operation than by simply sniping from the sidelines.

The issue is a real one, as the references to evolutionary biology and sociobiology in chapter 1 demonstrate. What is at issue is, at least in principle, the constitution of the collective wisdom by which our society organizes its affairs, and the willingness of anthropology to contribute to that wisdom. It is for this reason that I believe it worthwhile to work towards a 'natural science of society'. While I sympathize with those who prefer to adopt a humanistic rather than scientific model for anthropology, I believe that to do this is to accept a position for anthropology on the sidelines of our society and, in the process, to abandon a social role that it should be undertaking.

For me a general theoretical framework is not, as I hope I have made clear, an expression of a 'unitary and totalizing paranoia' (Foucault 1984: xiii). It is a tactical device. It is an intervention in an ongoing debate, and its aim is not to restrict debate by imprisoning it within totalitarian categories, but to open it up by providing the basis for challenging those categories. I develop this view a little further in chapter 12.

Anthropology and the people it studies

The question of the social construction of anthropological knowledge can be approached from another angle. The discourse of anthropology involves and constructs a particular relationship towards anthropology's subject-matter, the people whom anthropologists study. In the past, and often even today, these people have typically been members of other cultures, frequently preliterate and in no position to contest the way in which we present their lives and their experience. Both Scholte (1986) and Keesing (1987) have raised points of this kind about the discourse of anthropology, as did James Boon in his book *Other Tribes, Other Scribes* (1982). There is no doubt that there are some real and difficult moral issues involved.

Any text implies the author's relationship to his or her subject, whether this be the overt attitude of cultural supremacy found within the average nineteenth-century travelogue or the epistemologically questionable pose of objectivity implied by the traditional anthropological monograph. More specifically, the conventional monograph hides the context within which the knowledge it contains was produced. Observation and interview are represented, if at all, by selective quotation. The members of the society studied are given little chance to speak for themselves. Thus the issue of textuality becomes associated with a moral argument to the effect that anthropology, in effect, continues the tradition of colonialism by subordinating non-Western peoples to a Western mode of discourse (cf. Said 1979).

Various experimental modes of ethnography have been attempted in order to remedy this situation, many of them involving the presentation of autobiographical material from informants, inclusion of much more detailed primary source material than had previously been usual, and related devices (e.g. Crapanzano 1980, Colby and Colby 1981, G. Lewis 1980, Clifford and Marcus 1986). Where this line of criticism leaves the anthropological theorist is less clear. In practice, its end result is probably similar to that of the arguments considered in the previous section, except that the 'totalizing discourse' to be rejected is now seen as having colonialist implications in addition to its other dangers.

In so far as anthropology aspires, as I have suggested that it should, to be a science, then its mode of presentation has to be conceived within that perspective, and it cannot help but subordinate whatever ethnographic material it uses, non-Western or Western, to the purposes of that specifically Western enterprise. Anthropologists can aim to expand Western science to include modes of understanding that were previously alien or incomprehensible to it, but science remains an integral part of modern industrial society.

This is not intended to suggest that other forms of writing, in which, for example, the anthropologist acts simply as a translator of the 'native view', do not have their place.[11] It should be clear, however, that the present work is arguing for a role for anthropology that goes beyond translation. If the style of anthropology proposed in this book is of any assistance to the peoples whom anthropologists study, and I hope that it is, then it will be so through providing them with a Western scientific understanding of their own culture, and a formal language within which they can encode that culture's enduring values, rather than by claiming to present 'their own' view of the world. Ultimately, after all, they are the only people who can do that.

Increasingly, in any case, we are all part of the same world, and the boundaries between the peoples studied by anthropologists, and the peoples who supply the anthropologists, are blurring rapidly. As that process accelerates, anthropology as translation will become a less relevant activity, but anthropology as a science will have a new and increasingly important function. That function will be to include the values and modes of operating of all human societies within the repertoire of possibilities from which the world's future will develop. Given the extremely impoverished range of options within which most modern societies operate at present, it would be difficult to argue that such a project is unnecessary.

In chapter 3 we shall begin the task of developing the new framework with an examination of the resources available within the work of some contemporary anthropologists.

3   Starting points I

As I suggested in chapter 1, a basic issue with which the multimodal framework is concerned is the relationship between, in conventional terms, individual and culture (or society). In that chapter I spoke of Type I and Type II 'readings' of the 'social manifold', corresponding to what Popper, Agassi and others have termed 'individualist' and 'holist' perspectives, and I suggested that we might look for a third type of reading (Type III) that belonged to neither category.

Both Type I and Type II readings have been important in the history of anthropology and the other social sciences. To the extent that anthropology has been a study of 'cultures' and/or 'societies' rather than of individuals it has tended to Type II formulations. An insistence on Type II formulations was the essence of the Durkheimian position, and it is not surprising that Louis Dumont, in many ways a self-consciously Durkheimian anthropologist, declared this to be the central social-scientific insight, the 'sociological apperception' (Dumont 1970: 39ff.). He could as well have said the 'anthropological apperception', at any rate with reference to the British and French traditions of social anthropology, and to an influential part of American anthropology.

At the same time, it has been generally characteristic of anthropology that such theoretical work as has taken place within the discipline has been done by people who were also involved in ethnographic field research with specific human societies (as contrasted with, for example, sociology, where many of the most significant theorists have done little or no empirical research). The nature of anthropological field research, carried out for the most part in small communities in a face-to-face context, has meant that anthropologists necessarily spend much of their time dealing with people as individuals, and, necessarily, becoming aware of their differences. This

29

helps to explain why Type I formulations have also had an important presence within anthropology, particularly within the American tradition, where they have been reinforced by influences from the essentially individualistic (i.e. Type I) field of psychology.

Since Type II theorists were well aware of the reality of human individuals, and Type I theorists were equally aware of the importance of collective variables, the theoretical positions that developed within anthropology necessarily involved some kind of attempt at accommodation between the perspectives. In chapter 4 I shall examine some of the theoretical formulations that resulted from basically Type I perspectives, in the work of authors such as Anthony Wallace and Ward Goodenough. In this chapter I begin with some of the most influential formulations in recent years of Type II perspectives, those developed by the so-called *interpretive* or *symbolic* anthropologists such as Victor Turner and Clifford Geertz. In particular I shall discuss some of the suggestions of two critics of interpretive anthropology, Maurice Bloch and Dan Sperber, which seem to me to point to some of the central issues involved in the conflict between Type I and Type II perspectives.

Interpretive anthropology and its critics: Bloch and Sperber

The interpretive anthropologists came to prominence in the late 1960s and early 1970s. These scholars argued that 'culture' should be seen as an autonomous world of meanings. This world was constructed through the activity of cultural symbols and had a constraining and defining effect on the thought-processes of the members of any particular society. The emphasis on cultural *symbols* continued a major strain in Durkheim's own later work. Historically, interpretive anthropology was one of the high points of the anthropological assertion of the primacy of social or cultural (Type II) explanations for human social behaviour.

The central technique of interpretive anthropology was to treat human 'culture' as being externalized in cultural artefacts such as rituals, myths, works of art, items of language or sequences of social behaviour. These artefacts could be analysed as sequences of symbolic messages referring to matters such as ethos, purpose and the patterning of human relationship within society. Thus an analysis of these cultural items would enable anthropologists to connect structures of action, feeling and thought within a particular social group.

The emphasis on the unity of behaviour, ethos (emotion, personality) and cognition was a characteristic feature of the work of Clifford Geertz, Victor Turner and many other interpretive anthropologists. I regard this as one of the major insights of interpretive anthropology, and it is carried over into the MMF's central concept, the modal state. However, while the interpretive anthropologists rightly sensed that such a unity could be conceptualized, they were by and large unable to provide a coherent theoretical framework within which to place it. The difficulties centred on the relationship between individual and 'culture', in other words on the conflict between Type I and Type II readings.

Interpretive anthropology was by no means a unified position, especially if the term is used to cover Lévi-Straussian and other cognate approaches as well as the American and British symbolic anthropologists. Geertz and Turner, the two best-known figures in the latter group, came from quite different intellectual backgrounds (cf. Ortner 1984: 128–31). Although their initial formulations in the 1960s had many features in common, they subsequently moved in quite different directions. By the 1970s interpretive anthropology had become a family of only loosely connected approaches.[1]

Interpretive anthropology at its best produced an impressive series of analyses of the universes of meaning, feeling and behaviour found within particular societies. However, the incoherence of the general perspectives within which these studies were carried out gradually became apparent. A whole succession of anthropological critics have argued for the autonomy of the individual, or for the primacy of political and economic processes, as against the culturally defined universes of meaning posited by Geertz, Turner and their colleagues (e.g. Bloch 1976, Sperber 1975, Asad 1979, 1983, Austin-Broos 1979, 1981, 1987a, Keesing 1986, 1987, Scholte 1984, 1986).

Some of these critics confined themselves to demonstrating the limitations of the symbolic perspective. Others, such as Maurice Bloch and Dan Sperber, have outlined alternative theoretical approaches, and it is these that are of primary interest to us here, since they suggest how the insights of interpretive anthropology may be carried on into a more satisfactory framework. Nevertheless, neither Bloch's nor Sperber's suggestions appear to me to be satisfactory as they stand.

Thus, Bloch (1976), in an article that began as one of the Royal Anthropological Institute's Malinowski Lectures, claimed that the symbolic universes postulated by Geertz and his followers were simply part of a mystified view of the world, created for *ideological* purposes by the ruling classes of each society. Bloch analysed his own fieldwork material from Madagascar in these terms, suggesting that the relationship between people and ancestral spirits within Malagasy ritual was no more than a mystified projection of the relationship between people and tribal elders in village life (Bloch 1974, 1976).

If individual human beings were totally constrained by the power of such ideological constructs, there could be no possibility of social change. Bloch, therefore, postulated an ordinary *common-sense* view of the world, which he suggested must exist alongside the ideological constructions of cultural symbolism. This common-sense view was non-symbolic, it derived from an unmediated (and presumably trustworthy) perception of nature, and it was capable of seeing through the deceptions of ruling-class propaganda that anthropologists had been foolish enough to take seriously. It was on the basis of this common-sense view that individuals could mobilize to bring about social change. Despite the distortions of ruling-class propaganda, the masses knew, at least intermittently, what was really going on.

Sperber also attacked the closed symbolic universe, though from a somewhat different perspective. In his best-known work, *Rethinking Symbolism* (1975), he argued on the basis of his Dorze field material that one simply could not find the kind of coherence in culture presupposed by the proponents of symbolic modes of analysis.[2] If the realm of the symbolic was to have any coherent meaning, that meaning had to be individual rather than cultural, and it needed to be located in a theory of cognitive processes within the individual.

Sperber, therefore, suggested a model of the brain that included two different modes of processing of language and other data. These were the 'rational' and 'symbolic' mechanisms. Normally experience was processed by the rational mechanism. Symbolic processing took place only when the brain was confronted with data that could not be dealt with satisfactorily by normal rational processes. In Sperber's terms, such items did not fit into the 'encyclopaedia' of rational knowledge. Consequently, instead of being treated rationally, they became the object of the symbolic processes of 'focalization' and 'evocation', through which each individual built up the chains of association that constituted his or her personal symbolic universe (Sperber 1975, 1980, 1982, 1985b).

Both Bloch and Sperber, despite their very different starting points, attempted to remedy inadequacies within symbolic anthropology by introducing assumptions about the relationship beween symbolism and human thought processes. Both, too, argued in a more or less explicit way for a shift from a collective (Type II) to an individual (Type I) frame of reference. While these two moves have an obvious relationship to each other, they do not necessarily entail each other, and I shall discuss them separately.

Symbolism and the structure of thought: bimodal and multimodal models

Both Bloch and Sperber wanted to move away from a perspective in which individual thought was dictated by or derived in a strong sense from society, and to restore some degree of autonomy to the individual. Both, therefore, attacked the idea of the closed symbolic universe that they believed to be implied by the symbolic anthropologists (Bloch 1976, Sperber 1975).

Bloch and Sperber were surely right to reject this idea, although it is less clear whether any of the symbolic anthropologists actually believed in the closed symbolic universe in the very strong sense that their critics suggested. Geertz and Turner were certainly aware of the problematic nature of treating concepts as socially determined and culturally uniform.[3]

Nevertheless, the assumption of cultural unity was, as Bloch suggests, implicit in many of the writings of British and American anthropology since the 1930s, Geertz and Turner included. While it was easy enough to point out its limitations, for example in dealing with social change, it was more difficult to put something better in its place. In part this was due precisely to the resistance apparently felt by many anthropologists to introducing explicit assumptions regarding the mechanisms of thought.

While Bloch and Sperber deserve credit for their attempts to find a way out of this *impasse*, the models they employed in their critiques were far too simple. Neither Bloch's opposition of ideological and common-sense knowledge nor Sperber's contrast between the rational and symbolic mechanisms can stand up to much detailed examination.

Essentially both writers made a similar move. Faced with the difficulty of conceptualizing how human beings can be *both* cultural *and* individual at the same time, they attempted to segregate the cultural (i.e. symbolic) and individual into separate categories. Neither author was prepared to allow cultural influences any serious place in structuring rational thought. Thus, for Sperber the encyclopaedia of rational knowledge presumably contained culturally specific material, but this was not *structured* by the symbolic mechanism, which operated in a quite different area. Similarly Bloch held that common-sense thought went on outside the (for him very limited) realm of the symbolic. In seeking to escape from the apparent irrationality and rigidity of the cultural determination of thought, these authors ended up by asserting for human rationality a quite implausible degree of autonomy.

The difficulty results from the essentially *bimodal* nature of Bloch's and Sperber's models, in which common sense is opposed to ideology (Bloch), or rationality is opposed to symbolism (Sperber), as two alternative and mutually exclusive modes of human thought.

The primary difficulty here arises from Bloch's assumption of a sphere of realistic common-sense perception that can form the basis of a critique of the ideological realm, and from Sperber's similar assumption of a sphere of rational thought unpolluted by symbolism. There is little reason to consider that there is such a thing as realistic, innately valid, culturally independent common-sense rationality and plenty of grounds for supposing that there is not. Some of the relevant arguments have been rehearsed in chapter 2, in relation to the collapse of positivism, where it was pointed out that even scientific thought is necessarily pervaded by assumptions that cannot be justified purely on observational grounds.

Yet it seems equally problematic to imply, as some symbolic anthropology comes close to doing, that our thought processes are entirely dictated by our cultural context. We need to find some way of conceptualizing a situation between these two extremes. Bloch's and Sperber's difficulty came about, because their models of human rationality were too simple, operating in effect at only one level.

If Bloch and Sperber had looked at contemporary developments in the philosophy and sociology of science, they could have found models of a more sophisticated kind. Here at least one kind of thought, scientific thought, was increasingly being treated as 'rational' (in the sense of proceeding in a logically coherent manner) and as culturally structured at the same time. Thomas Kuhn's idea of the scientific paradigm was an early attempt to describe precisely such a situation. In more recent years, a substantial body of research has begun to demonstrate the degree to which 'cultural' materials underlie even those areas of natural science that seem well removed from strictly ideological concerns (cf. Mulkay 1979, Samuel 1985a).

What all of these authors do, in one form or another, is to distinguish between (i) underlying and mostly unconscious structures of thought (e.g. Kuhn's paradigms or Karl Popper's metaphysical assumptions) and (ii) rational thought as taking place *within* (in other words, in terms of) these structures. In the terms employed in chapter 2, these correspond to (i) the mapping conventions, by which certain things are agreed as being appropriate to represent upon the map, and ways of representing them decided upon, and (ii) the logically subsequent process of drawing a map. We can refer to models that allow for the coexistence of several different frameworks or paradigms, each of them culturally structured, as *multimodal*. The MMF is a model of this kind.

The distinction between (i) and (ii) is closely analogous to that made by the anthropologist Gregory Bateson between (i) the acquisition of the general 'contexts' of thought and behaviour ('Learning II' or 'deutero-learning') and (ii) the learning of individual items of behaviour within these contexts ('Learning I' or 'proto-learning', cf. Bateson 1973: 133–49, 250–79). Bateson's formulation was first presented in 1942 and substantially revised in the early 1960s. It is significantly more advanced from the anthropological point of view than the formulations of Kuhn and his successors, since it includes the unity of conceptual framework, ethos and behaviour that was to be developed by the interpretive anthropologists. It will be considered further in chapter 5 as an important precursor for the MMF.

The (i)/(ii) distinction also bears a significant family resemblance to the Freudian distinction between 'primary process' and 'secondary process' (cf. Bateson 1973: 111–13). These will again be discussed at more length in chapter 5.

Kuhn, Popper, Imre Lakatos and other philosophers of science disagree to some extent on how encompassing and exclusive the structuring of scientific thought by 'paradigms' or similar structures might be. Even in Kuhn's work the paradigm was not conceived of as totally rigid. It contains, as it were, the seeds of its own dissolution, since it ultimately proves inadequate in maintaining the processes of rational enquiry that it generates, and so it collapses. This brings about a period of competition between paradigms and the eventual emergence of a new paradigm (Kuhn 1970).

It should be noted that this aspect of the paradigm differentiates it from closed systems of rationality such as that postulated by Edward Evans-Pritchard in the case of Zande witchcraft ideas (Evans-Pritchard 1972).[4] While at any given time particular scientific fields or sub-fields may be dominated by a single paradigm, science as a whole contains many paradigms, often conflicting with each other.

The Zande case has occasionally been cited in the literature on the philosophy of science, and the anthropologist Robin Horton has attempted to contrast the relatively 'open' nature of modern scientific thought with the more 'closed' nature of traditional African thinking, on the basis of his own Kalabari field material (Horton 1967). As Bloch and Sperber suggest, and as Horton himself later accepted (Horton 1982), there are strong arguments against assuming total closure in any context, Western scientific or African. Horton's 1967 article is, incidentally, important in relation to the present book for its acceptance of the vocabulary of gods and spirits in African religion as a genuine explanatory system with significant truth-content. This theme is taken up in a rather different form to Horton's in chapters 8 to 10.

In fact, while Evans-Pritchard's Zande study provides a key example of a closed logical system, I do not think that we have to take his account of Zande witchcraft and sorcery beliefs as demonstrating the existence of an entirely closed symbolic universe. Evans-Pritchard himself noted that not all misfortunes were explained in terms of witchcraft and sorcery. If a pot broke during firing, witchcraft might be blamed, but Zande were equally willing to entertain the hypothesis that the potter was incompetent. For that matter, the two modes of explanation that Evans-Pritchard referred to as 'witchcraft' and 'sorcery' were in some respects competing, if closely related, explanatory paradigms.

What studies such as Evans-Pritchard's do suggest is that Bloch and Sperber are on the wrong track when they assume an unstructured model for 'common-sense' thought (Bloch) or 'rational' thought (Sperber). The complex of ideas in Zande society about witchcraft and sorcery undoubtedly reflected the indigenous power structure, as Malcolm McLeod has demonstrated, but it was also one of the standard idioms of everyday ('common-sense') Zande thought (McLeod 1972).

All this leads to one of the central assumptions of the MMF: that something akin to the paradigm model can be used as a description of everyday thought, not simply of specialized scientific thought. The MMF assumes that within any society there is a repertoire of such 'paradigms', each of them constituting a framework of concepts *within which* 'rational thought' may take place. It is further assumed that there is no rational thought (though there may well be something we might want to call 'thought') entirely outside such a framework.[5]

I find it difficult to imagine what rational thought *outside* a framework might conceivably be, although Bloch and Sperber apparently have no problems here. Any rational thought implies a series of initial assumptions and some rules at least for argument, and these assumptions and rules in effect define a 'paradigm' or conceptual framework.[6] Language itself, as has been frequently noted, already encodes an elaborate set of implicit assumptions about the nature of, and the relationships between, the entities it refers to. Here the work of George Lakoff and Mark Johnson on the symbolic (or metaphorical) structures underlying common-sense English-language statements has provided some excellent examples (Lakoff and Johnson 1980, cf. also Keesing 1986).

The MMF's device of a repertoire of culturally provided conceptual frameworks between which individuals switch is itself doubtless too simple to provide a full description of ordinary common-sense thought. It is presented in this book as a model that is nearer to the correct order of complexity (as contrasted with Bloch's and Sperber's simple bimodal models) and that can serve as a basis for further refinement. The MMF assumes that human beings in general have the ability to operate in *several* different 'modes', each involving a different culturally provided framework, and that individuals in some way select an appropriate mode and framework for the situation at hand.

Thus, rather than opposing a 'rational' (or 'common-sense') mode to a 'symbolic' mode, the MMF postulates a series of modes or states of human consciousness, all of which are both 'rational', in that they allow for rational thought, and 'symbolic', in that rational thought within them is culturally structured. It is these 'modal states', which, as was foreshadowed in chapter 1, are not just individual but cultural as well, that provide the variables intrinsic to the social manifold needed to set the Type III reading in motion. They are the central concept of the MMF.

It is probably clear that, if we are to use such a model, then the various 'paradigms' or frameworks used by a particular individual will not necessarily all be of the same degree of complexity. This is not a particularly worrying conclusion, since the same is already true within the more limited realm of scientific paradigms. It is also clear that we will need to allow for the possibility of influence on one framework by another. This is again a process familiar in the context of scientific paradigms, where it constitutes one of the major sources of theoretical innovation.

What the MMF offers us, apart from consistency with recent work in the philosophy of science, is a picture in which there is both structure and freedom. Structure exists at the level of the 'modal state' or conceptual framework. Freedom exists at two levels, that of rational thought within the framework and that of movement between frameworks. This is a substantial improvement on simple determinism or voluntarism, or on the bimodal models suggested by Bloch and Sperber, and it allows us to move on to a crucial next step.

If we are to regard such cultural structuring of thought as being, in effect, what the symbolic anthropologists are talking about, we need to make a linkage between the symbolic mechanism as employed by Geertz or Turner, for example, and the cultural structuring of these frameworks. This is not difficult to do. Geertz already posits a strong cognitive element for his symbols (e.g. Geertz 1973: 87–125). Sperber's processes of 'evocation' and 'focalization', once they are allowed to operate on the structure of rational thought rather than being confined to a special realm of symbolism, give at least an idea of how symbolism and cognition might interrelate.

The next step is to go beyond the simple cultural structuring of thought and to develop a conceptual framework within which we can relate this structuring of thought to processes of political and economic domination. In chapter 1 I cited the late Bob Scholte's observation that

> ...one cannot merely define men and women in terms of the webs of
> significance they themselves spin, since...few do the actual spinning while
> the...majority is simply caught.   (Scholte 1984: 540)

This observation brings us back to the issue of the individual's *manipulation*
of symbols, ideologies and structures of meaning.

Clearly Scholte's point is vital, if we are at all concerned about the
human implications of our theoretical frameworks. As will become clear,
the MMF goes beyond his remark to emphasize that being 'caught' is not
an entirely passive process. Indeed, it is because we collude in our captivity
that we have some hope of escaping from it. At any rate, if there are 'webs
of significance', we are not all in the same relationship to them. We would
seem to need a model of just how the webs are spun, and how and why most
of us simply become caught in them. It will be noted that there is more than
a suggestion in Scholte's formulation that some individuals (the spiders) are
engaged in purposeful spinning. It is hardly possible to say much about
such matters unless we give these individuals, as well as the flies they catch,
a more explicit place in our framework.

This brings us to consider the other implication of the work of Sperber
and Bloch: the move from a social to an individual perspective.

Moving away from cultural unity

I have already noted how Sperber's work moves our attention
away from the supposedly unitary symbolic system belonging to a culture.
In its place Sperber proposes systems created autonomously by individuals
on the basis of the (perhaps culturally given) symbolic material that they
encounter. Bloch's work would seem to carry the same individualist
implication, if less overtly, since it is individuals and groups of individuals
within his schema who are capable of seeing through the mystifications of
culturally prescribed ideology and thus of deciding to take remedial
action. A similar move from a social perspective to an individual perspective
has been urged in recent years by a series of philosophers of social science
whose work derives from Karl Popper's advocacy of 'methodological
individualism' (cf. O'Neill 1973, Agassi 1975).

There are some practical advantages to such a move, and it seems to me
that we need to consider the human individual more explicitly than in, for
example, Geertz's earlier writings (e.g. Geertz 1973: 87–125, 360–411).
Nevertheless, the *a priori* grounds for giving individuals special theoretical
status are no stronger than those for giving such a status to cultures or social
groups, and there are serious difficulties in doing any anthropological
analysis without concepts that operate at a cultural as well as at an
individual level. Those anthropologists who have worked in individualist

terms have in practice assumed some mechanism by which a more or less autonomous cultural level is generated (cf. chapter 4).

Sperber himself has recently sought to reintroduce concepts that operate at a cultural level in a lecture on the 'epidemiology' of cultural representations (Sperber 1985a). Here he seems in practice to be arguing for a position close to that of Geertz's well-known paper on the Balinese cockfight ('Deep play', Geertz 1973: 412–53). Both these papers suggest a kind of dissolution of culture into relatively free-floating cultural fragments, each of which has at least some structuring capacity in relation to human thought. Thus, Geertz speaks of culture as an 'ensemble of texts', while Sperber suggests that we pursue an 'epidemiology' (i.e. a study of patterns of distribution) of 'cultural representations'. The distance between the two models is not very great, if we leave aside the contrast between Geertz's basically hermeneutic orientation and Sperber's rationalism.

These two papers would seem to be on the right lines in looking for a level of analysis intermediate between society and the individual. We can begin to see here the outlines of an approach in which 'culture' (in the Geertzian sense) provides the individual with a series of frameworks that structure thought, feeling and behaviour. The individual uses these frameworks in order to make sense of his or her own life and also to manipulate other individuals. As we shall see in the next chapter, a similar proposal has been made, starting from a rather different direction, by Ward Goodenough, who speaks of individuals as having a range of 'operating cultures' (Goodenough 1963: 259–62 and 1981: 98–9).

Using the MMF's terms, one can speak of modal states at the (Geertzian) 'cultural' level, and of modal states at the individual level. Depending on the success or failure of the use of 'individual' modal states in interpersonal transactions, particular 'cultural' modal states may become more or less prominent within a social group, so that the 'culture' of that group (in the Geertzian sense) is affected over time by the agency of individuals. It is important to remember that both 'individual' and 'cultural' modal states are derivative quantities. The whole idea of a Type III framework such as the MMF implies that the modal states proper exist at the level of the social manifold, and that 'individual' and 'culture' are secondary and derivative concepts. Where necessary, the three types of modal states are indicated by the abbreviations MS_c, MS_i and MS_m for modal states at the cultural level, at the individual level and at the level of the manifold (the modal states proper).

In other words, the MMF as formulated in this book deliberately avoids treating either the individual or the group level as primary. The choice between the two is an impossible one, unless the question is begged by prior theoretical commitment to one position or the other, yielding a Type I or

Type II reductionism accordingly. This suggests that the question itself (i.e. of which level is primary) is wrongly phrased, and that we would do well to reformulate the problem. This is one of the major reasons for the move to a Type III reading.

The issues considered in the preceding sections are central to the theoretical argument of the book, and it is worth clarifying some of the issues involved by taking a different perspective.

Geertz and Bloch: contrasting structurings of the 'flow'

In chapter 1 I introduced the concept of the 'social manifold' as the most general conceivable description of the social universe, and I also presented the 'flow of relatedness' as an image of this manifold. The question of developing a theoretical framework can be phrased as follows: What kind of structure do we place upon this 'flow of relatedness' in order to describe it? Along with this goes a second question: What assumptions are implicit in the structure or construction that we place upon the flow?

Let us consider what is involved in the case of two of the theorists discussed above, Clifford Geertz and Maurice Bloch. We can say that the theoretical framework behind Geertz's works of the mid-1960s, such as 'Religion as a cultural system' and 'Person, time, and conduct in Bali', imposes a certain structure on the general field or flow of 'relatedness', emphasizing certain aspects of that flow. The framework underlying Maurice Bloch's critique of Geertz's articles implies a different structuring of the flow and emphasizes certain other aspects.

Each of the two frameworks builds in specific assumptions about the internal structure of the flow. These assumptions may seem so natural to the theorist (or the casual reader) as to be unnoticeable. This is one reason why discussions between people using different 'paradigms' tend to be unsatisfactory and inconclusive. However, when particular assumptions are brought into the open, their deficiencies and inadequacies may become more apparent.

We can spell this out more explicitly for the cases of Geertz and Bloch. The concepts used by these two theorists constitute reifications or 'crystallizations' of particular insights into the nature of the 'flow of relatedness'. These insights did not originate with Geertz and Bloch, although Geertz and Bloch formulated them in ways that are personal to each of them.

Thus Geertz's framework, as has been frequently recognized, was a reformulation of the insight whose classical exponent was Emile Durkheim: that ritual and religious symbolism, along with other aspects of human behaviour, operate so as to maintain the solidarity of the social group.

40

Geertz's primary concepts in the two papers mentioned differed considerably in detail but were identical in basic structure (i.e. in their underlying theoretical framework). In each case they encapsulated this particular insight. They highlighted those aspects of the flow that contribute to the maintenance of social solidarity, and they ignored or played down those that do not.

This was to some degree explicit, as in the famous definition of religion that forms the basis of 'Religion as a cultural system':

> Religion is a system of symbols which acts to establish powerful, pervasive, and long-lasting moods and motivations in men by formulating conceptions of a general order of existence and clothing these conceptions with such an aura of factuality that the moods and motivations seem uniquely realistic. (Geertz 1973: 90)

Here the maintenance of social solidarity and group cohesion is in the foreground. However, it should be noted that the static and collective nature of Geertz's framework was also present at an implicit level, in the concepts and in the way they were used. It belonged, in other words, to the theoretical framework, rather than to the specific theory about the nature of religion that was here being stated in terms of that framework.

Thus the definition did not necessarily imply that the moods, motivations and conceptions were uniform throughout a particular society. Nor did it state explicitly that they remained constant throughout time. Yet, this static and collective orientation was assumed in Geertz's usage of his concepts both in this paper and in 'Person, time, and conduct'. The whole idea of 'symbols' is, after all, that they constitute a means by which continuity can be assured.[7] The symbol does not change through time, and it is poorly adapted to cope with those aspects of the 'flow' that do change through time.

Consequently, at the end of 'Person, time, and conduct', Geertz was unable to say more about cultural change in Bali than that, once the symbolic constellation (the 'cultural triangle of forces') that he had outlined breaks down, the whole society would change drastically.

If we consider now Bloch's Malinowski Lecture, in which a critique of 'Person, time, and conduct' played an important role, it is evident that it was precisely these implicit characteristics of the Geertzian (and Durkheimian) structuring of the 'flow' that Bloch objected to. Yet Bloch, in his lecture, put forward a structuring of the field that was equally shot through with questionable implicit assumptions.

For Geertz, the aspects of interpersonal communication and of 'relatedness' that were of interest were those that maintained the solidarity of the society. For Bloch, the aspects of interest were those that maintained or subverted the class interests of individuals or groups within the society.

41

Bloch's intellectual lineage here went back not to Durkheim, but to Karl Marx, albeit in a vulgarized form.

Bloch's whole conceptual framework was intended to highlight those aspects of the onward 'flow' that were to do with the *manipulation* of ideas and concepts by the dominant group in order to maintain the power structure or by the subordinate group in order to attack it. Other aspects, consequently, were played down or dismissed. In order to maintain the simplicity and integrity of his own framework, Bloch had to deny the validity of Geertz's. Specifically, he was driven to treat the symbolic structuring of thought as peripheral to human consciousness, and he claimed that it applies only to a strictly limited realm of ideological thought.

This was because Bloch was unable (or unwilling) to see the symbols and concepts of religious or political ideologies as both providing a basis for unity and providing a basis for manipulation. It would appear that for Bloch manipulation had to be both deliberate and fully conscious. Consequently, a population had to be either in a state of confusion created by the power of ruling-class ideology over it or in a state of common-sense clarity. This false dichotomy led Bloch to treat religious concepts purely as a form of conceptual mystification that lay outside of the mainstream of human rationality.

I have already pointed out that Bloch's contrasting of ideology and common-sense rationality implied an over-simple view of human thought processes. One might indeed say the same of Geertz's framework, at any rate as presented in his 1960s papers. For one thing, functionalist idealizations apart, neither societies nor human beings are static. A more complex theoretical framework is evidently needed, one that is capable of considering both the structuring of the flow and the processes of manipulation within it: both 'process' ('agency', in Giddens' terminology) and 'structure'.

This is what the MMF is intended to do. At this point we can return to the idea of a body of 'modal states' and see how it offers the possibility of a degree of synthesis of the 'process' and 'structure' perspectives. Where Geertz saw 'structure' as being simply reproduced along the onward flow of the stream until it broke down irretrievably, and Bloch saw the flow merely as the result of conscious manipulation ('process' or 'agency'), we now have a less limiting alternative.

This involves regarding the character of the flow at any point as being describable in terms of the relative significance of the various modal states present within the flow. As we move along the flow, particular states become more or less significant, and the overall character of the flow can change more or less gradually. The *kind* of process or agency that can take place at any point depends on the particular mix of states at that point. In this picture there is room for both change and continuity. This is because it is a more general framework than that used by either Geertz or Bloch.

Geertz's position, in his mid-1960s writings, implied that at any time there was only one modal state of any significance present within a particular society, and that it could either reproduce itself without significant change or break down into a period of disorder. As Geertz himself had clearly realized by the time of such papers as 'Deep play', this was an inadequate picture, but Geertz's later work has offered little beyond the 'ensemble of texts' to put in its place. Indeed, Geertz in his more recent writings seems, as I suggested in chapter 2, to have renounced the whole project of an overall framework for understanding human behaviour.

In relation to Bloch's position the key point is that *any* modal state, through its associated body of concepts, highlights certain aspects of reality, while leaving other aspects invisible or only dimly perceived. Consequently all modal states involve some degree of mystification and confusion, and some degree of insight and clarity.

I am not asserting here that all 'paradigms' are equally mystifying, although the question of the extent to which we may be able to speak of degrees of insight is a difficult one that I shall not examine explicitly in this book.[8] I am merely pointing out that it is not necessarily true that rebellion against an established order arises from a clear-sighted vision of how things 'really are'. We may well abhor exploitation and injustice, but we are being naive if we choose to believe that revolutionaries always understand the structure against which they are fighting. Still less do we need to assume that the ruling class's ability to exploit implies that they can see, as it were, through their own ideological smokescreen. The MMF implies that insight within the 'flow of relatedness' is always partial. Indeed, as Bateson has argued, total insight may simply be incompatible with ordinary human functioning (1973: 114–16).

Our examination of Geertz and Bloch has highlighted the need for a more careful look at the kind of concepts we use in anthropology and the social sciences generally. The task of developing appropriate concepts seems indeed to be fraught with traps and pitfalls for the unwary. This is particularly so when we are concerned, as we will be in the present work, with concepts as rich in associations and as personally significant to many of us as equality, domination, ideology, hierarchy and the like.[9]

In chapter 5, we shall proceed, with due caution, with the development of the central concepts of our new framework, the MMF. Before doing so, it is worth examining how the problems discussed in this chapter have been dealt with by social scientists working within Type I (individualist) frameworks. This will be the subject of chapter 4.

4   Starting points II

In this chapter we examine some other developments in US cultural anthropology, sociology and linguistics that are relevant to the construction of the MMF. We will consider two main groups of social scientists. The first consists of cultural anthropologists active at the University of Pennsylvania, in particular Anthony Wallace and Ward Goodenough. The second is a more diverse group of sociologists, sociolinguists and other scholars including Erving Goffman, Albert Scheflen, Dell Hymes, John Gumperz, George Lakoff and Mark Johnson. Both groups of scholars worked in various ways on the description of cultural processes, and their approaches are worth considering both as prefiguring the MMF and in order to clarify where the MMF goes beyond and contrasts with their approaches.

Wallace and Goodenough

We begin with Anthony Wallace and Ward Goodenough. The contrast between interpretive anthropology and the kind of anthropology represented by these scholars emerges clearly in Goodenough's distinction between 'culture' and 'cultural artefacts' (Goodenough 1963: 265ff., 1981: 50), and in his associated rejection of Geertz's approach to culture in terms of symbols and their meaning:

> For Geertz, culture is both the acts as symbols and their meaning. He focuses on the artefacts – exposure to artefacts is what people share – and states that these artefacts as public symbols and the public meaning they have acquired in social exchanges constitute culture. We take the position that culture consists of the criteria people use to discern the artefacts as having distinctive forms and the criteria people use to attribute meaning

to them. We address the problem of how these criteria, which are individually learned in social exchanges, can be said to be public at all, a problem Geertz does not address.

If we stop where Geertz does, we cannot readily account for the fact that people experience novel events and find them immediately meaningful, like a newly devised trick play in football or a newly created poem or musical composition. Our approach goes further and is concerned with the cognitive and emotional factors that make it possible for the novel to be meaningful. These factors, which form the ultimate locus of culture, help explain how culture as Geertz defines it can exist at all.

(Goodenough 1981: 59)

For Goodenough in 1963 and 1981, as in Wallace's work in the 1950s and 1960s, culture was something that was learned by individual human beings. Where the interpretive anthropologists looked for culture as something public, as describable in terms of Type II quantities, for the Pennsylvania theorists culture was acquired and possessed by individual human beings, and ultimately described by Type I variables.

It is clear that what is at issue here is not simply the usage of that notoriously slippery term 'culture'. Goodenough's view of culture was premised on an entirely different approach to anthropological explanation. It was by no means a simple reaction to Geertz's work, but grew logically out of the kinds of theory he and Wallace had been exploring over the previous decades. Whereas the interpretive anthropologists' predilection for Type II explanation ultimately went back to Durkheim, with a lineage passing mainly through Talcott Parsons for Geertz, through Radcliffe-Brown and Max Gluckman for Turner, the Pennsylvania theorists' preference for Type I explanation was associated with a different, primarily American, theoretical background. A major constituent of this background was the American tradition of psychological anthropology, and of culture and personality studies, familiar through the work of cultural anthropologists such as Ruth Benedict and Margaret Mead, or through the cross-cultural research on child socialization of John Whiting and Irving Child. Another important influence was the social interactionist approach in American sociology, deriving from George Herbert Mead.

Consequently, anthropologists such as Goodenough and Wallace approached the question of shared human cultures from the opposite end to Geertz, Turner or Lévi-Strauss. Whereas the interpretive anthropologists were tempted to see culture as a unity existing at the social level and only gradually started to move towards a more fragmented approach in the 1970s and 1980s, the Pennsylvania theorists began at the level of individual psychology and gradually built up to some degree of unity at the social level.

Consider, for example, the extended theoretical statement that forms

Part 1 of Goodenough's *Cooperation in Change* (1963). This begins from the individual human being's 'wants' (desired states of affairs) and 'needs' (the effective means to achieve those states). Goodenough classifies different 'customs' as reflecting the ways in which individuals in different societies learn how to meet various 'universal needs' (chapters 3 and 4). Subsequently, he derives the common 'values' of groups from (individual) personal 'sentiments', and he explains various aspects of social life in terms of the need to deal with the conflicts between different sets of common values (chapter 5). 'Beliefs' are significant as providing a 'coherent cognitive organization of experience' (Goodenough 1963: 146) that is a necessary precondition for purposive human action.

> Ultimately all beliefs have some connection with behaviour... [T]hey provide the means whereby people orient themselves to their surroundings in ways they find gratifying. (1963: 157)

Beliefs for Goodenough provided the linkage between our perceptions of our environment and the specifically cultural explanations of the universe that we accept (cf. also Black 1973: 512–15, 521–3, 526). He saw them as closely connected with the coding of perception intrinsic in learning a language (cf. also Goodenough 1981: 63–74).

Goodenough criticized the suggestion that shared beliefs are necessary for social cooperation, citing Wallace's demonstration (Wallace 1966a: 29–41) that

> it is unnecessary for the participants in a social system to have the same conceptual picture of it or to believe the same things about matters of common interest for social relations to proceed harmoniously and for the social system to work smoothly. (Goodenough 1963: 172)

In a later paper Goodenough returned to this point, suggesting that the existence of multiple 'microcultures' was characteristic of human experience even in simple societies (1978). Here we can see, from another perspective, a development similar in its implications to Sperber's 'epidemiology' of cultural representations or to Geertz's 'ensemble of texts'. For Goodenough such a position was much less threatening than for the Type II theorists, since all through his work he has tended to consider social quantities as essentially derivative from, and secondary to, individual variables. As a consequence, their unity or diversity was for him not particularly worrying, whereas for the Type II theorists, as we have seen in chapter 3, it constituted a substantial problem.

The relative openness to biology of these theorists in comparison with their Type II counterparts is also worth noting. Anthropologists such as Wallace and Goodenough saw culture from the beginning as something that should in principle be integrated with biology. Thus, Wallace in *Culture and Personality* (1966a) viewed culture explicitly as part of the process of biological evolution. He gave an extended discussion of 'proto-cultural' systems among non-human animals and of the nature of the transitions to human cultural systems (1966a: 45–62). Wallace linked the transition to a dramatic increase in brain size in hominid species coinciding with the invention of stone tools, speculated on the factors involved (pp. 66–71) and proceeded to examine the general effect of culture on the genetic evolution of the human brain (pp. 72–83). Such questions were not even considered by British social anthropologists of the period or by their American 'Type II' colleagues.[1]

Identity, the self-image and the mazeway

One of the most significant aspects for the MMF of the work of these theorists is their interest in processes of identity formation and self-image, and particularly the relationship that they drew between these processes and social transformation. Wallace's work on the 'mazeway', and his account of mazeway resynthesis as a central aspect of societal 'revitalization' is worth special attention.

Wallace introduced the concepts of 'mazeway' and of 'revitalization movement' in two articles dating from 1956. The 'mazeway' was a concept intended to cover the individual's personal representation of the whole area of self, body-image, personality, and acquired cultural and social competence:

> ... as a model of the cell–body–personality–nature–culture–society system or field, organized by the individual's own experience, it includes perceptions of both the maze of physical objects of the environment (internal and external, human and nonhuman) and also of the ways in which this maze can be manipulated by the self and others in order to minimize stress. The mazeway is nature, society, culture, personality, and body image, as seen by one person. (Wallace 1956a: 264)

In his other 1956 paper, Wallace provided a more detailed psychological account of the mazeway (1956b); a further description can be found in *Culture and Personality* (1966a: 16–20).

Wallace used 'revitalization movement' as a general term for a range of processes of social transformation. These included 'cargo cults' and 'millenarian movements' as well as the prophetic impulses at the beginning of minor and major religious cults. According to Wallace '[b]oth Christianity and Mohammedanism, and possibly Buddhism as well, originated in revitalization movements' (1956a: 267). Such movements took place at a point where individuals within a society were no longer able to find an adequate response to the stresses they were undergoing. The members of the society responded by changing the mazeway, which in its turn generated an attempt to change their social and physical environment:

> The effort to work a change in mazeway and 'real' system together so as to permit more effective stress reduction is the effort at revitalization; and the collaboration of a number of persons in such an effort is called a revitalization movement.   (1956a: 267)

What Wallace provided in these papers was an account of how social change took place at the conceptual level, a solution, in fact, to the problem posed by Bloch some seventeen years later in his Malinowski Lecture (see chapter 3). Bloch was right (if not especially original) in pointing to the difficulty that Durkheim-derived approaches such as those of the Geertzians had in dealing with social change. Wallace's solution, unlike Bloch's own proposal, did not make the unrealistic assumption that social change derives from some kind of veridical insight into the nature of exploitation. It merely suggested that stress leads to a transformation in 'mazeway', which may, if widely enough supported, lead to social action and transformation.

Another aspect of Wallace's approach to revitalization movements was his emphasis on the role of dreams and visions in these movements. This is a theme to which we shall return in chapter 9:

> With a few exceptions, every religious revitalization movement with which I am acquainted has been originally conceived in one or several hallucinatory visions by a single individual. A supernatural being appears to the prophet-to-be, explains his own and his society's troubles as being entirely or partly a result of the violation of certain rules, and promises individual and social revitalization if the injunctions are followed and the rituals practised, but personal and social catastrophe if they are not.
>   (1956a: 270)

Wallace's suggestion that 'revitalization movements' generally originate in visionary revelations, rather than in mechanisms of pure rationality or common-sense, contrasts markedly with Bloch's assumption that such processes originate from common sense. In societies where the process Max Weber referred to as 'rationalization' is far advanced, programmes for social innovation may well have aspects of 'scientific' rationality, perhaps typified by the familiar figure of Karl Marx at his desk in the Reading Room of the British Museum. Yet if we look at the creation of new modal states in a more general cross-cultural context, the typical human agents are shamans and prophets rather than exponents of hard-headed common-sense rationality. Nor was Marx himself all that far from this tradition.[2] He was, after all, as has often been remarked, one of the most successful prophets in history.

The idea of mazeway resynthesis and of revitalization movements, adopted also by Goodenough (1963: 286–321), was still framed within the context of a normal static condition of society interrupted by occasional radical breaks. We might consider how far 'mazeway resyntheses' of greater and lesser degree form part of the ongoing process of society. Certainly some examples are more dramatic and larger in scale than others, but even movements such as the 'cargo cults' of Melanesia or the prophetic movements of the Southern Sudan are now beginning to look more like a regular mode of response to social change (cf. chapter 9). We are also becoming more aware that stasis is an exception, not a rule, in social life. Societies may indeed incorporate homeostatic mechanisms, as Wallace (1956a: 265) and others have suggested, but they nevertheless change, and not merely as a result of external pressure. In the MMF it is suggested that the creation of new modal states (which may be taken as roughly equivalent to Wallace's mazeways, in this context) and the growth and fading in importance of particular modal states, is a continuing process and corresponds to the continuing transformation of social life.

Goodenough also dealt with identity formation, self-image and self-worth at length in *Cooperation in Change*. This book constructed a close linkage between identity change and community development in terms close to Wallace's work on mazeway resynthesis (1963: 176–251). The emphasis on the self and its construction was entirely typical of this group of writers, and can be traced back to the interest in such questions by American sociologists such as C. H. Cooley and George Herbert Mead, and to Goodenough's predecessor at Pennsylvania, Irving Hallowell, who discussed the self at length in a major theoretical essay dating from 1951 (1955: 75–110 and 172–82). By contrast, the self as a subject of study for British and American anthropologists in the Durkheimian (Type II) tradition emerged only gradually and indirectly during the 1960s and 1970s, and it is only in the last decade or so that it has emerged as a major topic (e.g. Heelas and Lock 1981, Carrithers, Collins and Lukes 1985, Kapferer 1979; cf. also Ortner 1984: 151).[3]

Limitations of Type I cultural anthropology

There is much that is relevant and useful for the MMF in the work of Wallace and Goodenough and the American cultural anthropology tradition. In particular, their work on the construction of the self is of direct relevance to the concept of the individual modal state in the MMF (cf. chapter 6). The MMF treats values, beliefs, wants and needs (to keep Goodenough's terminology) as varying between individuals and avoids treating 'society' as any kind of assemblage of uniformly socialized people. In these respects, it is quite compatible with the work of Wallace and Goodenough.

Nevertheless, there are points at which the MMF diverges sharply from the work of Goodenough or Wallace. These are concerned, as might be expected, with the move from Type I to Type III variables and the whole question of the position of cultural, social and structural factors within social theory.

Goodenough regarded Geertz's account of 'culture' as essentially incomplete, as lacking any explanation (in terms of processes at the individual level) of why such a phenomenon should exist at all. The response of interpretive anthropologists to 'culture' as conceived of by Goodenough or Wallace would probably have been that the specifically social object of study in which they were interested had been dissolved into a mere assemblage of individual psychological processes. Even such an intrinsically social phenomenon as language is treated by Goodenough as an assemblage of idiolects (1981: 19–36). The fact of individual variation is not in question, but consistent reductionism of this kind makes it difficult to justify explanations or theories of an explicitly sociological kind. There is no doubt that the macrosystem takes second place in the work of Goodenough and Wallace. Sociological phenomena are regarded as emerging in some form from essentially individual variables.

The dichotomy between human agency and individual variation on the one side, system and structure on the other, is the essence of the conflict between Type I and Type II approaches, and it goes back to basic questions of the nature of scientific explanation. While it is conceptually possible to analyse, say, the laws of English grammar as a simple aggregate of the learned practices of hundreds of millions of individual English speakers or to treat a Tibetan ritual as a mere average of millions of ways in which that ritual has been and will be performed, it is hardly practicable, nor do Goodenough and his colleagues do so in their ethnographic work. Agassi's prescriptions for 'methodological individualism' raise the same problem (Agassi 1975).

I am unclear how far Goodenough's or Wallace's work derives from a philosophical commitment to methodological individualism. I suspect that the human individual in their writings had its central place more because of an implicit acceptance of human beings, as creatures with certain properties and capacities, as the appropriate starting point for anthropological theory. In either case, though, the assumption of the human individual as the basic explanatory unit is open to question. Its inherent plausibility derives from its closeness to the way in which human beings, and particularly human beings who have been socialized within a modern

Western society, learn to conceptualize their universe. However, that is precisely the problem behind accepting such an assumption at face value. It is for this reason that the idea of a Type III reading of the social manifold, and the MMF as an example of such a reading, is presented in this book.

This is one of the central arguments in the book, and it may be worth spelling it out in a little more detail. There are two parts to the argument:

    (i) anthropology as a consistent science needs to operate with variables that are all the same 'Type'.
    (ii) This type should be neither Type I, nor Type II, but Type III.

Part (i) of the argument derives from the idea of anthropology as a 'natural science of society', in other words as science-like in that it operates with a consistent body of concepts. If anthropology is a heuristic collection of techniques for describing variations between human groups, then there is no reason why it should not operate with an unsystematic mixture of Type I and Type II terms, incorporating, for example, both social factors and individual psychological and cognitive processes. There is no doubt that much good anthropological research has been done in this way.

Anthropology as a science, however, cannot operate in this manner. Social and individual factors are not part of the same domain of enquiry. They are incompatible terms. The locus of explanation has to be either in the individual (Type I) or in the society (Type II) or somewhere else, such as the 'social manifold' (Type III). It cannot be in two or three of these places at once.

Those theorists who have tried to construct a consistent theoretical approach using both social and individual terms have ultimately had to come down on one side or the other. The mixture of Durkheim, Max Gluckman and Sigmund Freud in some of Victor Turner's earlier analyses (e.g. *The Drums of Affliction*, 1968) might serve as a case in point, and it is clear from Turner's later writing (e.g. 1975: 29–33, 1985: 205–26, 249–90) that he found his approach in those earlier studies unsatisfactory.

Part (ii) of the argument is about on which of these three levels we should situate our basic terms. We have already seen, in chapter 3, that Type II terms, for all their attractiveness, do not provide a satisfactory basis for a social theory. The response of critics such as Sperber and Bloch, and of some of the interpretive anthropologists, including Turner (1985: 249–90), has been to turn to Type I terms and to seek to ground their theories, ultimately, in biological assumptions about individual human beings.

This is not really satisfactory either. Dumont was surely right about the fundamental 'sociological apperception'. Social scientists have come from necessity to accept the existence of forces that operate at a level beyond the individual and that affect and shape the individual (1970: 39ff.). Such forces cannot be adequately understood in a conceptual framework where some specific model of individuals, their structure and motivation is taken for granted, as has to be the case in any Type I framework. The mistake of Type II theorists was to locate the supra-individual forces within 'society', which turned out to be an even less coherent and satisfactory concept than that of the human individual. Where they should be located was first, I believe, pointed out by Gregory Bateson: in the relationships between human individuals, and between humans and their environment, in what he referred to as an 'ecology of mind' (1973) and I have spoken of in this book as a 'flow of relatedness'. This is the essence of a Type III framework.

Some theorists of social interaction and its communicative aspects

We now turn to examine a second group of social scientists, who have in common an interest in the analysis of social interaction and particularly of the role within social interaction of linguistic and paralinguistic processes. We begin with Erving Goffman, whose work, especially in its later phases, has many points of contact with the MMF, and we continue to examine some other analysts of communicative processes.

Goffman's early work, in books such as *The Presentation of Self in Everyday Life* (1959) and *Asylums* (1961), was part of an opening up of sociology to the detailed analysis of small-scale, face-to-face interaction. From the point of view of the MMF, these stages of Goffman's work are significant mainly for the attention they directed on the complexity of human interaction and on the kinds of resources used by individuals in bringing off interaction successfully.

Goffman, along with Harold Garfinkel and the ethnomethodologists, did much to demolish the apparent obviousness of everyday human life in Western industrial society and to constitute it as something that needed serious study. In this sense, his work has been described as a kind of ethnography, implying a parallel with the analysis of 'exotic' societies by anthropologists (e.g. Black 1973: 535). However, Goffman's close analysis of impression management, manipulative behaviour and game-playing in human interaction had few real precedents in ethnographic research by anthropologists.

In Goffman's later work, in particular the books *Frame Analysis* (1974) and *Forms of Talk* (1981), he developed the concept of the 'frame' in social interaction in a way highly suggestive for the MMF. We have already met, in chapter 3, the idea of human beings as shifting between modal states.

There I suggested that Bloch's and Sperber's criticisms of interpretive anthropology could be more satisfactorily met by this kind of model. Goffman's 'frame' corresponds closely to the conceptual aspects of the 'modal state', and his analyses of how changes between frames are signalled and managed is of direct relevance to the MMF.

Such processes are not carried out through ordinary language alone, but through paralinguistic cues such as stress and intonation. Goffman's work is highly sensitive to such mechanisms. There is an overlap here with the work of Albert Scheflen and others who have analysed the role of movement, gesture, facial expression and the like in human interaction (Scheflen and Scheflen 1972). Once again we find a continuum between 'mind' and 'body' in these processes, which are neither fully conscious, for the most part, nor entirely unconscious.

The linguistic and paralinguistic side of these exchanges and frame-transitions was also studied in some detail in the 1970s by sociolinguists and anthropological linguists involved in the area that Dell Hymes referred to as the 'ethnography of speaking' or (more generally) the 'ethnography of communication' (Hymes 1974a, 1974b, cf. also Gumperz and Hymes 1972). Elaborate processes of frame-shifting through metaphor, through shifts in language level or code or through the subtle manipulation of 'sociolinguistic rules' (cf. Erwin-Tripp 1972, 1974) were uncovered. This material provided both a substantial body of data about 'frames' (or modal states) and about transitions between them, and considerable information about how these states operate and are mobilized in sequences of human interaction.

George Lakoff's and Mark Johnson's work on metaphor in language, already mentioned briefly in chapter 3, shares several features with the ethnographers of communication. In particular, Lakoff and Johnson demonstrated in detail the often quite complex structures of explanation implicit in our ordinary use of language (Lakoff and Johnson 1980). Their work provides valuable support for the idea that the modal state has an intrinsic structure of reasoning associated with it, and for the whole idea of 'informal knowledge' (cf. chapter 1) as capable of being modelled by paradigm-type concepts.

Limitations of interaction theorists

The limitations of Goffman and the other scholars considered in the last sections, from the point of view of the MMF, are perhaps twofold. In the first place, they did not attempt to situate metaphors or frames in any kind of overall theory of mind–body functioning. Consequently, their work provides no clear picture of how the metaphors or frames are grounded in the individual as an active and creative entity. Goffman's image of the individual as an actor or game-player (cf. Geertz 1985) leaves a kind of gap at the core of the explanation. The individual has wants, needs, goals, patterns of action: but where do they come from? Here the cultural anthropologists, not surprisingly, have more to say, and some of Wallace's and Goodenough's most useful contributions (e.g. the mazeway) are in this area of theorizing the individual as a totality.

The other area of difficulty is that of the individual–society relationship, given little attention in general by Goffman or the linguistic scholars. In Goffman's case this goes along with the strong microsociological orientation of his work. Also, the emphasis on language and on other shared behavioural codes by all these theorists makes it easier to treat the individual–society relationship as uncontroversial and to take it, in effect, for granted.

The learning of a shared human language is not a perfectly understood process, by a long way, but it is not in question that it does take place and that we can define idiolects for each individual which are closely and systematically related to the language of the group. For 'culture' in general the situation is much more problematic. Sperber's critiques of symbolic anthropology made much of the argument that symbolism is *not* a language and so cannot be assumed to be shared in the way that languages are shared by their speakers.

The MMF implies that Sperber's view of language was too simple, as indeed does the work of Goffman, Lakoff and the others considered in the previous section. Language, too, is structured by metaphor and symbolism, by underlying frames and contexts. Nevertheless, taking language as a subject of study does make some of the difficult questions concerning the relationship between individual and society seem less urgent. Goodenough's emphasis on linguistic material and on the linguistic analogy (especially in Goodenough 1981) has a somewhat similar effect. This is not to say that language is not a vital part of human socialization, but to suggest that the acquisition of a shared language, and the relationship between that language and the ways in which its speakers use it, is in its way as mysterious and as poorly understood as the acquisition of other shared cultural material. The arguments presented earlier in the chapter for a Type III framework such as the MMF apply as strongly here as elsewhere.

Conclusion

In relation to the MMF, we can see that the theorists considered in this chapter have provided a variety of useful tools and parallels. These include the idea of alternating frames or paradigms of thought (Goffman), the idea of mazeways or other conceptual structures that are intimately connected to ethos and culture (Wallace, Goodenough), mazeway resynthesis as a mechanism for innovation (Wallace) and a general willingness to see human beings as shifting between a variety of conceptual-emotional frameworks (e.g. Wallace, Goodenough, Goffman, Lakoff). All of these are incorporated in various ways into the MMF. Their work also provides suggestions about how to deal with areas not discussed in any detail in this book, such as how transitions between modal states take place.

There is also at least a suggestion in the work of Wallace that mazeways or similar structures can be extended to cover body as well as mind (e.g. Wallace 1966a: 17–20). This suggestion is developed further and more systematically in the MMF through the concept of the modal state.

The other key proposal of the MMF apart from the modal state is the 'social manifold' or 'flow of relatedness' within which the modal states exist. The main subject of chapter 5 will be a detailed consideration of this 'flow'. In discussing how the modal state operates I shall make use of the ideas of one more theorist, Gregory Bateson, who has been mentioned briefly in both chapters 3 and 4. Bateson was connected with both British social anthropology (through his initial training) and the American cultural tradition (through his association with Margaret Mead and the culture and personality school), but developed in a highly individual direction. His emphasis on patterns of relationship and connectedness as the appropriate field for social analysis has been probably the strongest direct influence on the MMF, and especially on the 'flow of relatedness'.

5   Interpreting the flow

We have arrived at a point where we can consider the central concept of the MMF, the 'modal state', in rather more detail. In chapter 3 we have considered how different theoretical frameworks (Geertz's and Bloch's) placed different structures upon the generalized 'flow of relatedness' introduced in chapter 1. We also noted that the 'modal state' had some of the features of a scientific paradigm in the Kuhnian sense. It, too, in other words, places a 'structure' on the 'flow of relatedness'. In the present chapter we shall examine some of the implications of a concept such as the 'modal state'. What does it mean to say that the 'modal states' structure the 'flow of relatedness'?

Modal states at the individual level

This issue is initially simplest to approach in terms of the operation of the modal state at the level of the individual (the MS_i). At the individual level, the state's 'structuring' action functions so as to provide a structuring of experience for the individual who is operating in that state. The question of the structuring of experience has been explored in considerable detail by the anthropologist Gregory Bateson and some of his associates, and I now turn to look at some ideas from their work. This will also provide an opportunity to clarify where the MMF stands in relation to some other relevant ideas, such as the Freudian unconscious.

Bateson's work was referred to briefly in chapter 3, where it was suggested that the two contrasted terms 'Learning II' and 'Learning I' could be seen as parallel to (a) the acquisition of 'underlying and mostly unconscious structures of thought' (such as Kuhnian paradigms or the MMF's modal states), and (b) the operation of 'rational' thought within these structures. I referred to him again briefly in chapter 4 as suggesting the MMF's emphasis on 'relatedness'. Here we shall consider a series of concepts developed by Bateson as part of his account of the process of Learning II. These concepts are the 'context', the 'context marker' and, in particular, what Bateson calls the 'punctuation' of the stream of experience, a key element in various forms in much of his later work (Bateson 1973: 250–79, 1979, 1987).

A specific 'context' is in effect a way of seeing or interpreting the stream of ongoing experience. While that 'context' is in force, specific items within the stream of experience function as 'context markers', marking off significant sequences, and the stream is split up or 'punctuated' accordingly.

In an essay originally written in 1964, Bateson gave a highly abstract example of a sequence of interaction between two individuals A and B, consisting of a series of items of behaviour $(a_1b_1a_2b_2a_3b_3a_4b_4a_5b_5...)$ where A's action a_1 is followed by B's action b_1, A's action a_2 and so on. Bateson noted that there are three simple possible 'contexts' within which A may view any particular action. If we consider a_3, for example, A may take this as (1) the beginning of a sequence $(a_3b_3a_4)$; (2) the centre of a sequence $(b_2a_3b_3)$; or (3) the end of a sequence $(a_2b_2a_3)$. These correspond to ways that A may view his behaviour. In the learning-theory vocabulary that Bateson was then using, these can be stated as follows: A may view his action (1) as a *stimulus* for B, (2) as a *response* to B, (3) as a *reinforcement* of B's response to A's previous stimulus.

In addition, even within this very simple and schematic analysis, there are further possibilities, since A may simply not regard B's behaviour as relevant to A's behaviour and may analyse his actions within a framework that excludes B. Thus a_3

> may also be a stimulus for A; it may be A's reinforcement of self; or it may be A's response to some previous behaviour of his own, as is the case in sequences of rote behaviour. This general ambiguity [of how the sequence is to be punctuated] means in fact that the ongoing sequence of interchange between two persons is structured only by the person's own perception of the sequence as a series of contexts, each context leading into the next. (Bateson 1973: 270)

For Bateson, these contexts were acquired as part of the process of learning a particular culture, a process that he referred to as 'Learning II':

> The particular manner in which the sequence is structured by any particular person will be determined by that person's previous Learning II (or possibly by his genetics). In such a system, words like 'dominant' and 'submissive', 'succouring' and 'dependent' will take on definable meaning as descriptions of segments of interchange. (Bateson 1973: 270)

For example, Bateson suggests that we may speak of *A* dominating *B* in a situation where *A* and *B*

> show by their behaviour that they see their relationship as characterized by sequences of the type $(a_1 b_1 a_2)$ where a_1 is seen (by *A* and *B*) as a signal defining conditions of instrumental reward or punishment; b_1 as a signal or act obeying these conditions; and a_2 as a signal reinforcing b_1.
>
> (Bateson 1973: 270)

Even in Bateson's very simple and schematic example it is possible to see how the different logically possible contexts or frameworks have attributes that can be interpreted in terms of 'character' and that are concerned as much with the structure of *feeling* as with the structure of *perception*. Thus, the example demonstrates how a linkage can be made between feeling (character and ethos being terms that apply to consistently maintained patterns of feeling) and the application of a conceptual framework to the stream of experience. It was largely Bateson's work that led me to the original assumption that the modal state within the multimodal framework could be defined in such a way as to incorporate both these aspects.

This suggests that our central unit of analysis, the modal state, should refer neither to the conceptual level alone nor to the symbolic and affectual level alone, but to a larger and more complete unit of which both can be seen as aspects. The modal state, in other words, includes both 'feeling' and 'cognitive' elements and these are intimately related to each other.[1]

Scientific frameworks and modal states

A detailed treatment of these modal states is still some way ahead of us. For the present we note that the different contexts or frameworks should in principle be definable, as in Bateson's example, in terms of the structure of interpersonal behaviour; in terms of what I have called the 'flow of relatedness'. This, incidentally, is what generates the homology between what the subjects of social science (people) are doing and what social scientists do. Social scientists are also involved in imposing a context or framework upon the 'flow of relatedness'. So are all scientists, since the flow also includes human relations with non-human life forms and with the inanimate.[2]

The framework employed by the scientist has certain special features in comparison with those employed by human beings in their day-to-day affairs. These include, for example, its relatively explicit nature, achieved in part through the use of writing, its ideally objective and impersonal character, and the importance attached to logical consistency and to other criteria in its production. These points will be developed further in chapters

10 and 11. What is significant is that the scientific framework can be seen as a specialized case of the more general concept of modal state.

The coexistence of different modal states

I now turn to a second and slightly less abstract example. It is taken from the book *Pragmatics of Human Communication* by Paul Watzlawick, Janet Beavin and Don Jackson, three of Bateson's associates.

> Suppose a couple have [*sic*] a marital problem to which he contributes passive withdrawal, while her 50 per cent is nagging criticism. In explaining their frustrations, the husband will state that withdrawal is his only *defence against* her nagging, while she will label this explanation a gross and wilful distortion of what 'really' happens in their marriage: namely, that she is critical of him *because of* his passivity. Stripped of all ephemeral and fortuitous elements, their fights consist in a monotonous exchange of the messages 'I withdraw because you nag' and 'I nag because you withdraw'. (Watzlawick, Beavin and Jackson 1968: 56)

Unlike the participants in Bateson's example, the partners here have systematically different conceptual frameworks for dealing with the 'same' situation, and it is precisely these different views (or 'contexts') that keep the situation going.[3]

Watzlawick, Beavin and Jackson are talking about the pathology of human interaction, but I do not think that the maintenance of two or more substantially different conceptual frameworks (in our terms, modal states) within a single social situation is necessarily pathological. Such situations, on a much larger scale, are not uncommon within ethnographic contexts, particularly when the society at issue is highly differentiated. As I mentioned in chapter 4, Wallace and Goodenough have argued that the coexistence of different conceptual frameworks is characteristic of all human societies (Wallace 1966a: 29–41; Goodenough 1963, 1981).

One of the best examples known to me of the systematic maintenance of differing conceptual frameworks within a single social context is T. N. Madan's work on the differing perceptions of Kashmiri society by its Muslim and Hindu inhabitants (Madan 1972). The Hindu Brahmins studied by Madan formed only a small minority of a society of which almost all the remaining population was Muslim. They, nevertheless, managed to conceptualize their situation as if they were living in a standard Hindu caste society.

The Brahmins did this by treating the various Muslim sub-groups and occupations with which they had dealings as, in effect, separate castes. However, what were, for the Brahmins, *caste* distinctions were seen by the

Muslim population of Kashmir, in specific cases, as either status distinctions or as non-existent. The Muslims did not see their society as a caste society, but there seems to have been little or no direct confrontation between Hindu and Muslim perspectives. The two groups managed to coexist in terms of two different social realities within a single society.

A significant aspect of this example is that the apparent conflict of conceptual frameworks between the two communities did not lead to overt conflict, at any rate until the whole area became enmeshed in recent years in the wider conflicts between India and Pakistan.[4] This situation was perhaps more common in pre-modern times than we might imagine. The great commercial centres of the Middle East, Eastern Mediterranean and North Africa, cities like Istanbul, Alexandria, Smyrna and Damascus, appear to have had, until recent times, very much this pattern of coexistence of culturally quite diverse groups within a single community.[5]

Much the same is doubtless true of the divergent constructions of the world typical of men and women within a single society, or of ruling-class and working-class groups in a modern capitalist economy. In such situations, where groups with contrasting interests and orientations coexist within a single social structure, we typically find a core of shared 'conceptual frameworks', along with other 'frameworks' that are group-specific. Yet, for the most part, the apparent conflicts between group-specific frameworks do not emerge into open conflict, or even into visibility.

There are several reasons why this is so. In some cases, contrasting frameworks are employed in group-specific situations (men talking to other men about women, women talking to other women about men). In others, there is sufficient sharing of conceptual material that the contrasting value-orientations behind that material cause no serious problems.

Thus, Paul Willis reported that both working-class and ruling-class youth in British society employed a distinction between 'mental' and 'manual' labour, while applying different valuations to the opposed terms. Working-class youths regarded manual labour, with its associated factory shop-floor culture, as 'real' work, an indication of personal worth. Mental labour was effeminate and devalued. For the ruling-class youths, mental work was highly valued and manual work was thought of as inferior. Such a system can absorb a considerable amount of rebellion of a petty kind without the overall structure being threatened (Willis 1978).

More generally, human language operates so as to maintain a considerable degree of compatibility between contrasting frameworks. A comprehensive analysis of language lies outside my present framework, and I present the following fairly simple argument (cf. also Goodenough 1981).

If we assume that there is some kind of internal representation or process corresponding to each of the various lexical items, semantic and syntactic features of a language (whether in terms of the mind or of the brain and central nervous system is irrelevant here), then we have no reason to assume that the representation or process is identical, in any meaningful sense, for any two speakers of a given language.

In fact, it is hard to conceptualize what we might mean by identical, but this, if anything, strengthens the argument. We have considerable reason to assume that the mental representations and the corresponding states of the brain and central nervous system for two individuals are not identical. My concept of a tree is formed by the oaks, elms and horse-chestnuts I knew as a small child in a Yorkshire garden; my students in Australia grew up with their own individual and various combinations of eucalypts, figs, jacarandas and other non-European species. As for subtler matters, such as the way in which different individuals understand time, the situation is more complex again.

What we *can* say is that our concepts (and our internal states) are somehow intersubjectively translatable, and that our language usage is such that for the most part we can employ language *without* the conflicts between our internal representations coming into conflict. Indeed, it is not at all necessary that members of a particular linguistic (and cultural) community build up the 'same' internal representations. All that is required is that the degree of conflict between their representations is not such as to render language usage (and, more generally, social action) impossible.

This line of argument suggests that two or more people who are sharing a single 'modal state' may have substantially different 'internal representations' of that state. There is no *a priori* reason why we should not regard the unhappily married couple cited by Watzlawick, Beavin and Jackson as representing complementary aspects of a single modal state rather than as having different modal states. It is only when we move to the derivative level of individual modal states (MS_i) that they would necessarily be seen as contrasting (if still complementary). The general question of the delimitation of modal states is raised below at the end of chapter 6. Here, it might be said that it depends primarily on the nature of the problem being addressed in any particular instance.

Modal states and the Freudian unconscious

One issue that has been implicit in some of the above discussion may be puzzling some readers. What relationship do the various frameworks, states and contexts employed in the argument so far have to human consciousness?

Bateson spoke in the quotations given above of A's 'seeing' or 'perceiving' behaviour in a particular way. Yet, as my subsequent examples illustrated, this 'seeing' or 'perceiving' would not in general take place within the full conscious awareness of the person concerned. The nagging wives and withdrawing husbands, caste-bound Brahmins and caste-free Muslims, working-class lads rejecting 'mental' labour as effeminate and ruling-class youths studying conscientiously for their exams, are not fully aware of the assumptions behind what they are doing. We are talking about a hidden structure that gives shape to perception, rather than the conscious content of perception. It is only in exceptional circumstances, if at all, that these structures are seen as such by the person whose perception they ordinarily form. The whole point about rose-tinted spectacles and similar visual aids is that the wearer is unaware of using them.

The same surely applies, to some degree at least, to scientific theories. One of the major features of the Kuhnian paradigm is that during periods of 'normal science' it is not questioned and, for the most part, not even seen.

Elsewhere in his writings Bateson is explicit about the unconscious nature of these structuring contexts, and he identifies them, by implication at least, with the material of what is called in Freudian language *primary process*; the content of dreams and of the 'unconscious' mind in general (e.g. Bateson 1973: 111–15). This is a fascinating and suggestive equation, which ties together some quite disparate areas of scientific endeavour. Precisely because of its great power, it needs careful examination.

This is particularly so, because this concept of an unconscious mind, in a more or less Freudian sense, has attained considerable familiarity within our own cultural context. It has become a basic conceptual element within the frameworks many of us use to make sense of our lives (Cunningham and Tickner 1981).

At the same time, it is worth pointing out that the Freudian unconscious, historically, opened up a crucial space for the social sciences. If the work of Durkheim and his followers can be seen as stressing the ways in which human social behaviour was affected by processes *other than* simple rational self-interest, the Freudian unconscious provided a field within which those processes could act. Many social theorists in the twentieth century, perhaps most notably including the major figures of the Frankfurt School, have attempted to utilize this possibility.[6]

The MMF is not a straightforward translation of Freudian theory, but it provides an anthropological framework within which certain aspects of Freudian theory can be easily represented or mapped. In order to facilitate the discussion at this point, I will need to say rather more about the 'modal state of the individual' (MS_i) than I have had occasion to do so far.

I have already suggested that the cognitive frameworks of everyday life are linked to other aspects of human functioning, aspects that correspond to emotional states and personality attributes. I treat these aspects as forming a totality, which can be considered, in effect, as a *state* of the total human organism (body and mind). It is this that the concept of 'modal state of the individual' (MS_i) refers to. The general idea here is that each of us acquires a repertoire of such states, initially as part of the process of socialization within a particular culture, and that the human organism in the course of everyday life can be described as switching continually between these states (or combinations of them).

Like the wider modal states of which they are derivatives, the 'modal states of the individual' (MS_is) are essentially relational in nature. Our personal repertoire of modal states is our individual collection of ways of partaking within the 'flow of relatedness'. While the modal state proper refers to the level of the social manifold, the MS_i refers to the individual level.

If the modal state proper is in essence an elaboration of Geertz's symbolic texts and Sperber's cultural representations, it would seem appropriate to treat it, as I have already suggested, as having a body of associated symbolism. I assume that the same is true of the MS_i. I assume that each of us has an individual body of symbolism that is built up to a greater or lesser degree from the shared symbolism of our social context, and that the shared symbolism of a social group is capable of being affected in its turn by the individual symbolism of the individuals composing it.[7]

Given these suggestions, it now becomes possible to reinterpret what is happening in Freudian 'primary process'. This process, which becomes conscious, in part, through dreams and various culturally prescribed visionary techniques, can be understood as being concerned with switching between and manipulating MS_is, and also, at least on occasion, with the creation of new MS_is. This, incidentally, clarifies why, as suggested above, conceptual innovation (as in a revitalization movement) is not in general a 'rational' process. Rationality, at least in the sense in which I shall use it, is what happens *within* a particular MS_i; in Freudian terms, it corresponds to secondary process, not primary process.

Two levels of operation within the flow

The argument of the last section has clarified the relationship between two kinds of thought and behaviour; one kind that takes place *within* an MS_i and another that involves the manipulation of MS_is. The former appears to correspond to what we generally refer to as 'rational' thought and 'rational' action (the results of Freud's secondary process), and the latter to dreams, visionary techniques and 'analogical' processes in general (Freudian primary process).

This relationship can be refined somewhat further with the aid of the three Batesonian theorists who were introduced earlier in the chapter. Watzlawick, Beavin and Jackson summarize the argument of *Pragmatics of Human Communication* in the following series of 'tentative axioms' concerning human communication (the numbering is mine):

> 1. One cannot *not* communicate.
> 2. Every communication has a content and a relationship aspect such that the latter classifies the former and is therefore a metacommunication.
> 3. The nature of the relationship is contingent upon the punctuation of the communicational sequences between the communicants.
> 4. Human beings communicate both digitally and analogically. Digital language has a highly complex and powerful logical syntax but lacks adequate semantics in the field of relationship, while analogic language possesses the semantics but has no adequate syntax for the unambiguous definition of the nature of relationships.
>
> (Watzlawick, Beavin and Jackson 1968, pp. 48–67)

A fifth axiom, to do with the 'symmetrical' or 'complementary' nature of relationships, is not of direct concern here.

Watzlawick's, Beavin's and Jackson's dichotomy between 'digital' and 'analogic' is introduced in the specific context of communication, but it is evidently closely related to both the distinction between secondary and primary process, and to my own contrast between operations *within* an MS_1 and operations *with* MS_1s. Similar formulations have become common in the social science literature in recent years. Among them may be mentioned the structuralist opposition between 'syntagm' and 'paradigm' (e.g. Kronenfeld and Decker 1979), Edwin Ardener's contrast of 's-structures' and 'p-structures' (Ardener 1978), Julia Kristeva's usage of 'symbolic' and 'semiotic' (Kristeva 1984, Gross 1986), and Roy Wagner's distinction between the 'conventional' and 'tropic' use of metaphor (Wagner 1975, 1978). I shall return to the last of these in chapter 11. However, the clarity of Watzlawick's, Beavin's and Jackson's presentation, and its explicit introduction of the question of *relationship*, makes it especially useful for my present purposes.

As I have said, Watzlawick, Beavin and Jackson are dealing in the first place with communication, and it is easy to see what their axioms mean when applied to the processes of human communication. The rational content of speech corresponds, for example, to the digital aspect of communication; it is here that we find the 'complex and powerful logical syntax' of the fourth axiom.

The rational content of speech is of little use in defining the relationship between speaker and listener, because how it is interpreted will depend precisely on the nature of that relationship. It is the non-rational aspects of speech, such as imagery, choice of words, stress and intonation, that defines the relationship, along with the elaborate 'language' of non-verbal communication that accompanies spoken language (e.g. Goffman 1974, 1981; Scheflen and Scheflen 1972). Such communication, as the fourth axiom reminds us, is never unambiguous. It is always open to varying interpretation.

If we consider *written* communication, we can find the same duality of 'digital' and 'analogic' aspects. Considering the variety of written communication, it is apparent that the relative importance of these two aspects may vary considerably. There is a wide variety of language forms varying from those (the telephone directory, the technical manual) where 'digital' communication is paramount and 'analogic' communication muted, to those (the Romantic poem, the love letter) where 'analogic' communication is of primary importance and the literal, 'digital', meaning of the words secondary. At the same time, the nature of the analogic communication is never unambiguous. We may be reasonably certain that we are correctly interpreting the content aspect of a telephone directory, but we can never be sure that we know what a poet meant to convey through imagery and choice of phrase.

In extending the digital and analogic distinction to social life more generally, the example of written communication is worth bearing in mind. In a face-to-face interaction, analogic communication is always present, although perhaps not always with the same intensity. In the more general case, a particular action may be performed (or perceived) primarily in terms of its analogic significance, or primarily in terms of its digital or rational significance. The *proportion* of analogic significance can vary from a great deal to very little.

Thus, we can say that there are two *levels* of operating with the 'flow of relatedness'. One level consists of action (or interpreting the actions of others) within a given, temporarily fixed framework of relationship (the modal state of the individual or MS_i). At the second level, we operate with the MS_is themselves and move between possible frameworks of relationship.[8]

Semioticians are notoriously accused of regarding the world as consisting exclusively of messages (meaning, of course, analogic messages). Watzlawick, Beavin and Jackson help to clarify the situation: while anything and everything may potentially be analogic communication, whether it is or not in any given instance depends on whether the human participants in the situation regard it as such. In Bateson's terms, what is at issue is whether the participants are operating in such a way that they perceive 'context markers' in the event. The flight of a crow may constitute a vital piece of analogic communication in some cultures and be meaningless in others (Laufer 1914). A similar point has recently been made in relation to cultural symbolism by Roger Keesing (1986).

As far as human behaviour goes, certain ways in which human beings behave undoubtedly have a strong content of analogic communication in normal human interchange. In other words, they help to define relationships. They have an effect on the 'flow of relatedness'. Some of these modes of behaviour are doubtless built up on a genetic basis, in part shared with other higher primates, but they have been elaborated culturally and given specific cultural meaning. I have in mind here the whole 'vocabulary' of interpersonal movement and gesture referred to in chapter 4 and analysed by authors such as Albert Scheflen (Scheflen and Scheflen 1972). At the same time, many human actions are more appropriately analysed as rational ('digital') activity *within* a particular modal state (MS_i).

Recognizing this dual aspect of human activity helps to avoid the instrumental reductionism characteristic of some modern social scientists and exemplified in the ideal of the perfectly rational human actor (*homo oeconomicus*). The point has been made elsewhere, for example by Martin Southwold and Roy Wagner (cf. chapter 11, below). By *defining* rational activity as activity that takes place in a particular modal state, we are able to give rationality a place within our analysis of social life, without conceding to it an unwarranted dominance over the analysis of human thought and behaviour.

In this chapter we have examined various aspects of the MMF and of the modal states and, I hope, come to a clearer understanding of the nature of the new framework. In particular we have examined the questions of how the flow of relatedness is analysed by human consciousness, and of how 'rational' and 'analogical' interpretations of that flow are integrated into a total process of consciousness. We are now ready to look at the multimodal framework as a whole and to examine the concept of 'modal state' in detail. This will be the subject of chapter 6.

6 The multimodal framework

The present chapter provides a detailed presentation of the MMF. First we might recall three general features of the MMF:

1. THE MMF TREATS HUMAN THOUGHT AND BEHAVIOUR, WHETHER 'INDIVIDUAL' OR 'SOCIAL', AS DERIVATIVE FROM TYPE III VARIABLES (I.E. VARIABLES DESCRIPTIVE OF PROCESSES WITHIN THE 'SOCIAL MANIFOLD'). These variables are the 'modal states'. Individual and social descriptions and variables are explicitly derivative from these states. In this way, the MMF avoids accepting any conventional dichotomy between 'individual' and 'society'.

2. THE MMF TREATS BODY AND MIND AS COMPONENT PARTS OF A MIND-BODY UNITY. In other words, the MMF avoids assuming a dichotomy between body and mind. This is a necessity, if we are to have proper integration between anthropological and biological modes of explanation. The 'modal state' encompasses aspects of both 'body' and 'mind'.

3. THE MMF IS ESSENTIALLY RELATIONAL IN NATURE. In other words, its central concepts, in particular the 'modal state', are intended to describe patterns of *relationship* between the individual and his or her environment, physical and social, rather than aspects of the individual as a closed system. The modal state, in terms of the 'flow' metaphor used in chapters 1, 3 and 4, is not about what human beings are as separate 'individuals', but about how human beings orient themselves to the flow of the stream, that is to their social and physical environment, which includes their own biological organisms. No ultimate separation is assumed to exist between human beings and this environment. It is this relational aspect that makes the modal state into a quantity within the social manifold rather than an attribute of how human beings physically function.

It should be emphasized that the MMF is a model, a theoretical construct that is intended to represent the real world in a simplified form. It is a set of quantities and relationships on to which the 'real world' can be mapped (Samuel 1985a). Its status is hypothetical, and it is open to falsification and to competition with alternative models. It is assumed that it is only one of a variety of possible models, each of which are capable of capturing different aspects of that 'real world'.

In other words, the MMF is not based on positivistic assumptions, and to ask whether the modal states 'really exist' is to miss the point. Consequently, the important question to ask about the MMF is not 'in what ways is the model inadequate?' but 'in what ways can we do better?' In other words, this social scientific framework should be treated as theoretical frameworks are treated (or at least as they are supposed to be treated) in the natural sciences – as a basis for developing and testing hypotheses, with the aim of improving the framework.

The modal state, a central concept within the MMF, has already been introduced in part in the previous chapters. A complementary concept, the modal current, was mentioned briefly in chapter 1. These two concepts, which are closely interrelated, are analytic tools for grasping hold of the patterns of flow within the 'flow of relatedness'. We have already been presented with the idea of the modal state as describing a pattern of relationships that can be viewed at either individual or group level, but that has its primary locus in an autonomous sphere of explanation outside (or between) individual and group. The modal current is simply this pattern seen as a process, as an object developing and changing through historical time. Modal state and modal current define a level of analysis that is *neither* that of the purely social *nor* that of the exclusively individual, and that can be read in synchronic or diachronic form.

The modal currents that flow through space and time correspond to modal states at the synchronic (cultural and individual) levels. These are momentary or continuing 'states' of the minds and bodies of the human beings that make up society. I emphasize again that the states are states of both mind and body. Within any society, several modal states will be active at any point in time and at any given location in the social system. Alternatively, we might say that several modal currents are flowing through that location, and providing a corresponding dynamic to events at that location. A location here is defined not merely by place but by factors such as the age, gender, social position, occupation and so on, of the individuals at that point.

'Culture' can be seen as constituted by the ebb and flow of these currents. Within each individual the currents manifest in the form of the

MS_i (individual modal states), structures of conceptualization, feeling and intentionality within which each of us acts and chooses and behaves.

Modal currents are not envisaged in the MMF as permanent, although specific social and biological mechanisms, some of which we shall consider shortly, may lead to particular currents becoming relatively stable and long-lasting. I assume that currents that represent major and typical modal states within a given society have become stabilized by some kind of 'feedback' process. Even so they are not eternal and undergo processes of growth, transformation and decline, corresponding to the growth and decline in significance of the corresponding modal states.

What replaces a particular current depends on the individual creativity through which new states are constructed. This creativity works on the basis of the states (currents) already active at that point, but through it the currents themselves are affected, in a small or large way.

Within the MMF, the ability to create new states must be regarded as a human universal, since it forms a necessary part of the process of socialization or enculturation. In the MMF, rather than this process taking place through the simple imposition of modal currents on a *tabula rasa*, socialization involves an active response on the part of the individual. The child creates a personal repertoire of states in response to the material situation and to his or her position, as it were, within the flow.[1] I would suggest that this is a basic human activity, most familiar to us as 'play'.

The MMF leaves a number of matters incompletely specified. How rigidly does the cultural material condition the states that are formed? What kinds of 'cultural' material are involved in this process, and what are their relative importance? How far does a particular modal state dictate a specific response in a particular situation? How does the creation of new modal states take place, and how different can the new states be from those previously in operation?

The MMF as presented here is deliberately agnostic about these questions. Its intention is not to answer them, since at this stage we simply are not in a position to be able to answer them, but to provide a language within which they can be asked. To make the same point in Popperian terms, if the framework is accepted as providing a metaphysical basis for research, such issues become questions for investigation. In Kuhnian terms, they are questions *within* the new paradigm.

Appropriate experiments for testing them empirically could be devised, at least in principle. I would expect that the answers to some of these questions would vary substantially between societies, currents and individuals.[2]

This relationship between a structure of metaphysical assumptions (or 'paradigm') and questions for empirical investigation forms part of a widely shared common ground within contemporary philosophy of science. My usage of it here, as in chapters 1, 3 and 4, suggests the lines along which I believe that anthropology, and the social sciences more generally, can look for a genuine unity of method with the natural sciences.

Modal states and modal currents

By now it can be seen how modal current and modal state are simply two aspects of the same concept, seen in the one case in a historical perspective and in the other in synchronic terms. Within the individual (Type I) perspective, we can say that at any given point in time or space the growing individual is confronted with a variety of cultural material on the basis of which the individual modal states are built up. This material amounts, in a sense, to a body of modal states of the manifold internalized selectively by the individual. We could think of these as 'root paradigms' in the sense used in some of Victor Turner's later works (e.g. 1974: 67–8) or as 'cultural scenarios', using the term in a general and metaphorical sense. The individual is presented not only with a set of possible roles and patterns of interaction from which to construct his or her own identity but also with ways of feeling about those roles, sets of values connected with the roles, and so forth. All this is, for the most part, unconscious.

What is most centrally at issue here are patterns of *relationships* between the individual and his or her natural and social environment. The MMF does not make any assumptions about the process by which these states are internalized by the individual. It merely assumes that some mechanism generates a series of analytically discrete modal states within any particular population such that the different states (MS_is) of any individual are, in most cases, systematically related to those of other individuals. This can be rephrased as the assumption that there are analytically discrete modal states pertaining to the *group* (the MS_cs) that are 'realized' through the individuals belonging to that group. *These are two equivalent statements*. Neither individual or group descriptions are primary; both are derivative, as far as the MMF is concerned, from the modal states within the social manifold. These states (the MS_m) pertain to both group and individual, and their real domain is the relationships between individuals (the 'flow of relatedness').

The MMF does not assume that all individuals within a society have the same set of states. Nor does it assume that the states form a relatively harmonious and mutually consistent set. Functionalist anthropologists such as Victor Turner have argued, in effect, that both these assumptions are true to a considerable degree in the case of a traditional preliterate society such as the Ndembu (e.g. Turner 1968). As Turner himself argued in his later work, it would seem unlikely that the same would be true of a society such as our own (Turner 1979: 11–59 = 1982: 20–60). As Wallace and Goodenough's work implies (cf. chapter 4), any society is likely to contain a variety of states, and the degree of consistency and harmony between them remains to be established in particular cases.

The assumption behind the MMF is that the states in all societies are always in the process of change, that there is always some conflict and tension between them, and that individual state repertoires are never identical with each other. The states are not so much a closed and harmonious system as a set of ways in which individuals within the culture learn to operate. A set that is too limited, consistent and parsimonious would be unlikely to be adaptive over a long historical period.

In general, and particularly in situations of culture-contact within the modern world, a wide variety of modal states may be operative in a particular group. In a situation where individuals are exposed to material from more than one cultural repertoire, it is open to those individuals, as far as the MMF is concerned, to build up their modal states on the basis of whatever is available to them. This leads to a series of questions concerning boundary-maintenance mechanisms and the preservation of group identity. Clearly, in such contexts social and cultural mechanisms *do* operate in varying degrees to constrain the individual's freedom to select at will from all the available material.

The modal currents are, simply, the modal states seen as part of the onward cultural flow, rather than as realized through specific individuals at a given point in that flow. The modal current is in some ways not an unfamiliar idea. Fields such as the history of art or the history of ideas have traditionally operated in terms of similar concepts. Protestantism, cubism and functionalism all correspond to aspects of modal currents or of families of these currents. Here, however, we are concerned with the total structuring of the human mind and body, rather than with the more limited areas of aesthetic or intellectual activity. We will be able to see more clearly what matters might be included within the concept of modal current by turning to examine the modal states of the individual (MS_is) in more detail.

The modal state of the individual (MS_i)

Seen within the individualist (Type I) perspective, each human being develops a personal repertoire of modal states (MS_i) throughout his or her life. This process is presumably most active in the early years, but continues throughout the individual's lifetime. At any one time the individual has access to a limited personal repertoire of states and is relating to his or her environment through one or another of these states. The modal state governs the individual's relationship to the surrounding people and to other aspects of the social and natural environment.

The modal states are states of both mind and body. I assume that mental states correspond to physical states, and that modal states also correspond to specific states of the brain and of the central nervous system as a whole. Since the states are states of both mind and body, the possible states that an individual can manifest at any given point will depend on that individual's physical condition. A person who is starving or exhausted has limited freedom of action (a limited repertoire of available states).

In chapter 1 I presented a list of features of the individual modal state. I shall present it again here, with some comment on the various features included:

(1) The MS_i (modal state of the individual) has a cognitive function. It splits up or interprets the individual's stream of experience in characteristic ways, so that certain features of the external environment and of the body's internal processes are consciously perceived and others are not.

(2) Each MS_i is associated with a set of images or symbols, in part shared by individuals within a given cultural context, by which that MS_i may be referenced or evoked.

(3) Each MS_i corresponds to specific moods, motivations, feelings and emotions.

These first three characteristics are commonplaces of symbolic anthropology. They are found, for example, in Geertz's classic definition of 'religion' (but really of 'culture', using the term in Geertz's sense) in 'Religion as a cultural system' (Geertz 1973: 87–125). With less stress on the symbolic mechanism, they may equally be found as constituents of Wallace's 'mazeways' and similar concepts. The rephrasing of the cognitive function in (1) in terms of the punctuation of the 'stream of experience' is borrowed from Bateson. Its purpose is to give a more precise and, at least in principle, empirically testable description.[3]

(4) Each MS_i corresponds to a particular decision structure. Within it the individual will respond in certain ways to certain events, will subjectively find certain goals attractive and others unattractive.

This is a similar reformulation of (3), but it has been placed separately for clarity. The concept of a 'decision structure' is borrowed from computer programming, where it refers to the series of *choices* implicit in a particular program; these correspond to branches in a flow-chart.[4] It is introduced here in order to bring *behaviour* (including social behaviour in particular) explicitly into the modal state definition.

(5) Each MS_i corresponds to a particular subjective sense of self and a particular way in which the individual perceives of his or her relationship to other individuals and other aspects of the environment.

This is another reformulation of (3). The question of the subjective sense of self has been explored by some symbolic anthropologists, including Victor Turner and also Bruce Kapferer, who has analysed Sinhalese exorcistic ritual as operating on the sense of self.[5] Introducing this explicitly 'subjective' quantity here may also prove useful in constructing linkages with psychoanalytic theory (cf. below). It may be noted that (5) is closely linked to (1), the punctuation of the stream of experience. Both are concerned with *how* the ongoing stream of events is made sense of.

(6) Each MS_i corresponds to certain physiological correlates, such as posture, muscle tension, blood pressure, and the like.

This is introduced in order to make a direct linkage to those areas traditionally considered as somatic rather than psychic, body rather than mind. It would seem a plausible component of the modal state, since it is well known that the 'emotional' variables dealt with in (3) and (5) have physiological correlates.

(7) MS_is differ in terms of possible transitions to other MS_is. They may be more or less well connected to other states. They may also allow for more or less innovation in the creation of new states.

This last characteristic of the modal state is a direct consequence of the overall framework as presented earlier, but it has been stated explicitly here for clarity.

It will be noticed that the state includes aspects of human behaviour that are in a normal individual more or less conscious along with others that are partially or wholly unconscious. It includes aspects relating to the 'mind' as normally conceived and aspects relating to the 'body'. No assumptions are being made about directions of causality within the modal state. Conscious and unconscious, mind and body are interrelated aspects of a unitary system, rather than one being dependent on the other.

As previously stated, a major purpose of the MMF is to move us away from culturally constructed dichotomies such as those between mind and body, or conscious and unconscious. These dichotomies can be a major obstacle to understanding cultures and modes of being where these dichotomies are constructed differently or do not have the same central role that they do for us. The human organism in this framework is a unity upon which we construct the distinctions between mind and body, conscious and unconscious.

The modal state is a key term in the MMF, and it carries a good deal of weight and significance. I have discussed some reasons for choosing to group together the various aspects listed above within a single over-arching concept. In particular, aspects (1) to (6) would all seem to be in some sense or another acquired culturally upon a biological and genetic base, and it makes sense to consider this acquisition as a single process.

The concept of modal state also makes considerable sense in terms of our everyday experience. We are conscious of being in different moods and states at different times, and conscious, too, that our perceptions and our behaviour vary with these changes of state. It does not need much observation of ourselves or of others to convince us that these states have physiological concomitants as well, in terms of posture, muscle tension, facial expression and the like.

In principle, each momentary state of each individual is unique, since the total situation is always unique. Nevertheless, it seems that similar states recur. We can recognize the 'same' moods over and over again in ourselves and in people we know well, and may be able to predict quite accurately what state people will adopt, and so how they will react, in a particular situation. The idea of the repertoire of modal states would appear to be a reasonable tool for describing human behaviour, at least at a first approximation.

Ultimately, while there are arguments for combining this particular set of variables in a single over-arching concept, the real test of the framework has to be whether it is useful in understanding human society. In chapters 7 to 12 of this book I hope to show that it *is* useful, by demonstrating the light that it can cast on some central issues of anthropology and of social theory. In the remainder of this chapter, rather than attempting to argue further for the plausibility of the framework, I shall explore some of its implications.

How do individuals acquire modal states?

We have gone some way towards specifying what modal currents and modal states consist of. It would be helpful if we had some idea of how individuals acquire their repertoire of states, and of what mechanisms might in practice account for the persistence of currents linking the states of different individuals through space and time. While, as I have said, the MMF as such makes no assumptions about these matters, it would evidently fit better with certain kinds of theories than with others.

The process that the MMF describes in terms of *state acquisition* has been investigated at some length within anthropology by culture and personality theorists, interpretive anthropologists and others. At this stage of our knowledge it would seem plausible that the states are conveyed through cultural 'symbols', using that term in Geertz's very wide sense to include not only specifically designed 'symbolic' devices but, for example, words and grammatical structures, types of clothing and of housing, aspects of technology and subsistence, myths, dramatic and literary forms, to which might be added the whole range of body techniques, gestures and movements (cf. Geertz 1973: 87–125, Mauss 1979). Such items constitute a body of cultural material from which, in association with the natural environment, the material conditions of existence and the structuring provided by human biology, the individual constructs his or her repertoire of modal states.

In Goodenough's or Wallace's terms, we would presumably speak not of cultural symbols but of 'cultural artefacts'. Goodenough's own description of the acquisition of culture by individuals may be found in his book *Culture, Language and Society*, in which, as the title suggests, a major emphasis is placed on the role of language in this process.

It is not being suggested here that all of this material exists exclusively or even primarily in order to provide the basis for modal states. Much of it surely does not. Language, for example, also has a primary purpose of communication. However, whatever practices a people adopts for subsistence or other pragmatic purposes will have their effect on the individual growing up among those practices.

In addition, most – perhaps all – societies do have a body of practices whose main purpose appears to be the maintenance of modal states.

It was this body of material that Geertz emphasized in his well-known (and controversial) essay on religion as a cultural system (Geertz 1973: 87–125; cf. Austin-Broos 1979, Asad 1983). I see no reason to reject the idea that what we refer to as 'religion' is in many societies largely concerned with maintaining such states. In literate and technological societies like those of the modern Western world, where 'religion' in the traditional sense is a marginal activity, other practices such as literature, sport, theatre, cinema and advertising may be more central to the generation and maintenance of typical modal states (see chapter 11).

To develop these suggestions into a detailed account of the process of socialization in human culture would be a major undertaking. While many past studies might be reinterpreted so as to assist in writing such an account, extensive additional research would probably be needed before a detailed picture could be arrived at. The project is not one that can be attempted here in any detail. Nevertheless, we can imagine that such an account might be written, and we can speculate a little on what it might be like.

Consider, for simplicity, a dyadic situation: a newly born baby with its mother. From shortly after birth, both baby and mother are in a sense experimenting, through mutual play, in order to find appropriate ways of behaving towards each other.

The MMF assumes that once we get beyond very basic behaviours, such as those associated with feeding and crying, the genetic code provides the baby with general strategies and structures, rather than any specific patterns of behaviour. The mother, however, brings an already developed repertoire of states to the initial situation. Even if she is dealing with her first baby, she has been a baby herself, has usually experienced other babies, has watched other mothers with babies and in various ways acquired a body of conventional wisdom relating to babies.

Over time the situation of the mother–child dyad stabilizes. We could speak of an 'attunement' taking place between mother and child. Extending the acoustic metaphor, we might say that the *system* composed of mother and child has developed a series of preferred 'modes of vibration', ways of behaving that mother and child now 'naturally' fall into. As a first approximation, we can decompose each of these states of the *system* into an individual modal state (MS_i) of the mother and an individual modal state of the child. The baby's states are newly formed; those of the mother have undergone at least some change through her experience with her baby.

One purpose of introducing this little domestic scene is to stress again that the states are always *relational* in their origins and nature. They are always states of the system rather than of the participants. In reality this system would extend beyond mother and child to include any other human beings involved in the interaction, as well as the physical environment, other animals and objects (the family cat, the child's toys).[6]

We can imagine how children growing up in a particular society will gradually acquire a repertoire of modal states appropriate to their milieu, in the sense that they correspond to the standardized kinds of interactions that take place around them. These repetitive learning situations themselves occur precisely because previous generations have similarly acquired appropriate repertoires of modal states and continue to behave in terms of them.

I have emphasized the central role of 'play', or creative imagination, in the process of modal-state acquisition (cf. Roberts and Sutton-Smith 1962, Bateson 1973, esp. 150–67, Turner 1986: 262–6). The framework assumes that the process of acquiring or modifying a state is never a passive one. It demands the participation of the individual. Even if the social milieu provides the basic scenarios, we have to learn how to act our own part in them. (I make no assumptions here about how this 'imagining' relates to our conscious awareness.)

As we grow up, our repertoire of states becomes larger, more complex and more differentiated. We can manage quite well in most situations with the repertoire we have already acquired, and when new occasions arise we may tend to use existing responses with as little modification as possible. In principle, though, and this is a point of some importance, the MMF assumes that we are always capable of transforming the mode in which we are attuned to reality.

It seems natural to ask why people often appear to be locked into modes of behaving, modal states in the present model, which appear inadequate and self-destructive. In an article some years ago on ideology, Ernest Gellner argued that an effective ideology needs a 'bait' to make it attractive (Gellner 1978). Ideologies in Gellner's sense are a special class of modal states, and I would suggest that the same is true, more generally, of the modal states themselves. Every modal state has an attraction, a potential pay-off for the individual, or it would not survive.

A suggestion as to how this operates may be found in Victor Turner's illuminating analyses of African ritual symbolism (cf. chapter 7). Turner placed great emphasis in his writings in the early 1960s (*The Drums of Affliction, The Forest of Symbols*) on what he called the 'bipolar' nature of Ndembu ritual symbols (which I would treat as 'markers' of culturally prescribed modal states). What he meant by this was that the symbol linked significant aspects of social behaviour to imagery that was immediately physiological (mother's milk, blood) and so aroused strong positive or negative emotional associations. The symbol thus redirected powerful and potentially socially destructive human motivational states for the good of the social group (Turner 1968: 18–22, 1970: 28–9).

We can leave aside the functionalist implications of Turner's argument, and the more simplistic aspects of his psychology, about which he himself later expressed doubts.[7] There, nevertheless, seems to be an important suggestion here that, as Turner recognized, goes well beyond the confines of a single Central African society.[8] If we assume that the states built up in early life, at the period when the child is reaching an initial orientation towards social life, carry strong emotional affect, and that later states are built up through elaboration, modification and combination of these states, we can gain some idea of the kind of 'bait' or 'pay-off' involved in states that are apparently counter-productive for the individual.[9]

The precise details of how the states are acquired and of how they function in emotional terms is clearly a matter for further investigation. Nevertheless, we can assume that the adult repertoire of modal states develops from basic states associated with the early socialization period, and that those basic states must incorporate responses to universal features of the human situation.[10]

The discreteness of modal states and currents

Up to here I have spoken as if the question of identifying a modal state or a modal current, that is of determining what behaviour or knowledge forms part of one state or current and what forms part of another, is unproblematic. Yet it is not obvious where in practice we would draw the line between one state and another, or between one current and another, and the reader may well be confused about this aspect of the framework.

The apparent conundrum is clarified somewhat if we bear in mind that the multimodal framework is an analytical tool rather than a statement about what 'really is'. What states or currents we identify will depend upon the purpose of the analysis. A particular social milieu does not 'have' or 'consist of' twenty-five discrete modal currents. It is rather that it is convenient in the context of a particular analysis to treat it as being defined by twenty-five currents. A different analysis, for different purposes, might arrive at five, or fifty, currents, depending upon what contrasts are significant in relation to the problem at hand. In the following chapters some examples are given that will help to clarify this point.

This concludes my presentation of the central concepts of the MMF. In chapters 7 to 11 the framework will be applied to some familiar and less-familiar ethnographic data. In the process we will see what it has to say about a number of important issues in anthropology and social theory.

7   The Ndembu modal state repertoire

The first six chapters of this book have introduced the 'modal state' and other basic elements of the multimodal framework (MMF). In the remaining six chapters the MMF will be applied to some ethnographic material and some of the consequences of adopting it will be explored.

In the present chapter we consider a single body of ethnographic material: Victor Turner's work on the Ndembu of Central Africa. A central question will be the existence of mechanisms within societies for creating and maintaining a specific repertoire of 'modal states' among their members. As I emphasized in chapter 6, the MMF itself does not make any assumptions about how modal states arise within individuals, beyond the implicit assumption that the process has ultimately to be explained in 'relational' terms (i.e. in terms of processes within the social manifold). Turner's research, when translated into the terms of the MMF, amounts to a *theory* about such processes. This theory states that Ndembu ritual can be understood as a series of mechanisms for creating modal states and maintaining them in a condition of 'balance'.

Turner's analysis, especially in his earlier works, has many of the features of the functionalist school of British anthropology. Ndembu society is treated as a coherent whole whose unity and stability is constituted precisely by the rituals we are about to examine. One of the major reasons for introducing the MMF was to allow for processes of change over time that are difficult to theorize adequately within functionalist or structuralist frameworks. In translating a functionalist study into this new vocabulary, with its explicit assumption of change, we are therefore subjecting its central terms to a subtle alteration. Turner's ritual complexes no longer attain their justification from their ability to maintain the coherence and permanence of Ndembu society. Instead, they become generators of modal states, presenting, at most, conditional elements of stability within an overall situation that is not assumed to have any great degree of permanence. Even where they appear to cohere into larger patterns of significance and order, such patterns are themselves only aspects of the modal states, with a similarly conditional degree of long-term stability.

However, we should recall that functionalist and structuralist frameworks have, for all the faults pointed out by their critics, been fruitful in explaining many features of human society. That they have been so suggests that the assumption of relative stability built into functionalist and some structuralist frameworks has considerable validity. It may well be true, in other words, that Ndembu society functions to maintain its central repertoire of modal states relatively constant over substantial periods of time.

Ndembu rituals I: introduction

The Ndembu are an agricultural society in Central Africa, living in small villages based on matrilineal kin groups. Turner studied these people in the 1950s. Much of his work with them was concerned with their complex ritual life. Turner classified their rituals under two major types, 'life-crisis rituals', which were performed to mark the transition between stages in human life, and 'rituals of affliction', which were performed in response to illness or misfortune.[1]

These two types of ritual can be taken to correspond to two functions that are analytically separate; reproducing the society's modal states in each new generation of individual members and keeping the states in balance within each village community.

Ndembu rituals are structured around 'ritual symbols', a phrase that Turner uses to translate an indigenous Ndembu term (*chinjikijilu*, 1970: 48). The 'symbols' are material objects, in most cases consisting of, or made from, trees and other common plants in the Ndembu environment. As Turner's analysis makes clear, individual tree species are associated, because of various physical and other properties, with different aspects of Ndembu life. They are seen as potentialities or ways of being, which can be invoked and so created in the course of ritual.

This 'language of trees' provides a set of resources for the construction of modal states. Thus, the *mudyi* (Transvaal Rubber Tree, *Diplorrhyncus condylocarpon*) is a tree of central importance to the Ndembu ('it is our flag'), and it receives extensive treatment in Turner's work (e.g. 1968: 17–20, 1970: 52–8). This tree has a white latex that appears in milky beads if the bark of the tree is scratched. The Ndembu associate this white latex with mother's milk, and the tree therefore represents breast-feeding, the mother–child link and, by extension, the matrilineal descent groups. These groups of people who share a common mother, mother's mother or more distant matrilineal ancestor are basic units of the Ndembu social structure. In the next section we can see how this tree forms the central symbol of one of the most important Ndembu rituals, Nkang'a.

Ndembu rituals II: becoming a woman

Nkang'a is performed when a girl reaches puberty. It is one of the two main Ndembu puberty rituals (the other, Mukanda, for boys, is described in the next section). For the Ndembu, puberty is marked not, as in many societies in Africa and elsewhere, by the girl's first menstruation but by the growth of her breasts, so linking up with the milk-breast-motherhood symbolism of the *mudyi* tree. The Nkang'a ritual sequence culminates in the consummation of her marriage, so the explicit purpose of the whole ritual is the transformation of a young single girl, still a member of her natal family, into an adult married woman, ready to start her own family (1968: 198–268, cf. also E. Turner 1987).

As the following brief description of Nkang'a illustrates, this series of rituals presents a central matrix of relatedness within Ndembu social life, spelt out in terms of relationships between the girl, her mother, her future husband and the other women of the girl's matrilineage. The focus is on the new modal states (MS_is) to be acquired by the girl, and to a lesser extent by the husband and the mother. These modal states are presented in a social and relational context, rather than as isolated roles.

The first major phase of the ritual is carried out at the base of a young *mudyi* sapling, which explicitly represents the girl; its leaves stand for her future children. The girl remains motionless at the foot of the tree (the 'place of suffering') throughout a whole day while the women, and later all the villagers, dance and sing around her (1968: 205–27). Immediately afterwards, she is taken to a hut of *mudyi* wood at the edge of the village where she is secluded for some weeks. During this period she is given instruction in dancing and sexual techniques as well as moral advice on conducting herself as an adult married woman (228–49).

Finally she is 'brought out' as the central figure at another large-scale dance (1968: 249–51). That evening her marriage is consummated. The bridegroom has played some part in the proceedings so far, for example in building the seclusion hut, but the major part of the girl's transformation into an adult woman is conducted by the elder women of her own matrilineage, in particular an instructress, who is never the girl's own mother.

The bridegroom's role is still somewhat provisional until this point. The consummation of the marriage acts as a test of the bridegroom's virility, and the bride is able, at least in theory, to reject him as inadequate (1968: 259–61, cf. also 1970: 231). While it seems that the social and financial interests of the families in the marriage make this an extremely rare occurrence in practice, the idea, along with the girl's preparation for her adult sexual role, makes a point about the Ndembu construction of male–female relationships. The groom stays at his wife's village, working for his parents-in-law for another two weeks; Turner comments that 'in the past he might have been obliged to remain for a whole year' (1968: 263). After making a special final payment to his parents-in-law (additional, that is, to the bridewealth proper) he takes the bride home to his own village.

This brief description omits numerous illuminating details, many of them interpreted by Turner as relating to what he sees as the basic structural conflict within Ndembu society, that between *matriliny*, in other words the significance of matrilineal descent groups and matrilineal kinship links, and *virilocality*, the principle that a woman goes to live in her husband's village, away from her matrilineal kin. It is, nevertheless, clear from the account above that the girl is being inducted into a state of being and a way of behaving, that of an adult married woman in Ndembu society, a state that is constructed around the symbol of the *mudyi* tree. That state also implies a particular kind of relationship to her future husband.

Turner's analysis focused on the transformation of social relations around the girl. He interpreted the ritual as taking the girl away from her mother, who is excluded from significant stages of the ritual as well as from the role of instructress, and as establishing the new link to her husband. He also saw it as being concerned with the relationship between the girl's matrilineage and her husband's, and between men and women in general. The ritual restructures the social relations with which the girl is involved to correspond to her new status.

At the same time, the ritual also operates to transform the girl's own *understanding*, intellectual and emotional, of her situation so as to correspond to the new place she is to occupy. This is plain enough from the explicitly instructional aspects of her seclusion. Rites of passage of this type are regularly compared by members of the societies that perform them with Western-style schooling. In the Ndembu case, the death–rebirth symbolism of the 'place of suffering' where the girl lies all day, naked except for a blanket, in a position at once representing a corpse and a foetus, underlines this aspect of what is happening.

The modal state helps us to conceptualize as a single whole these two aspects, the 'sociological' and 'psychological' as it were, of what is happening. In general, Turner's analysis in *The Drums of Affliction* centred on the transformation of social relations, while giving some attention also to the changes being brought about in the girl's understanding. Other analyses of similar rituals, for example Suzette Heald's study of the Gisu circumcision ritual, a corresponding rite of passage to adulthood for boys, have placed more emphasis on the 'subjective' transformation (Heald 1982), as did Turner's own later work at times (cf. Turner 1975, preface). These two aspects are clearly part of a single process.

What is being presented to the girl in Nkang'a is not an isolated role but a pattern or matrix of relationships that involves her, her future husband and the children she may have, her mother and the village community as a whole. Most of these are present and involved in the ritual, and they, too, are presented with new understandings of who they are in relation to the girl. The individual modal state (MS_i) she internalizes is a personal version of this pattern of relationships, centring upon her specific identity and self-concept, but also necessarily including the whole set of reshaped social relationships that is implied by that new self-concept.

This matrix of relationships, incidentally, may be quite general in nature, but it is worth bearing in mind that the girl and the other participants are not simply being presented with the general form of the relationships, but with those relationships in the context of the specific actors present in the ritual. Typically these persons will already have been closely involved with one another as individuals. This is one reason why I assume that the MS_is corresponding to a given modal state in the social manifold (MS_m) are not simply identical 'realizations' of that MS_m. Each girl undergoes a different Nkang'a, since the situation, age, personality and social relationships of the various individuals involved will never be the same in two cases, even if the ritual is performed in exactly the same way, which is unlikely in a preliterate society.

The cultural symbolism employed to transmit the modal state is of considerable interest. In Ndembu rituals there is always one primary 'ritual symbol' (in the Ndembu sense), in this case the *mudyi* tree. Other symbols have a secondary part in the ritual symbolism. Each ritually conveyed modal state is built up from a sequence of operations with a specific group of symbolic objects.

Ndembu rituals III: becoming a man

We can see how a number of ritual symbols are used in sequence in the other major Ndembu puberty ritual, Mukanda. Mukanda is the boys' circumcision ritual and corresponds structurally to Nkang'a for girls. Mukanda is performed for a small group of young boys rather than for an individual child as is the case for Nkang'a (cf. Turner 1962, 1970: 151–279, E. Turner 1987).

Here we consider mainly a single central ritual sequence of Mukanda. In this sequence, several trees are played off against each other to represent the relationship between male and female roles within the overall pattern of Ndembu society (Turner 1962). The circumcision itself takes place under a *mudyi* tree that, as in the girl's ritual, serves as the 'place of suffering' and dying to the life of childhood. The boys are then taken over a sapling of the *muyombu* tree (White Syringa, *Kirkia acuminata*). This tree, with its white bark and colourless gum, which the Ndembu interpret as representing tears, is used for shrines to the ancestral spirits. In the context of Mukanda, according to Turner, it stands for death.

The boys are then seated on logs made of *mukula* wood, where the older men feed them as if they were infants. *Mukula* (Kiaat, *Pterocarpus angolensis*), is a red hardwood that exudes a red gum. Red stands for blood in Ndembu symbolism and so for the meat of wild animals, for hunting, a prime male activity, and for the male role in general, although *mukula* is in other contexts associated with menstrual blood and is used in the Nkula ritual to cure menstrual disorders. Its red gum coagulates quickly, which makes it appropriate to the context of Mukanda, where it is desirable that the boys' circumcision injuries heal quickly.

Turner analyses this sequence as representing the separation of the boys from the mother–child linkage symbolized by *mudyi*, followed by death (*muyombu*) and rebirth in terms of the new male imagery of the *mukula* tree. This kind of playing off of symbols against each other, performed in words rather than acted non-verbally, is very similar, incidentally, to the underlying structure that Lévi-Strauss indicated for myth in his *Mythologiques* (e.g. Lévi-Strauss 1969b).

In this Mukanda sequence *mudyi*, *muyombu* and *mukula* are used, along with other symbols, to construct the specific modal state appropriate for the boys as they enter adulthood. The three trees, along with many other symbols, are employed to construct the two sets of MS_is, one for men and one for women, which are really two complementary aspects of the same underlying MS_m.

There are other levels of symbolic coding involved in Ndembu ritual. For example, every ritual has a characteristic drumbeat, which provides a further level of association for the corresponding MS_i. (The Ndembu term for ritual is the same as the word for 'drum', providing the pun in the title of Turner's book *The Drums of Affliction*.) This musical or sonic aspect to the encoding of modal states is found in many cultures. The widespread use of characteristic drumbeats, dance-rhythms and songs in Africa may be paralleled by the use of musical modes, or complexes of modal fragments, as in the Arabic *maqam*, the Indian *raga* or even (a very simple example, with only two terms) the Western major/minor distinction. Other sensory modalities, such as characteristic smells or tastes, may also help to build up the symbolism of particular modal states.

Turner suggested that there is also a more basic level of symbolic coding that underlies Ndembu tree symbolism. This is a ternary division into red, white and black symbols. *Mudyi* and *muyombu* are white, *mukula* is red. Turner discussed this ternary classification at length, drawing parallels from throughout and beyond Africa, including the well-known Indian scheme of the three *guna* or basic qualities (*sattva, rajas, tamas*) underlying the universe (Turner 1970: 59–92).

The entire range of significant Ndembu trees and plants is quite large. Turner has mentioned at least a hundred in his various writings, although some are clearly more important than others. They can be regarded as forming a kind of analogical catalogue of Ndembu culture, a vocabulary out of which modal states are built, and they are used in ritual to evoke and create the appropriate modal states in the participants.

Male and female socialization: some comments

It will be noticed that what Nkang'a and Mukanda are doing, in my interpretation of Turner's analysis, is to create (or recreate) a modal state within the local social manifold (MS_m) that represents, as it were, the ideal average adult male and female roles for the Ndembu. The individual modal states created in men and women through these rituals are both derivative from this underlying state of the manifold. Thus, the MS_m is 'realized' as tens of thousands of slightly or markedly differing individual modal states (MS_is) of Ndembu men and women; to the extent, that is, that the rituals 'work'.

The ritual is by no means the only basis on which Ndembu boys and girls learn to be adult men and women. It is not even necessarily the most important. Turner's analysis emphasized the constructive and effective role of the ritual, and it seems reasonable to assume that these lengthy and complex rituals do have significant effects on those who take part in them, above all on the boys and girls who are at their centres. We should remember here, too, that any individual Ndembu woman or man will not merely undergo a single Nkang'a or Mukanda as central figure. She or he will witness as a more or less closely involved participant a whole series of Nkang'a and Mukanda rituals for many girls and boys. A girl will typically act as assistant for an older girl who is going through Nkang'a before she undertakes the ritual herself. A boy will both go through Mukanda with a small group of other boys and then take the male (bridegroom's) role in his future wife's Nkang'a. Both will attend Nkang'a and Mukanda rituals for other children in the neighbourhood.

For all this, there are many other factors that will certainly have a bearing on the constitution of the MS_is of adult male and female Ndembu. These include the culturally specific patterns constantly being reinforced through sequences of social interaction, through the adult male and female roles that the growing child sees all around himself or herself.

The specific genetic endowments of each particular individual will presumably also have a bearing on their particular 'realization' of the basic modal state. The MMF does not regard the modal states as being imposed upon any kind of *tabula rasa*. They are being acquired in a creative and interactive manner by an individual who has a specific and constantly developing and changing body, female or male, and who is in a specific and also constantly transforming pattern of social relationships with immediate family and community members.

Thus, the most that can be expected of even the most effective and psychologically penetrating ritual is that it helps to direct and shape these factors in a particular way. Nkang'a and Mukanda may do little more than subtly shift the emotional balance and the central common-sense assumptions of Ndembu society in a particular direction. This may still be enough to make a very substantial difference in the day-to-day happiness and fulfilment of individual Ndembu, and in the viability of their society as a whole.

Male and female roles among the matrilineal Ndembu appear to be less unequally valued and to involve a more positive appreciation of femininity than is the case among many human societies. Ndembu men and women are, nevertheless, not equal either in the duties they are expected to perform within the household and the general economy or in their access to the relatively limited roles of political leadership and authority within traditional Ndembu society. Here, as elsewhere, the reproduction of society, in the form of the reproduction of cultural modal states, is the reproduction of difference. We might choose to regard the difference in the Ndembu case as being relatively benign. Elsewhere it can be much less so.

Ndembu rituals IV: healing and balance

I shall now go on to apply this idea of taking the rituals as creating and representing modal states in the case of the 'rites of affliction' that form the other major category of Ndembu ritual. The Ndembu suppose that illness, death and misfortune frequently result from the action of the ancestral 'shades', that is the spirits of ancestors in the last two or three generations (i.e. the grandparental or great-grandparental generation). Specific ancestors from this group become upset or annoyed at the acts of their descendants and indicate their displeasure through causing the affliction. The ancestral spirit or spirits are thought to attack the living through a particular named mode or aspect of affliction, such as Chihamba, Nkula and so on. Each of these 'modes' can be dealt with by an appropriate ritual.

These modes of affliction, and the corresponding rituals, involve a wide range of illnesses as well as other kinds of misfortune. They centre on the areas of reproduction (for women) and of hunting (for men). They can be seen as reinforcing additional, supplementary modal states focusing on specific male and female roles or on more general issues of social relationships within Ndembu society.

These rituals, the 'rites of affliction', all have the form of rites of passage, or initiation rituals, like the girls' and boys' rituals described above. The patient who is diagnosed as being afflicted by an ancestor, for example in the mode of Chihamba, must be initiated into the cult of Chihamba, becoming a 'novice' and then an 'adept' in that cult. He or she is assisted to do so by other Ndembu who have previously passed through the same experience and who are now adepts in the cult in question.

Turner analysed these rituals of affliction at several different levels. For Chihamba, for example, he focused in one study on the way in which the ritual acts as an initiatory process for those undergoing it and conveys a central insight about the nature of reality (Turner 1975). Elsewhere he discussed Chihamba in terms of its effect in repairing the network of social relations within and surrounding a Ndembu village, and pointed also to the social value of the ties formed between Ndembu who have undergone the ritual together (Turner 1957).

Within the MMF, these different levels of analysis can again be seen as part of a unity. Chihamba, as with all these rituals, represents both the cultural and the individual modal state. It acts at once on both group and individual. The patient's illness and the general malaise in the community leads to the diviner being consulted and to a performance of Chihamba being undertaken.

The Chihamba ritual can be seen as an attempt to correct a *lack of* or weakness in the modal state that Chihamba represents and inculcates. In slightly different words, we could say that the negative aspect of the modal state (the lack of 'Chihamba feeling') is the cause of the problem. This negative aspect is represented by the ancestor-spirit acting in the 'mode' of Chihamba. It is of some interest that in this limited context the Ndembu can be said to use a language of 'spirits' to refer to modal states, because in chapters 8 and 9 I shall suggest that this is an example of a more widespread usage and that references to 'spirits' in non-Western societies can often be interpreted as speaking about modal states.[2]

When a diviner diagnoses an illness as the result of a particular male or female ancestor attacking the community in the 'mode' of Chihamba, the effect is to prescribe a ritual that will presumably strengthen the positive modal state associated with the Chihamba ritual. The identification of a particular ancestor here is not arbitrary since, as Turner noted, it specifies the composition of the social group that will be responsible for organizing and performing the ritual.

The modal state in chapter 6 was defined as referring to the physical state of the body as well as constituting an experience of the external world. Consequently, Chihamba must also imply a way of feeling about one's own body. The ritual can be expected to transform the patient's attitude to the illness, both by explaining it and by strengthening a positive modal state whose essence is health and well-being. Western medicine has begun in recent years to appreciate the significance of the patient's 'subjective' approach to illness or injury, and to see the healing process as involving a transformation at this level as well as physical intervention through drugs or surgery.

The multimodal approach gives some indication of how such transformations are brought about in non-Western cultures. Here again Lévi-Strauss's classic study of shamanic healing, with its emphasis on mythological language as enabling the patient to make sense of and so control what would otherwise be inchoate and unbearable sensations of pain came close many years ago to this mode of analysis (Lévi-Strauss 1972: 167–85).

The language of conventional Western medicine, with its rigid body–mind dichotomy, by contrast confines the 'patient' to the passive role that the word implies, with no possibility of influencing the outcome of the condition. Western or 'allopathic' medicine treats the ailment rather than the patient; it identifies particular syndromes (diseases, malfunctions of various organs) and deals with them individually through standardized techniques.

The assumption of replicability within Western medicine, basic to the scientific method, encourages the doctor to see the problem as physical, and as a repetition of some known and analytically discrete physical problem. It should always be possible to find a specific remedy for a specific physical problem, although in any particular instance the situation may be complicated by the interaction of two or more discrete problems, not to say by the side-effects of the remedies used.

By contrast, medical procedures in Ndembu society, as in many non-Western societies, give as much or more priority to the restoration of balance and harmony in the patient. This state of harmony is a function of the organism as a whole (the MS_i in MMF terminology) and indeed also of the patient's social context and thus the MS_m. This emphasis is not necessarily due to a lack of medical technology, since many of these non-Western societies, including the Ndembu, have a moderately sophisticated pharmacopoeia of herbal and other natural medicines. When access to Western medical facilities becomes available in such societies, they are generally welcomed as an addition to ritual techniques, but not as a replacement. The performance of ritual continues to be regarded as a vital part of treatment.

The MMF helps to explain why and how these rituals can have an important effect in restoring health. The Ndembu procedure of freeing oneself from the negative effects of a modal state by becoming an adept in the cult associated with that state is a suggestive one. As Turner himself stresses, it is not just the individual patient who is healed, but the entire social group that is being brought back into balance.

Ndembu diviners are a characteristic example of the kind of religious specialist to be found in such societies. They become diviners through another 'ritual of affliction' specific to the calling of diviner, and they practise while 'possessed' by a diviner-ancestor in the 'divining' mode (Kayong'ù).[3] Generically, such specialists can be referred to as 'shamans', a term that will be considered further in chapter 9. Their occupation is normally a part-time one. Turner gives a detailed discussion of one form of Ndembu divination, that using a basket of assorted 'symbols' that is shaken by the diviner and then examined to see if it reveals significant combinations of the objects (Turner 1968: 25–51; 1975).

The basket here constitutes another kind of inventory of symbols for constructing the modal states of Ndembu society. It is, as Turner notes, somewhat different from that represented by the trees and the rituals, since it is used in an analytic rather than a synthetic way.

One might say that the diviner has to enter a mode of thought in which anything (within the total range of Ndembu culture) is possible, in order to find the appropriate modal state for the situation at hand. In other words, he is engaging in the 'analogical' type of thinking discussed in chapter 5. Generally speaking, all of the various divination techniques found in different societies, including those such as astrology, tarot and the Chinese *I Ching* within complex literate societies, share this characteristic of permitting analogical thought about the range of possible modal states to apply to the situation at hand, although the actual methods used can be quite various.

System and meaning in the catalogue of modal states

I have suggested that, if Turner's analysis is correct, the rituals of Ndembu society create and maintain a series of modal states within that society. It is important not to overstate the systematic nature of this set of modal states. Rituals are not static. Especially in a preliterate society, each performance is a re-creation. The interpretation of a ritual is by no means fixed; as I emphasized above and in chapter 6, cultural material is internalized by individuals in unique and personal ways.

Turner gives enough details of how individual Ndembu understood the meanings of different trees and plants to make this clear. Most Ndembu could provide some associations for at least the major symbols, but individuals such as Muchona, one of Turner's main informants and a kind of Ndembu anthropologist *manqué*, had developed much more elaborate personal understandings of a more systematic nature (Turner 1970: 131–50). There is no overt conflict between different interpretations, and in many such societies it is only the presence of an anthropologist, with the specifically literate techniques of recording and comparing variant interpretations, which makes the variety of personal understandings clear.

We should beware of over-systematizing sets of symbols such as those encountered here. These sets cannot be expected as a general rule to exhibit formal coherence or closure. The Ndembu are not concerned with developing a 'complete' set of symbols according to any arbitrary rational criterion. The set is complete only in the sense that the Ndembu succeed in constantly changing it to meet the demands of social life over the years.

In general, I would suggest that it is wrong to look for too much order or systematization in the analogical thought of preliterate societies. Order and system can be found, as in the ternary scheme of white, red and black symbols underlying Ndembu symbolism, or the 'mandala'-type schemes found in Native American and Aboriginal Australian cultures.[4] Individuals within such a culture may produce personal schemes of a much more systematic nature, but in the absence of writing these remain personal schemes. Jack Goody has rightly emphasized the importance of literacy in the creation and development of elaborate classificatory systems, a topic that will be further considered in chapters 10 and 11 (Goody 1968, 1977).

It is this lack of system that often confused early investigators of the religious and philosophical ideas of small-scale preliterate societies. An absence of formal doctrine does not imply an absence of philosophic thought. On the contrary, one often finds that members of such societies are constantly playing with the analogical resources of myth, ritual, proverb and everyday life in order to make sense of their world (Wagner 1978). It is precisely the lack of prescribed doctrine, of pre-given explanations, which makes such 'play' possible and necessary.

One writer who has made significant observations about the nature of this kind of thinking is Pierre Bourdieu. His discussion of the 'fuzziness' or 'indeterminacy' of logic among the Kabyle people of Algeria emphasizes the vital point that symbols in such societies are defined by their use, not by their position in an abstract system. No such abstract system exists outside the context of use (Bourdieu 1977: 109–14, 123–4, 140–3).

The set of modal states defined by the rituals in a society such as the Ndembu is unsystematic and incomplete in another sense. We have no reason to assume that all the modal states of Ndembu culture are included in this set. There is good reason to suppose that they are not.

The complete repertoire of Ndembu modal states is formed by all the material presented to individuals in the course of life (in relation to their genetic structure). What the rituals do is to present a set of states by which Ndembu ideally can manage to conduct their social life; and these rituals, we presume, are to some extent at least positive and eufunctional.

Modal states representing selfishness, malice and the like also exist in Ndembu society; they are explicitly represented by the diviner's symbols. These states are not inculcated in rituals, although they may be represented in other ways, as through the set of beliefs and practices associated with sorcery in Ndembu society. The major rituals present socially positive renderings of Ndembu experience. They are, however, not so much representations of how the Ndembu should behave as procedures that (ideally) influence Ndembu behaviour (in other words, the prevailing MS_ms of Ndembu society) in a particular and socially constructive direction.

Ndembu sorcery

The question of sorcery is worth giving further consideration, in order to see how the ways in which it is conceptualized might fit into the MMF. Turner, as far as I know, did not treat sorcery itself in great detail in his writings, although it turns up frequently as a subsidiary theme, most notably in the various episodes of the 'social drama' of *Schism and Continuity* (1957) and in relation to the craft of the diviner. Sorcery fitted rather poorly with the positive and eufunctional tone of Turner's analysis, although he did his best to incorporate it within the functionalist picture of his main Ndembu writings, and he presents enough material to make its place in Ndembu society evident.

Sorcery accusations are, it seems, a regular part of Ndembu village life, but they become validated, if at all, when they are made in public by a diviner. Diviners are on the whole unwilling to find sorcery, since the accused party will probably be present at the consultation and may attempt violence against the diviner (Turner 1968: 31). Where there is a possibility of bringing about reconciliation and harmony within a village, according to Turner, the diviner diagnoses affliction by an appropriate ancestral 'shade', with the concomitant prescription of the corresponding 'ritual of affliction'. He diagnoses sorcery where the split in the village community is irrevocable. The accusation of sorvery thus legitimates and justifies the tensions within the community and at the same time brings them to bear on the single divide between the alleged sorcerer's party and the rest of the village. Its normal consequence is that the village splits up along this divide.

What we have here, as Turner made clear, is the social recognition of a negative and socially destructive modal state or category of modal states. Turner portrayed this as a last resort. If the emotions and tensions within the community can possibly be channelled into a 'constructive' modal state, then this is done. However, there is also a place within the system for when this is not possible (1968: 43). We will see further variations on this issue of the conceptualization of 'evil' in later chapters.

8   Sociocentric modal states

The treatment of the Ndembu in chapter 7 was not intended to imply that the Ndembu are a 'typical' society, or even a typical small-scale, preliterate, low technology society. Its purpose was simply to demonstrate that the MMF provides a convenient and practicable language for describing at least some aspects of one human society. At the same time I introduced the theme of societal mechanisms for creating and maintaining modal states, along with a number of related issues. In this chapter I shall follow up some of these issues further through shorter discussions of several other societies.

To begin with, let us return to the Ndembu analysis. Note the way in which the multimodal framework, when applied to the Ndembu material, groups together the 'individual', 'group' and 'societal' aspects of Ndembu rituals and their symbolism. It is not coincidental that this grouping appears to make so much sense when applied to the Ndembu data. It corresponds to what Turner himself was doing in his classic studies. Turner, in his writings of the 1960s, was struggling against the nature of the categories available to him at that time. His works represent a significant attempt to *fit together* what those categories separate.

This, it seems to me, is the point of Turner's emphasis on the 'bipolar' nature of Ndembu ritual symbols, a theme explored at length in his writings of the early 1960s. He argued repeatedly that symbols like the *mudyi* tree had both a sensory, physiological, 'orectic' pole and a cultural, ideological pole (Turner 1968: 18–22, 1970: 28–9, 54–5; cf. also 1985: 269–71). In the case of the *mudyi* tree, the first pole was represented by the image of milk and breast-feeding with its connections to early childhood experience and its presumed ability to tap into deep and powerful emotional drives. The second pole was constituted by the *mudyi* tree's use to signify the *social* link between mother and child, especially mother and daughter, the socially defined matrilineal descent categories and 'Ndembu tradition' as a whole.

Turner developed this argument further in passages such as those in *The Drums of Affliction* where he analysed the effects of the Nkang'a (girl's puberty) ritual (1968: 234–9, 264–8). Because the *mudyi* tree, the central symbol of Nkang'a, had this bipolar symbolism, because it operated at once on the sociological and the psychological level, it could tie together emotion and social structure. In this way it could redirect the potentially anarchic and anti-social tendencies of human emotions to socially constructive ends, specifically the 'making' of a new adult Ndembu woman, with the attendant reshaping of social relationships about her and her husband. Similarly the rituals of affliction, as in the culminating acts of the 'social drama' portrayed in *Schism and Continuity*, could reshape the strained and conflicting emotions of the strife-torn village community, reasserting their essential unity and restoring at least some temporary measure of harmony and co-operation among them. As Deleuze and Guattari remarked in relation to the activity of the diviner in another of these 'rituals of affliction' described by Turner,

> [i]t is not only a question of discovering the preconscious investments of a social field by interests, but – more profoundly – its unconscious investments by desire, such as they pass by way of the sick person's marriages, his position in the village, and all of the positions of a chief lived in intensity within the group.　　　　(Deleuze and Guattari 1984: 168)

As with many of Turner's most vital contributions, his arguments strike me as both deeply problematic and, in some basic sense, right. Turner, as often, was on to something that went beyond the ability of the vocabulary he had at his disposal. We are, I think, missing Turner's point if we accuse him of being, in effect, an 'idealist' who is claiming an unwarranted power for symbols over human life (cf. Austin-Broos 1981). His central problem was precisely to *break down* the artificial barriers between ideas, emotions, and social life. Unfortunately, he had to do this in terms of a pre-given (Manchester-school functionalist) theory of the social domain and an equally pre-given (sub-Freudian) psychology. It is clear from Turner's later writings that he himself was well aware of the difficulties. He continued to look for new conceptual frameworks that could aid him in resolving them, right up to such late papers as 'Body, brain and culture' and 'The new neurosociology' (Turner 1985: 249–90).

Much of the problem arises from the continuing dominance of a rigid mind–body dichotomy in Western thought. This division still pervades our intellectual categories, a century after the theology that provided it with such strong ideological underpinning ceased to be intellectually respectable and more than half a century after the conversion of theoretical physics to a conceptual framework (quantum theory) quite inconsistent with both mind–body dichotomizing and with the positivism that traditionally accompanies it.

Really hard-headed scientists, provided that they are ignorant enough of modern physics and the other post-positivistic disciplines, often claim that they no longer believe in the mind, but only in the body, which is identified with physical 'reality'. This dispiriting move in no way affects their commitment to a body–mind dichotomy. It simply asserts that the domain of 'mind' is not to be discussed, leaving mental activity free-floating and untheorized except for a dogmatic assertion that it *must* be reducible in some ultimate way to the physical.

Assertions of this kind have not been productive in anthropology, despite occasional claims made for cultural materialism and some of the more reductionist versions of Marxism. Nevertheless, theorizing a genuine *unity* of body and mind is not an easy business.

Turner's problem here is a case in point. He was attempting to put together what his society's categories of thought kept apart. Fortunately he had a major resource in the thought and practice of the Ndembu themselves, who insisted in talking and acting as if there *was* no rigid mind–body dichotomy. Nkang'a operates on both levels at once, and if we decide, as Turner did, that its effects are real, we are driven towards constructing a non-dichotomizing social theory to explain them.

The MMF provides a language within which such a theory can be put forward, although in chapter 7 I did little more than demonstrate that Ndembu practice can be represented easily within its categories. A full-blown theory might, for example, go on to investigate in detail the processes by which Ndembu ritual operates, in terms of a vocabulary of modal states present within Ndembu society, and to attempt to evaluate what kinds of transformations, if any, it brings about.

Similar conceptual problems arise with the other dichotomy that has raised such drastic problems for the social sciences, the dichotomy between individual and society (self and other).[1] Here again a reductionism that blindly asserts that one category exists and the other is a mere epiphenomenon will not get us very far, whether we select the 'individual' or the 'society' pole. Ndembu ritual operates at both levels, and we need categories (such as the modal state) that do the same if we are to study what is going on effectively.

I am not suggesting that the Ndembu are incapable of distinguishing individuals from each other or that they cannot tell at least as well as we can when they are day-dreaming and when they are perceiving a 'real' event in the external world. In some measure they, like all human beings, need to make these distinctions. What is at issue is the kind of *significance* that

95

is attached to the dichotomies between individual and society, body and mind.

The typical distinctions of modern Western society are not universal, and we cannot afford to have an overall theoretical framework that is tied to the local and parochial assumptions of our own society. Our overall framework should have assumptions that are as limited as possible, as explicit as possible, and that are always open to alteration. I have tried to meet these demands in the case of the MMF, which is in part an attempt to see how far it is possible to get with a deliberately parsimonious set of basic postulates.

Non-dichotomizing strategies in social life

I hope that the above comments on the problems of Western dichotomizing thought have clarified the situation a little. In saying such things I occasionally have a feeling of stating the obvious, but there is no doubt that the point has yet to be assimilated by many social scientists. I have referred several times to the absence of such dichotomies in much contemporary theoretical physics, but one can look around the sciences more generally today and find frameworks that do not take the body–mind or individual–group dichotomies as ultimate.

Thus Maturana's and Varela's attempt to reconceptualize perception, behaviour and reproduction in terms of the unified body–mind process of 'autopoesis' (1980, 1988), Karl Pribram's holographic model of the mind-brain (1971), and Rupert Sheldrake's rethinking of the development of species in terms of 'morphogenetic fields' through which 'individual' defines 'species' and *vice versa* at the same time (1987) are all of this kind, as are a whole series of other new theoretical approaches that have arisen over the last few years in areas such as biology and ecology. The point here is not whether specific theories of this kind in their present form will prove adequate, but that scientists are now relatively free to develop such theories.

It is true, nevertheless, that many of these approaches have been attacked precisely *because* they overstep the sacred dichotomies, and that the mind–body and self–other distinctions are very deeply embedded in the way we speak, argue and think.[2] Even those who are prepared to accept the reality of body–mind *interaction* are often much less prepared to accept the conceptual shift that is implied by that interaction.[3] As for attacking the individual–group or self–other dichotomy, that seems to be, if anything, even more threatening to the carefully cossetted and protected Western ego.

To point, as I am going to, to a mode of thinking in which these distinctions are systematically denied can thus still strike an uncomfortable note, especially as it may seem to revive memories of Lévy-Bruhl's primitive mentality and other dubious items in the anthropological broom-cupboard. However, it seems to me more or less incontrovertible that such modes of thinking exist and that they are of importance in many human societies. In considering them, we should always bear in mind that in the very nature of the MMF we are never talking about 'what natives think' but about only one of a number of possible modes of thinking within a society.

To start with, let us reflect a little more on the significance of the non-dichotomizing concepts found in Ndembu ritual. What is really at issue here is a kind of confidence-trick, or a mass act of self-hypnosis, at the basis of Ndembu society as in varying degrees of all societies. It is the confidence-trick that Emile Durkheim recounted in the *Elementary Forms of the Religious Life,* by which people come to value their society or community more highly than their own individual existence (Durkheim 1976). We are now in a somewhat better position to see how it is done.

It is not, it should by now be apparent, simply an 'ideological' process. To describe it in this way explains nothing and threatens to take us back to Maurice Bloch and his unviable opposition between 'ideology' and 'common-sense'. What is going on is more complex and more far-reaching, since the process is operating not merely with how the Ndembu (for example) *see* the world but also with how they *feel* about the world and with how they feel about themselves.

One cannot separate a particular orientation towards the social group from a specific perception of the nature of 'reality' and especially from a specific construction of the sense of self.[4] The ritual operates on all of these at once; it operates on the modal state (of the group and of the individuals composing that group).

It can succeed in doing this because the specific modal state it is operating with does not incorporate the self–other dichotomy. By this I do not mean simply that the modal state operates on both self and other, individual and society, because this is true by definition of all modal states. The point is that the modal state itself does not involve such a dichotomy in the way in which a person who is 'realizing' it perceives the world. Seeing and feeling the world through that modal state, the barrier between individual and society, self and other does not exist. The individual, the self, is part of the larger social group.

Such modal states could be described as 'non-egoic', since they deny the self–other boundary, or as 'sociocentric', since they emphasize group rather than individual. I shall adopt the term 'sociocentric' here and shall contrast these states with 'egocentric' modal states that assert and emphasize the separateness of the individual. These 'sociocentric' states will acquire some importance over the next couple of chapters. It would seem likely, for a start, that they have a bearing on the notorious problem of 'altruism' that has so concerned many sociobiologists (e.g. Alexander 1982).

One can, of course, maintain order within society, impose the subservience of individual to group, without employing sociocentric modal states. Armies do quite well, at least in the short term. So do egocentric modal states, provided they are of the right kind. Modern industrial societies generally do involve sociocentric states (they can be seen in full fling in the football crowd and at the patriotic parade) but they appear to be less important than other, thoroughly egocentric, modal states, under whose influence the individual is more or less successfully convinced that his or her personal welfare is best promoted by behaving in a relatively orderly and socially-constructive manner. I shall have more to say about this fascinating class of egocentric states and about the mechanisms by which they are directed (in particular, advertising and the media) in chapter 11. Clearly, they correspond to a 'psychic economy', a contrasting construction of the self, somewhat different to that found in a society such as the Ndembu.

Egocentric states do not necessarily represent a 'problem' for orderly social existence. They are basic to much human functioning. The process of recognizing ourselves as discrete individuals distinct from other people, from other living species and from the environment is part of how our species operates, and it is hard to see how we could do without the ability to do this altogether while continuing to live within society. To a certain degree private good is bound to contribute to public good, in that these states at least motivate us to look after our survival, health and shelter.

It would seem, though, that it is problematic for human societies to have their entire population spending all of their lives in egocentric states. Human beings live in groups, and group living requires some willingness to care for others. It would seem reasonable to assume that the human biological basis allows for the formation of sociocentric states as well as egocentric states.[5] Modern industrial societies may be unusual in the low frequency of such states, a situation that may reflect the need to maintain a constant demand for industrial products among their populations. As John Berger has suggested, advertising works by creating the essentially egocentric states of personal lack and inadequacy as a basis for the desire for consumption (Berger 1972).

Modern industrial societies, as I have implied above, also have ultimate recourse for the purposes of maintaining order to the use of superior physical force, in the shape of police and the military, along with the associated apparatus of law-courts, prisons and the like. Preliterate, stateless societies rarely have such civilized amenities at their disposal and have little choice but to do their best to ensure their members' voluntary co-operation. Here it becomes important for them to encourage sociocentric modal states and to prevent egocentric states from becoming too strong.

Restraining the ego: Semai, Temiar and Chewong

We shall now look at some further examples of the small-scale preliterate society, to gain some idea of the variety and nature of these strategies involving differing types of modal states. Our first case comes from the highlands of peninsular Malaysia and concerns various social processes found among several related peoples, including the Semai, Temiar and Chewong.

These are closely related tribal groups living in the forests of Northern Malaya. Their economy is based on shifting agriculture in forest clearings, along with some hunting and fishing. These Malaysian aboriginal peoples are notoriously peaceful, co-operative and non-aggressive, and the processes at issue seem to be closely concerned with how they are socialized into this unusual way of behaving.[6]

These processes have been analysed by Robert Dentan and Clifton Robarchek for the Semai. The Semai, according to Robarchek, have a concept, *pehunan*, which refers to 'a state of being unfulfilled, unsatisfied, or frustrated in regard to some specific and strongly felt want' (Robarchek 1977: 767, cf. also Dentan 1968). Being in such a state renders one liable to illness and misfortune. There does not seem to be any specific mechanism postulated for how the misfortune operates – it just happens – but in two more specific kinds of frustration there are definite spirit-entities that are brought into effect. Thus *srnglook* is a highly dangerous and malevolent spirit-being who will cause illness and sudden death in the case of failure to keep a promised appointment, while another such spirit is involved in cases of *sasoo*, where one partner fails to turn up for a sexual assignation or where any individual's sexual desire for another person is frustrated.

In all these cases, it is the person whose desire is frustrated who is at risk. Thus a Semai 'shaman' is reported as saying: 'One should not want a [particular] woman too much or think about her all the time, there is danger of *sasoo*' (Robarchek 1977: 771). The implication is that excessive or uncontrolled desire can lead to disaster for society. Since it is considered socially irresponsible and improper to cause someone to be attacked in such a way, Semai are extremely careful in interpersonal relationships, going to great lengths to avoid stating requests directly and never making explicit demands on other people.

The Chewong, according to Signe Howell, have a similar set of concepts, including a term, *punen*, that is presumably cognate with Semai *pehunan*. *Punen* may be set into motion if a hunter fails to share out equally among the community any food he has caught. It may also be set off if someone expresses the hope that he will have a good catch when hunting. Any emotional display in the case of an accident or a personal loss can also cause *punen*.

Punen leads to an attack by a scorpion, millipede or snake either in material or spirit form, with consequent illness. Similar concepts are associated with incest, with the failure to offer hospitality and with disrespect to affines and to animals, and with expressing one's emotions in major life crises (Howell 1981).

Howell interprets such terms as a kind of negative way of conceiving of the *emotions*. She points to the limited emotional vocabulary of the Chewong, much of it derived from the dominant Malay population of the peninsula, and suggests that these are people who learn to live their lives at a low level of emotional affect. Jealousy, envy, intense desire are states to be avoided within this society, and they are symbolized by this vocabulary of dangerous states and beliefs about their consequences.

It is clear, though, that neither the Semai nor the Chewong terms are referring simply to individual emotions. They can more appropriately be interpreted as referring to intense egocentric modal states. Such states are regarded as a social hazard in a society that survives by a deliberate avoidance of interpersonal hostility, and it is not surprising that they are imagined as leading to illness and misfortune.

These terms are in some respects analogous to Ndembu and other African concepts of sorcery, witchcraft and the like, but they seem to lack the individual focus on the witch or sorcerer typical of these. 'Jealousy' here is not an emotional state pertaining to an individual, as it would be for us, but a kind of generally malign force, which the community has to be constantly on its guard not to invoke. Here the stress is not on creating sociocentric states, but rather on *not* invoking those (egocentric) states associated with intensified ego-boundaries.

These Malaysian highland peoples, at any rate the Semai and their neighbours, the Temiar, also have ritual cycles of song and dance that can be seen as attempting to create positive and constructive sociocentric modal states. The rituals are thought of as bringing about the 'coolness' associated with well-being, with the forest-spirits and, it would seem, with the lack of intense feeling.[7] I shall have more to say about these rituals in chapter 9.

We now move on to another society, or group of societies, for which sociocentric states have been described at considerable length, though not always with much comprehension of what was being described. I refer to the Australian Aborigines and to the set of ideas generally known as the 'Dreaming' or 'Dreamtime'.

Rethinking the Dreaming: the Australian Aborigines

Australian Aboriginal kinship systems comprise a series of categorizations that divide the social and natural universe into classes. The classes are both descriptive and prescriptive in nature, and by definition interrelated by mutual obligation and need. These categorizations include various moiety, semi-moiety, section and subsection systems. Moiety systems divide society and the external universe into two classes, semi-moiety and section systems into four classes, and subsection systems into eight classes. These classes are defined variously on a patrilineal or matrilineal basis.[8]

A single community may contain several of these divisions; the Gunwinggu of Arnhem Land, for example, have matrilineal moieties, matrilineal semi-moieties and patrilineal subsections ('skins'). Animals such as the various kangaroo and goanna species, dugong and fish, plants and natural phenomena, such as winds and rain, are all assimilated into these schemes, and until recently most Aborigines would be well aware of the categories into which most items in their environment fitted (Berndt 1970: 65–6). Indeed, they had to be, because these categories defined to some extent their relationship to the item in question.

Another system is perhaps the most important of all. This is the system of associations between social group, 'ancestral' beings, plants, animals and geographical region ('country' in Aboriginal English) centring about the various myths and songs of the Dreaming. This, above everything else, defined who a person was in Aboriginal society and did so in a way that was explicitly non-dichotomizing. To be an 'individual' in Aboriginal society is to be part of a unity that is trans-human and trans-temporal.

Adult males in ritual re-create the Dreaming directly by dancing and singing the creative travels of the Dreaming beings, of whom they are the contemporary representatives. All these systems work through saying, in effect: 'There are certain possible alternative patterns, such as *A*, *B*, *C*, each of them built up through a network of analogical associations within itself and between it and the other patterns, and the appropriate pattern for these individuals in this situation is (for example) *B*.' Put in other terms, *B* is the way in which those individuals should participate in the total pattern by which human life should be lived; what Australian Aborigines refer to in English as the 'Law'.

Lévi-Strauss was surely right to argue that the most significant feature of 'totemism', of which the Australian Aborigines are a classical example, is the use of a set of different animal or plant species to represent and construct a set of different social groups. The resemblance of goanna people to goannas and kangaroo people to kangaroos is entirely secondary to the argument that goanna people and kangaroo people *differ* as do goannas and kangaroos (Lévi-Strauss 1973).

The symbolism, nevertheless, has a life of its own, since the symbols are real rather than abstract. One could also say, after all, that goannas and kangaroos differ as do the corresponding human social groups. For us the goanna–kangaroo distinction may be phylogenetically prior to the distinction between goanna and kangaroo 'people'. It is not ontogenetically prior for the Aborigines, who in the course of their individual life-cycles may well learn these two parallel distinctions alongside each other.

The net result of the bringing together of all these sets of associations and relationships between symbols is the construction of a series of complex entities that are *neither* human *nor* animal *nor* territorial *nor* mythological in nature, but a combination of all of these, in which each component helps to define how the other is to be seen. These complex entities can be mapped quite directly on to the modal states of the MMF, as further examples of sociocentric states. Here, again, we can see how an indigenous concept that fitted notoriously badly into conventional anthropological categories can be represented very naturally within the MMF.

Aboriginal and other non-linear senses of time

There are some further interesting aspects of Australian Aboriginal thought, especially in relation to the question of time, and these lead us to consider the general question of creativity and change in the system of modal states. As is well known, the Aboriginal Dreaming, from which all these modal states ultimately arise, is only in an approximate and unsatisfactory way to be regarded as an event in historical time. It can be seen more accurately as one of a range of concepts found in many societies that imply in various ways realms of being 'outside' ordinary linear, historical time, which for traditional Aborigines would have been very shallow, at most three or four generations in effective depth.

Attempting to specify such concepts in terms of our own concepts of temporality, which are dominated by a linear, historical time sense of very great depth and an omnipresence of clocks, calendars, dates, timetables and other cultural items that reinforce this linear mode, can pose real problems. Nevertheless, there seems little doubt that such non-linear views of time exist and are important. Among classic analyses of such situations we may include Benjamin Lee Whorf's and Edward Sapir's work on Native American populations (Whorf 1956), the accounts of Bali by Gregory

Bateson (1973: 80–100) and Clifford Geertz (1973: 360–411) and W. E. H. Stanner's short description of the Aboriginal Dreaming itself (1979).

The Geertz reference here is to 'Person, time, and conduct in Bali', which has already cropped up in chapter 3 as the main case-study in Maurice Bloch's attack on interpretive anthropology (Bloch 1976). Bloch was particularly opposed to Geertz's assertion of a 'detemporalized' sense of time for Bali, an assertion that Geertz linked closely to a sociocentric sense of self. It was this central 'cultural triangle' of detemporalized time, sociocentric personhood and valuation of social role over individuality that Bloch attacked as mere 'ideology' and contrasted with a common-sense world in which individualistic, competitive Balinese lived in linear, historical, purposive time just like everybody else.

As my discussion of Bloch in chapter 3 indicates, it is more plausible to assume a variety of Balinese modal states and to treat none of these as directly linked to some kind of common-sense reality.[9] Some or many of these states may well incorporate Geertz's 'detemporalized' sense of time or something like it. This still leaves us with the question of what these strange, detemporalized senses of time are about and why they appear to be associated with sociocentric states.

I think that it is precisely this association with sociocentric senses of self and the opposition of such states to ideas of agency, conscious purpose and linear, historical time – features stressed by Geertz and Bateson respectively – which help to give the game away. Societies that emphasize and deliberately 'create' sociocentric states have a certain problem, which is at its most acute when the question of *change* in those states arises. This problem is, quite simply, 'Where do the states come from?' or, equivalently, 'By whose authority are the rituals that instill the states performed?'

This second formulation is the crux of the matter, because the whole point of such a modal state is that no single individual within normal, historical, linear time is generally in a position to impose any absolute personal authority. The rituals (and the states) are more powerful, more authoritative than the individual, and this can scarcely fit with the right of any individual to change them on his or her personal authority. The realm of the Dreaming and other concepts of Great Time or Mythological Time are significant primarily as legitimating and allowing the establishment of rituals and other fundamental practices of the society *outside* normal historical time and the process of ordinary human agency.

Here we should bear in mind that while the modal states of such societies may give the impression of constituting a rigid and inviolable set of categories within which the universe is perceived, this is generally very far from the case. The categories are categories to think with and act through. They are not inviolable laws, however much they may at times give the appearance of the latter, and they are constantly changing and being renegotiated and reinterpreted.

It is worth giving some examples of change from Australian Aboriginal society, since that society offers especial temptation to view its categories as eternal or at least as handed down from the very distant past (40,000 years is the currently fashionable figure).

> (i) The eight sub-section system has in recent times considerably expanded its area of influence, and been adopted by societies with other kinship systems. (Stanner 1936–7)
> (ii) In situations where two or more groups have been relocated on a single settlement, the groups concerned have rapidly negotiated equivalences between their sub-section and other categories, so as to enable normal social relationships to take place between members of the different groups. (Tonkinson 1974)
> (iii) The process by which songs and rituals are revealed through dreams, taken up by one community, and passed on to others, where they rapidly become regarded as having been handed down from the Dreaming, has in some cases been traced. (Tonkinson 1974)
> (iv) Major rituals such as the Kunapipi have spread within the last fifty years to areas where they were not previously performed, replacing older rituals that have disappeared. (Berndt 1951, Stanner 1959–63)

There is no reason to suppose that such things have not always been happening. The relationship between the permanence that the sets of states are assigned within the society, and the fluidity and change that they display to an outside observer, is worth examining more closely and will bring us to consider the nature of innovation within such societies.

Aboriginal rituals and kinship systems come and go, Semai song cycles (cf. chapter 9) and Balinese deities (cf. Bateson 1970) rise and fall, but the members of these societies are alike in viewing rituals, Dreaming beings, deities and other labels of modal states as having existed from eternity. They are 'given' by tradition, in the primal time, in the Dreaming, or in any of a variety of equivalent ways.

What is meant by these various assertions, and what are the mechanisms by which change actually comes about within these systems? In general, change is mediated by some individual who is regarded as a channel or medium for communications from the 'other realm'. This 'other realm' is, in effect, the realm of the modal states themselves and is occupied by their symbolizations and personifications, who are often and misleadingly rendered into English terminology as 'gods' or 'spirits'.

The precise nature and degree of formalization of this role of medium or channel varies from one society to another, but what is critical is that change is not presented as taking place on the individual's own authority. Typically, in these societies, individuals simply do not *have* such authority.

Instead, change results from a communication from the 'other realm', more specifically from the entities operative within that realm.

This does not necessarily mean that such communications must be or will be obeyed. Even (and perhaps especially) in societies where they are taken very seriously, it is rarely true that messages from the spirit-realm are automatically accepted as authentic. They have to be acceptable to the informal processes of decision-making within the community. One might suggest that it is only in a situation (such as that of a 'millenarian movement') where many people are ready to contemplate drastic changes to remedy a disastrous situation that persons communicating such drastic remedies are likely to be taken seriously.

These procedures may be referred to as a class as *shamanic mechanisms*. In chapter 9 we move on to a more detailed examination of how they work.

9   Shamanic mechanisms

In this chapter, the mechanisms for creativity that were briefly introduced at the end of chapter 8 are considered in more detail. Generally, I refer to these procedures as *shamanic mechanisms*, and to the individuals who carry them out as *shamans*. The term 'shaman' is not used consistently in the anthropological literature. Some of the areas of disagreement are

(i) whether the term should be restricted to its original Siberian context and to probably historically related systems such as those of Mongolia and Korea or whether it should be used more widely;

(ii) whether the term 'shamanic' should be restricted to practitioners involved in individual healing or extended to those involved in wider social processes;

(iii) whether soul-flight, spirit-mediumship and spirit-possession vocabularies should all be classed as shamanic, or only the first.

In each case I opt for the more extended usage. The restricted usage at (i) would deny any analytic (as opposed to descriptive) usage of the term, whereas that at (ii) makes little sense within the MMF, given its general position on the individual–society dichotomy. With regard to (iii), there are undoubtedly social contexts where distinctions between different vocabularies are significant, but this does not seem to me to be sufficient justification for abandoning a useful comparative term.

It may be noted that my usage has considerable precedent, particularly in American anthropology. Thus, Anthony Wallace defined *shamanic institutions* as a subset of cult institutions within which

> an individual part-time practitioner, endowed by birth, training, or inspirational experience with a special power, intervenes for a fee with supernatural beings or forces on behalf of human clients ... Shamans are to be found not only in the northern circumboreal and circumpolar regions

(whence the term 'shaman' derives), but also among most other communities, including our own. They act as shamans proper (in Siberia), as diviners, as magicians, witch-doctors, medicine men, mediums and spiritualists, palm-readers, astrologers, and so forth.

(Wallace 1966b: 86)

Around twenty years later, Ruth-Inge Heinze gave the following definition or description of shamanism in her introduction to the *Proceedings* of the Second International Conference on the Study of Shamanism:

(1) shamans have access to alternate states of consciousness and can produce these states at will, (2) they fulfill needs of their community which otherwise are not met, and (3) they are mediators between the sacred and the profane, they are the interpreters and image-makers.

(Heinze 1985: iii)

The Soviet anthropologist V. N. Basilov has given a similar definition:

[shamanism is] a cult whose central idea is the belief in the ability of some individuals chosen by some spirits to communicate with them while in a state of ecstasy and perform the functions of an intermediary between the world of spirits and the given human collective (collectivity).

(Basilov 1981)

I take this definition from Ioan Lewis's recent book *Religion in Context*, where it is quoted with approval (I. Lewis 1986: 92).

While the definitions given by Wallace, Heinze and Basilov are all slightly different, and all offer some problems, they are all 'extensive' rather than 'limited', in relation to points (i), (ii) and (iii), and they all in practice delimit an area similar to that covered by my own usage. In this book a 'shaman' is any of the many types of ritual specialist found within human societies who are concerned with the manipulation and balancing of modal states and/or with the introduction of new modal states, such processes involving communication with some supposed other mode of being or realm of existence. The Ndembu 'diviner' in chapter 7 is an example of such a specialist, although Turner (like other British Africanists) did not himself use the term shaman in reference to the Ndembu.

Visionary states

We can go on to speculate a little about how these practitioners operate. Some 'communications' from the other realm are no doubt partially or wholly fraudulent, in other words, the practitioners in these cases are engaged in processes of conscious rational invention of messages from the other realm. Nevertheless, there is no reason to suppose that most or all shamanic practice is fraudulent. Within the MMF, 'genuine' shamanic practice presumably involves shamans moving into special MS_i that are different from the normal body of modal states within the social group. These MS_i enable them to see the normal body of states in symbolic form from the 'outside'.

This implies that shamans must learn in some way to dissociate themselves from the more or less automatic succession of modal states that takes place through habitual associations in the course of ordinary human life.

Different cultures have evolved a variety of means to aid this process, and the means employed, such as the induction of trance through drumming and singing, or the use of psychotropic drugs, support the suggestion that shamans learn to enter special modal states not normally accessible to the individual. I refer to such special states as 'visionary states'. The variety of mechanisms used to induce them suggests that we are dealing not with a single type of 'visionary state' but with a whole family of perhaps related states. It seems likely that, in some cases at least, these are associated with common mechanisms in terms of chemical processes in the body.[1]

I have assumed that a vital feature of 'ordinary' modal states is the set of established linkages between the concept-frame (the cognitive aspect) and the motivational and physiological concomitants that accompany that particular way of seeing the world. In the 'visionary states', these linkages are temporarily broken, and there is the possibility of new linkages being formed. Each set of linkages, each modal state, is tied up with a particular sense of self, and it therefore makes good sense that learning to be a shaman commonly involves some kind of death and rebirth experience. Shamans do indeed need to die to their ordinary sense of self, as part of the process in which they learn to go beyond and to perceive in symbolic terms modal states that involve a variety of particular senses of self.[2]

Within the MMF, however, the 'visionary state' is itself another modal state and so corresponds to a particular sense of self. Presumably this sense of self is wider and more inclusive (more sociocentric) than the ordinary senses of self. In so far as the shaman is expected to act on behalf of the whole society, rather than his or her personal interests, it would be natural for the sense of self in the 'visionary state' to be seen as corresponding to some entity more inclusive than the ordinary ego and thought of as being concerned for the social group as a whole. Here we can perhaps see the logic behind the various vocabularies of spirit-possession and shamanic journey vocabularies.

Precisely how shamans in particular societies conceptualize their 'visionary states' is likely to have a considerable effect on how the shaman acts in relation to society. Societies where shamanic procedures are commonplace are frequently concerned about the possible use of shamanic powers for selfish and destructive purposes. The shaman may have to transcend the states of the ordinary individual, but the 'visionary states' open up possibilities for good or bad.

Conceptualizations such as the Aboriginal Dreaming, which we examined in chapter 8, can now be seen as a way of talking about the relationship between the world of everyday reality and the 'other' world in which the modal states are symbolized or hypostatized. They may also be in part a reflection of how that other world is experienced by shamanic practitioners. At any rate, there is no reason to regard them as simply illogical or prescientific.

Shamanic concepts are, no doubt, easier to maintain in societies that lack the universal measure of linear time associated with literacy and with clock time. These same factors make it correspondingly difficult for us to make sense of shamanic language. We take it for granted that clock time is real, and that our subjective perception of time is secondary and deceptive. We also take it for granted that the pattern of society is the result of action by human individuals in historical time. Consequently, for us a perception of time radically different from ordinary time must necessarily be illusory, and the suggestion that the social pattern is laid down by entities operating at this different level makes no conceivable sense.

For a society without historical records or clocks, these obstacles do not exist in the same way. I am in no way suggesting that members of these societies are incapable of perceiving time in a linear and causal sense similar to our own. It is unclear in any case how far the non-linear time corresponds to an actual *experience* of time as non-linear, although it seems likely that some sociocentric states and particularly 'visionary states' involve non-linear experiences of time.

The shamanic approach

For shorthand, I shall refer to societies where such mechanisms are common as employing 'shamanic strategies' or the 'shamanic approach,' and occasionally speak of them as 'shamanic societies'. We should remember that such societies are not all alike and that most generalizations about them are likely to fall down. What they have in common is at a fairly abstract level. If it is possible to present a picture of the way in which time is typically perceived in such a society, this is at best a kind of amalgam of a large number of ethnographies of different societies.

We might, nevertheless, note that in many of these 'shamanic societies' linear, historical time gradually merges at a distance of a few past generations into the mythological Great Time. Beyond a certain point the sequence of events is no longer clear. Everything in mythological time in a sense happened at once, and attempts to sort out the events of myth into a linear sequence are neither possible nor relevant. We are familiar with these kinds of problems from the myths of our own religions, in the apparent inconsistencies of the creation accounts in Genesis for example. They arise through attempting to force the simultaneous statements of an analogical argument into a linear historical sequence.

The events of the Aboriginal Dreaming and similar conceptions are not really in the distant past. They are now, because their whole purpose is to constitute the structure of experience in the present. It is because they are about the way in which the structure of perception itself is formed, in that they define the modal states within which all perception takes place, that they have to be in a sense both pre-given and outside time. They are the preconditions of experience, including the experience of time itself, so their creation can hardly take place within any linear sequence of time.

Changes in the system of modal states cannot be seen as an event in time of the normal kind. How such changes are conceived varies from society to society, but there is always the quality of a revelation from another world outside the normal constraints of time and causality. What is revealed has been true from the beginning, but not previously known. Alternatively it may be obtained from spirit-beings who are themselves outside the everyday world. The 'visionary states' are culturally appropriate modes by which such revelations may take place.

This does not imply that innovation necessarily takes place through an actual 'visionary state' in any particular circumstance. New ideas and ways of operating may also come, for example, through contact with other societies. It is worth noting that Western science still lacks an adequate account of the creative process. Recent attempts to conceptualize creativity show some similarity to the present description, in that they generally involve movement *outside* the frameworks of normal thought (e.g. Koestler 1964, de Bono 1970, Bohm 1976).

We can also note that there are countless cases of peoples who are aware of possible technological changes or innovations, in that neighbouring groups are already employing the new practices, but who do not choose to adopt the new practices themselves. It would seem that it is not enough merely to witness a technological innovation being used by another people. Before it can be adopted, it has to be incorporated into the group members' own repertoires of modal states.

The introduction of major societal innovation is an exceptional event. It is particularly interesting because it raises the whole problem of change in society, and it will be explored further in the course of this chapter. It should be remembered, though, that everyday shamanic activity is much less spectacular. It is typified rather by the Ndembu diviner and tens of thousands of spirit-mediums, village healers and the like around the world whose communications with the spirits are for the most part to do with unspectacular matters such as a sick child or a lost animal. These interventions achieve at most a kind of fine-tuning of the community's system of modal states, preventing them from being thrown out of balance by the series of minor crises that social life generates.

More dramatic changes do occur, however, and in the following sections we look at two contrasting societies where they are found: the Nuer of East Africa and the Semai/Temiar of peninsular Malaysia.

Shamanic strategies for change: the Nuer

Our first example is one of the classic tribes of British anthropology, the Nuer of the Southern Sudan (Evans-Pritchard 1940, 1956). The Nuer are, on Evans-Pritchard's account, a sober, commonsensical people, and spirit-revelations and shamanic procedures generally are relatively marginal to their way of life. Their significance in my argument is as a kind of base-line for the use of such mechanisms. The Nuer employ them when they have to, as a way of dealing with unusual and extreme situations.

The Nuer, according to Evans-Pritchard, are a strongly independent people, without chiefs or leaders of any developed kind, living through a mixture of cattle pastoralism and some agriculture in country partly marshy, partly fairly arid, along the upper reaches of the Nile. At the time of Evans-Pritchard's visit in the early 1930s, they had just been involved in a lengthy, though ultimately unsuccessful, war against the government of what was then the Anglo-Egyptian Sudan.

Much of Evans-Pritchard's classic book on the Nuer, which appeared in 1940, is concerned with how these people, despite their emphatic rejection of any person's authority over anyone else, and the lack of any kind of formal leadership beyond the village level, nevertheless had an effective political structure that enabled them, among other things, to gather together in military campaigns on a very large scale (tens of thousands of individuals). Evans-Pritchard showed how the Nuer kinship system, which was structured in terms of patrilineal descent groups, extended throughout the whole Nuer people and formed the basis on which large-scale political action could take place. Nuer society, in Evans-Pritchard's phrase, was an 'ordered anarchy' (1940: 181).

The segmentary lineage system answers the question of how it was that the Nuer managed to take concerted action on a large scale. It does not answer the question of how that action was originated, particularly when the situation was outside the normal experience of Nuer life.

A case in point is the concerted Nuer reaction to Arab and European slave-raiding and military incursions in the later nineteenth and early twentieth centuries. Action in such cases came about through the intervention of a special class of individuals, whom Evans-Pritchard refers to as 'prophets' (*guk*). They formed a subdivision of a more general class of religious specialists known as 'possessors of spirit' (*gwan kwoth*). Evans-Pritchard describes them briefly in his 1940 book (1940: 185–8) and somewhat more extensively in a later work specifically on Nuer religion (1956: 303–10). Subsequent reanalyses of Evans-Pritchard's material have suggested that he deliberately played down their importance, and particularly their political role, possibly in order to protect the Nuer from interference by the colonial regime (Arens 1983).

For the most part 'possessors of spirit' were minor ritual specialists with a relationship to the spirit of crocodiles or of certain birds. The prophets, however, were connected with the major spirits of the air. These spirits could possess a man, causing him to fall ill, experience severe sickness and behave in unusual ways. When he recovered they remained with him and spoke through him. The vocabulary is very similar to that of shamanic specialists in many cultures. The prophet was able to predict and divine, to heal and to exorcise, and also to curse with efficacy.

It is these people who organized large-scale action, such as fighting against the neighbouring Dinka people and against European and Arab aggression. The spirits gave them instructions about when and how the Nuer should attack; the 'prophet' might also perform sacrifices before battle. It was, in other words, not the prophet but the spirit who predicted, and it was the spirit speaking through the prophet who was obeyed.

Since it was the spirit rather than an ordinary human being who was speaking, obedience did not conflict with the strong Nuer values of individual autonomy. Evans-Pritchard gives little information about precisely *how* the spirits spoke through the prophets, although the idiom appears to have been that of possession by the spirit. This is a pattern that occurs with minor variations in many parts of Africa, Asia and the Americas (cf. Halifax 1980, I. Lewis 1971).

Nuer society used spirit-revelations to generate new modal states at a few critical points. It seems that the Nuer did not employ such procedures much in their ordinary, day-to-day life. When the society came under threat through external military action, epidemic disease of cattle or human beings, or other abnormal situations, the mechanism of the prophet allowed new patterns and ways of behaving to enter.

In a society that operated successfully in a difficult environment through respect for strongly defined traditional norms, the occasional use of these shamanic mechanisms provided a way of dealing with exceptional situations. It is understandable that Nuer employment of shamanic procedures appears to have involved little formal training. Since the primary need was to introduce fantasy and variety into the culture, any state that worked would do, and apprentice shamans could be left to develop their own procedures. By contrast, in societies with well-developed shamanic roles, such as Tibet, we often find elaborate formal training in a series of specific types of alternate states (cf. Aziz 1976, Stablein 1976, Samuel 1984, 1985c, 1989).

Shamanic strategies for change: the Semai and Temiar

Our second example of shamanic processes is taken from a people or group of peoples, the Semai and Temiar of Malaysia, sometimes known collectively as the Senoi, among whom these mechanisms are much more widely used. I referred to these people in chapter 8 in relation to their conceptualization of negative, excessively egocentric states. Here we look at the positive role of dream-revelations in Semai and Temiar societies.[3]

These peoples have acquired some notoriety as a result of Kilton Stewart's writings on their usage of dreaming as therapy (Stewart 1969). Stewart's work, unfortunately, turned out to be largely spurious (cf. Faraday and Wren-Lewis 1984, Domhoff 1985), but the Semai and Temiar have been studied in detail by several anthropologists and ethno-musicologists, and a more accurate picture of the role of dream-revelations in their society has emerged. The Semai and Temiar do indeed take dreaming very seriously, if not quite in the way described by Stewart (cf. Dentan 1968, Oesch 1973, 1974, Benjamin 1979, Roseman 1984).

Like the Nuer these peoples are or were non-hierarchical. Unlike the Nuer, who are physically quite assertive, the Senoi are non-violent to a remarkable degree. Senoi lack of aggression has been a prime focus of several studies of these people (Dentan 1968, Robarchek 1977, 1979, Robarchek and Dentan 1987, Royce 1980, Knauft 1987, Betzig 1988). The Senoi shamanic complex, which centres about the use of the dreaming state, can perhaps be related to the general situation of these people, who have taken refuge in the forest and agriculturally marginal hill-country from the more technologically advanced and aggressive Malay culture in the lowlands.

Like the Mbuti pygmies of Central Africa, described by Colin Turnbull, the Senoi cope with the surrounding Malay and Chinese not through physical force, where they are at a disadvantage, but by the essentially shamanic strategies of showmanship, deception, conciliation and adaptation (Turnbull 1962, 1965, 1983). The apparent success of the Semai at keeping good relations with both government and communist forces during the 1940s Malayan insurgency is a good example, although some of the Temiar groups were less fortunate during this difficult period (Dentan 1968: 80–1).

Dreaming for the Semai and Temiar is a state in which it is possible to communicate with the spirit-world. All Senoi are believed to have the ability to do this to some extent, but some have much more than others, and these people, mainly adult men, take a leading role in the community in consequence of their ability, which is callèd (with some variants) *halaa'*. People who have or are *halaa'* are good at establishing communication with the spirit world in the dream state and can derive healing powers from the spirits.

One of the main things that the spirits do is teach songs and dances to the people they favour. That is, the dreamer is taught a song and the dance that goes with it. While these dance-songs are a form of entertainment, they are also of ritual significance. They establish a channel through which cool spiritual essence, associated by the Senoi with the mountains and rainforest foliage, is conducted and distributed throughout the members of the community. The language of the songs is poetic and allusive; the singing is led by the shaman who received the song and echoed by a (usually female) chorus (Roseman 1984).

In addition to this generalized ritual function, Senoi dream revelations have political and social aspects that parallel Nuer prophecies. H. D. Noone gives examples of the tiger spirit instructing the villagers where to make a new settlement, and of the spirit of the wind among the bamboos explaining that it is wind that makes aeroplanes fly! An especially dramatic example is that of a cycle of dance-songs that originated in the 1930s at a time when the morale of the Temiar was particularly low. There had been an influenza epidemic, a crop failure, and there were problems about relationships between Temiar and surrounding Malay and Chinese populations.

This song-cycle (Chinchem) was revealed to a leading Temiar shaman by the spirit of his dead wife, and it was intended, according to his wife's spirit, to drive out the dark forces of disease and calamity. The spirit instructed the Temiar to stop eating pigs and rodents, this being an activity that led to Malay prejudice against the Temiar. H. D. Noone refers to this song-cycle as 'the symbol of a new order of life growing out of the traditional tribal pattern' (Noone and Holman 1972, Noone n.d.).

While the songs and dances revealed by the spirits are undoubtedly appreciated for their aesthetic qualities, the shamanic complex from which these songs and dances derive is part of the Senoi adaptation to their environment. The Senoi are limited in their ability to control their physical environment directly and unable to meet the threat posed by the lowland peoples through force. Their extensive use of shamanic 'visionary states', in this case a form of controlled dreaming, appears to be a way of maintaining both group morale – seen in terms of the constant infusion of cool spirit essence – and preserving the adaptability necessary for the success of their non-violent lifestyle.

Shamanic mechanisms and cultural creation

We can move on from these two examples to a general consideration of the relationship between shamanic vision and goal-directed behaviour. It will be recalled that in chapter 6 a particular goal structure was assumed to form part of each modal state.

Consider the situation where a new modal state is created through shamanic vision. While its creator, the shaman, is in the visionary state in which the discovery takes place, the question of the material advantages of the new modal state is temporarily in abeyance. Once the state has been, as it were, 'revealed' and enters the general social arena, it offers possibilities for use and manipulation for the goal structures already implicit in the social group. In other words, members of the society may internalize and accept the new state because it allows them to pursue various goals (for the individual or the social group) more successfully. For all the authority of the other realm, it is unlikely that a shaman could continue to act as a source of cultural change and innovation unless members of the society see some gain in terms of their personal goal structures in the new modal states.

It should be pointed out that the development of new modal states would not *necessarily* involve their conscious origination by some individual member of the culture. They might result simply from individual reactions to changed material circumstances. All that the MMF implies is that new patterns of behaviour require the development of new modal states at the individual level and cultural level.

It is only, I assume, in exceptional circumstances, as in the so-called 'millenarian movements', that individuals on a large scale seek consciously to bring into existence a new modal state. Such movements generally have a strong moral component; people actively seek to acquire new patterns and styles of behaving. We are here in the realm of Wallace's 'revitalization movements'. As Wallace suggested, many of the world's major religions appear to go back to such origins (Wallace 1956a: 267; for Buddhism cf. Samuel 1989).

Societies certainly vary in the degree to which they are open to such innovation. People like the Senoi (Semai, Temiar) of the Malaysian rain forests are perhaps at one extreme, with the deliberate cultivation of dream-revelations by all members of society, leading to a continual flow of new ritual songs and dances. In Senoi society these are conceived of as gifts from the spirits (Noone and Holman 1972, Benjamin 1979).

The Nuer may be more typical. The role of 'prophet', to use Evans-Pritchard's term, is an uncommon one, and it is only in extreme circumstances, such as organizing resistance to the Sudanese government, that major innovations take place. The prophet is a medium for one of the *kuth nhial* or 'spirits of the air', who are, according to Evans-Pritchard, aspects of the more general concept which he translates as god or spirit. The prophet's statements are communications from that aspect of spirit (Evans-Pritchard 1940, 1956).

Thus, among societies that employ shamanic mechanisms, there are some where a large proportion of the population learns the conscious use of the alternative, analogical mode of thought, and others where it is a comparatively rare procedure; some where practically everybody is a shaman to some degree and others where the shaman is an exceptional being.

The encounter with technologically superior societies often seems to have provoked an outburst of 'shamanic' activity, as in the witch-finding cults common in Africa after European contact, and frequently seems to have been interpreted as a response to the changes flowing from that contact. To some degree this is the case for the Nuer themselves. In the case of the Senoi, a technologically simple society with a long history of interaction with the materially more advanced Malays, the ubiquity of 'shamanic' activity might be considered a social adaptation to an enduring contact situation. If so, there are parallels elsewhere; the Amerindian populations of the Amazon basin regions of Colombia and Ecuador appear to be in a similar situation that goes back for several centuries (Taussig 1981).

The responses by 'shamanic' societies to the drastic impact of European society provide an illuminating range of illustrations of how innovation takes place. To the extent that these processes have been noticed by others than a few anthropologists or specialists in 'primitive' religion they have mostly been misinterpreted. Thus in Melanesia the more bizarre manifestations of such changes were classed as 'cargo cults' and the less conspicuous ones, many of them taking place under the umbrella of Christianity, ignored. On closer examination both the 'cargo cults' and much of Melanesian Christianity form part of a process going on throughout Melanesia and indeed throughout the world. The cultural idiom in Melanesia is mostly one of revelations through dreams. Elsewhere possession or Siberian-style shamanic journeys provide similar channels by which the society can introduce and experiment with new modal states.

Societies such as the Senoi suggest that shamanic 'visionary states' can be learned by most or all human beings. There is another reason for supposing that this is so. The shamanic 'visionary state' can be seen as an extension and development of a universal human ability, that of play.

It is through play that we first acquire our repertoire of modal states. In the case of a shamanic society where the 'play' results in a new way of doing things or a rearrangement of the old modal states, the level is societal not individual, but there is in general no compulsion in a shamanic society to accept any individual's revelation. The individual shaman's revelations may be accepted, or not; there are always grounds for deciding that a revelation may not be genuine or simply may not be particularly significant.

In the case of a small child, the modal states have not yet become as rigid and all-encompassing as in later life. There is still scope to try out new things. There are still large areas of behaviour that have not yet been learned and so not yet incorporated into modal states. Learning to walk, for example, involves acquiring new modal states, and those modal states will have much to do with the child's eventual relationships to the body as an adult.

The shamanic 'visionary state' may be considered as an extension and development of this childhood play, although in the case of an adult there are certain important differences. In the first place, there are pre-formed modal states to be dissolved and transcended. Also, the shaman's innovations may be innovations for the society as a whole, rather than for himself or herself as an individual, although within the modal state approach this cannot be an absolute difference. Even a small child necessarily has to invent roles for its mother and siblings to play as well as for itself.

The shamanic society can be seen as the exemplification of a particular approach to life. The emphasis is on maintaining the appropriate mood and style, as defined by the prevailing set of modal states. If these fail to meet the situation, they are transformed. Rational thought is limited to the context of particular states, rather than elevated into a general principle dominating the entire system (cf. Wagner 1978).

This can be illustrated by the approach in such societies to the settlement of disputes. The emphasis is typically on mediation, on creating a solution that will be acceptable to all parties concerned, rather than on the imposition of a solution by authority in accordance with the dictates of a body of law and of precedent (e.g. Bohannan 1957, Gulliver 1963). Correspondingly, the 'typical' shamanic society is relatively non-hierarchical and in anthropological terms 'stateless'. To use Weberian terms, authority is either 'traditional', that is deriving from the governing of relationships by the system of modal states, or 'charismatic', which can be equated with the innovatory authority of the shaman.

There is no scope here for the rational authority of the bureaucratic ruler, who introduces changes through personal dictate. The settlement of disputes by institutionalized authority in such preliterate but hierarchical societies as, for example, the South African Barotse (Gluckman 1967), is already a marked departure from the shamanic norm. In Barotse (Lozi) society the existence of institutionalized authority extends to the arena of political as well as legal decisions, and the organization of social life is well on the way to being considered as human creation rather than divine revelation.

The typically shamanic process of dispute-settlement, through mediation and through discussion among the parties concerned, can be rephrased as involving the attainment of agreement about the modal state to be applied to the situation. In the case of the legal procedures of a modern hierarchical state, the modal state is given by the written body of law and precedent. The one is primarily an exercise in analogical thought, the other in rational thought, although as always the distinction is not absolute.

A conspicuous feature of many shamanic societies is the similar use of analogical methods of modal state manipulation to manage the relationship between the human social group and the total ecological system. This has been described in the case of hunting and gathering societies such as the South American Tukano Indians (Reichel-Dolmatoff 1976) and the Mbuti Pygmies of Central Africa (Turnbull 1962), and for small-scale agricultural societies such as those in the New Guinea Highlands (Rappaport 1967, 1979).

The shaman and the trickster

Shamanic societies deal with the problems of everyday life through the manipulation of modal states. This is the primary function of the shaman. It is also the principal purpose of ritual in shamanic society as elsewhere; ritual creates and stabilizes a particular modal state within the participants and so reorients them to the business of everyday life. One could imagine making such comments about ritual within modern Western societies, in relation to, for example, the Christian Mass, the Saturday afternoon football match or watching one's favourite TV serial.

Nevertheless, there is an important distinction to be made between such kinds of ritual and the rituals of shamanic societies. Shamans operate within a system of thought where they can prescribe the correct ritual to maintain the balance of society. We participate in the rituals of modern industrial society out of habit, out of liking or because they are the appropriate behaviour for that occasion. There is no equivalent to the shaman, continually modifying and fine-tuning the rituals performed to maintain a particular kind of 'balance' within society, a particular structure of interpersonal relationships and often a specific ecological balance with the surrounding natural environment.

In shamanic society any illness or other mishap is a sign of an imbalance. That imbalance is at once in the individual, in society and in the cosmic order. Within the non-dichotomizing language of the shamanic visionary state, there is no real distinction between them, and the mechanisms for restoring balance likewise are thought of as operating in all these spheres at once.

The 'psychic economy' of shamanic societies implies that all their members have a weaker sense of the discreteness and separateness of the individual self than is found in modern Western societies. This is the reverse side of the 'individualism' so often diagnosed as a characteristic of modern Western societies. For the shamans themselves the implications are more radical. The shaman, to operate properly, has to see the system as a whole and has to avoid identification with any of the potentialities within it. The shaman's ability to act as a genuine innovator, as a channel through which new patterns and states can enter society, depends upon the objectivity with which he or she is able to regard the current patterns of society, and on the degree to which a state of 'play' can be entered within which those patterns can be shuffled around and changed.

It is this ability to play with the patterns and to transform the world as a consequence that accounts for the behaviour of the various 'trickster' figures who are the representations in myth of the shamanic role. Coyote and similar creatures in Native American myth, Anansi the Spider in West Africa and the Caribbean, and their countless equivalents around the world all have this quality of play both destructive and creative. They have no respect for society, but paradoxically they are responsible for many of its institutions, and their activities provoke an awareness of the mutual dependence upon which all social life rests (Radin 1955, Grottanelli 1983, Koepping 1985, Turner 1985: 263–4).

The inequalities of shamanic society

It can be tempting to idealize shamanic societies, with their absence of political hierarchies, their highly developed and subtle approaches to human and ecological relationships, the apparent absence of the *anomie* and the existential disorders of modern society. That we have something to learn from these societies is undoubtedly true. Yet, if we are to make intelligent use of their knowledge, we should also be aware of its limitations and its more problematic aspects. The technological limitations of shamanic societies are well known and need little discussion, but it is worth giving some attention to the moral limitations of the shamanic approach.

It should be appreciated that the shamanic approach to societal problems, with its emphasis on discussion, negotiation and, where appropriate, more or less radical innovation, within a relatively small social group, may allow for far greater participation by most members of the group than does our own system, but it in no way guarantees human equality. The 'big man' in a shamanic society does not have the backing of formal political office to enforce his suggestions, but those suggestions will still carry more weight than those of others. The role of kinship ties and of networks of economic obligations can be of great significance here and have been studied in considerable detail by anthropologists. Physical strength and skill in fighting and warfare can also lend force to an individual's arguments. While shamanic societies may well include mechanisms that inhibit the growth of political domination and state power beyond a certain degree (Clastres 1977, Deleuze and Guattari 1987), they cannot and do not deliver total equality.

This is particularly notable when we look at the relations between men and women. Gender inequality is present in most shamanic societies, with the bulk of physical labour often falling on the women of the group. There are shamanic societies that approach more closely to gender equality than any centralized state society, but there are others where violence and exploitation of women are regular features of life. The great power of the old in some shamanic societies, as in the 'gerontocracies' of Aboriginal Australia, also carries its dangers; and many shamanic societies regard and treat members of societies other than their own as less than fully human.

All these are possible, but not necessary, outcomes of the shamanic approach, and it has always to be remembered that our view of these societies is clouded both by the arrogance and contempt with which they have been generally viewed by members of technologically superior cultures, and by the romanticizing of 'primitive' life that has emerged, from time to time, as a kind of countertheme to that arrogance. The ideal is not to take sides but to learn from both sides. In chapter 10 we move on to look at human societies where shamanic mechanisms have a less dominant place and consider how these societies deal with the basic problems of human social life.

10   The growth of the clerical approach

In chapters 7 to 9 we examined a particular mode of organization of society that I called the *shamanic approach*. This approach is defined by the extensive use of *shamanic mechanisms* to maintain and balance the modal states within the social group and to bring about processes of social change where needed.

We should be wary of erecting 'the shamanic society' into a well-defined type. Many different human societies operate in this manner. They are not necessarily alike in other respects. While it has been argued that pastoral nomadic societies are particularly likely to employ shamanic mechanisms (Hamayon 1978), our examples of societies using the shamanic approach also include hunter-gatherers such as the Australian Aborigines and agricultural peoples such as the Ndembu. Forms of group organization and of kinship vary widely. So, as we have seen, do the details of the shamanic mechanisms employed.

It is also probably best not to think of the shamanic approach as representing an earlier stage in the evolution of human societies. We are in no position to know whether early human societies had developed shamanic mechanisms comparable to those of modern shamanically oriented societies. There are particular historical sequences (cf. Tibet, discussed later in this chapter) where shamanic mechanisms have decreased in importance over time. However, there are also historical sequences where they have become more significant. Examples include the 'shamanic reactions' to the colonial impact mentioned in chapter 9 (including perhaps the Nuer prophets) and the 'maraboutic crisis' in fifteenth- to seventeenth-century Morocco (Samuel 1982). Shamanic and non-shamanic modes of organization have coexisted for thousands of years, and the shamanic approach as we know it today may have developed in reaction to contrasting non-shamanic approaches (see below).

In this chapter we shall look at some examples of societies where shamanic and non-shamanic approaches coexist. We shall be considering three main case-studies: Tibet, where there is a history of mutual accommodation of shamanic and non-shamanic approaches; the 'traditional' states of Buddhist South-East Asia, where shamanic mechanisms became 'encapsulated' within a basically non-shamanic state structure; and West Africa and Latin America, where shamanic approaches have transformed in the context of modernizing societies. A fourth case-study, in which we look at modern Western industrial societies, will follow in chapter 11.

Shamanic mechanisms, mediation and hierarchy

I suggested in chapter 9 that, for all the differences between individual shamanic societies, they do have certain features in common at the level of decision-making and dispute settlement, in other words in their political and judicial mechanisms. The shamanic approach goes along with an emphasis on mediation and consensus. Shamanic societies are typically stateless; there is a relative absence of individuals with formal decision-making roles. Instead, we find decisions made collectively by the adult members of the group as a whole or by a sub-group such as male elders. Where formal chiefly titles exist, as with the Ndembu, these carry little or no political authority. [1]

The point here is clearly not that shamanic societies lack all appointed or hereditary leadership; they manifestly do not. The distinction being suggested is a more subtle one.

Consider the concept of mediation, which I have suggested is a key characteristic of the shamanic approach, and the normal mode of reaching decisions and settling disputes in societies where it is dominant. One can construct a Weberian ideal type of mediation in which the mediator (or the group of mediators) is detached and impartial with respect to the positions of the parties being mediated. This does not imply 'objectivity' in the sense of treating the parties in terms of some abstract code of regulations. Indeed, a good mediator needs to be able to identify with the modal states within which the parties operate, since the function of mediation is to help the parties to construct a shared modal state in which they concur and which is characterized by friendliness or at least mutual toleration.

Ideally the mediator's own purposes within the situation are restricted to bringing about such a positive outcome; the modal state of the mediator does not include any manipulation of the parties involved for his own purposes. This, presumably, is why the Ndembu characteristically go to a diviner who is living some distance from their village (Turner 1968) and so is uninvolved in local disputes, and why Tibetans frequently choose lamas or hermit yogis, supposedly free from this-worldly concerns, as mediators.

It is of the essence of mediation of this kind that the parties involved are free to choose a mediator acceptable to them. Mediators who display obvious self-interest will soon lose their reputation as appropriate persons to choose. The idiom of divination, where this is employed, helps to protect the mediator from suspicion of bias by both representing his or her decisions as coming from the eternal world of the Dreaming, or its local equivalent, and providing non-human sanctions against self-interested practitioners. Appeals to proverbial wisdom and traditional sayings can have something of the same implication.

A society such as the Tiv, in Nigeria, represents a step from the model of pure mediation towards that of political hierarchy. The Tiv have 'moots' (to use Paul Bohannan's term), meetings of male elders who resolve disputes brought before them through a process, essentially, of mediation (Bohannan 1957). At any given time the body of elders in a particular community is relatively fixed, and disputes within that community will go to them for resolution.

The ambiguous way in which such a status is viewed within what is in many ways a classic stateless society is shown by the Tiv belief that the elders possess *tsav*, the 'witchcraft-substance' enabling those who have it to kill by non-physical means. The elders are supposed to employ their *tsav* for the good of society, but they are, nevertheless, held responsible for all deaths within the community, if only for the reason that they must have allowed them to happen (cf. Edwards 1983, 1984).

It is easy for a particular elder to become suspected of using his *tsav* improperly for his own ends and so to become excluded from the moot. As Charles Keil has noted, this way of conceptualizing power is radically different from that of modern Western societies:

> Tiv are always ready to unmask god the father; we are not. Tiv ostracize or punish a greedy elder swiftly and efficiently; it took us a long time to retire LBJ, longer to impeach our mad Quaker captain, even longer to put his Christian Scientist assistants – Haldeman and Erlichman – in prison. Having viewed one of the most popular American films of all time, we come away from three hours of bloody manslaughter deeply satisfied, despite ourselves, with the young godfather's growing ability to survive. We identify with the survivor; Tiv do not.   (Keil 1979: 19)

The forms of chieftainship and political office in African societies ranged from relatively stateless societies, such as the Tiv or the Nuer, to states whose rulers were invested with what at first resembles absolute power (cf.

Mair 1962, Schapera 1967). The Tiv can be contrasted with the Barotse of Southern Africa, mentioned above, who had regular courts made up of hereditary chiefs (Gluckman 1967). Their decisions were made in accordance with precedent and a recognized body of oral law, and they were enforced by the chiefs' retainers. In this they differed from the decisions of the Tiv elders, which could be enforced only by general agreement.

Nevertheless, even the most hierarchical of these societies had real limitations to their power, and this would have been even more true in the days before the availability of guns and other sophisticated weaponry. The king, to quote a common African proverb, was a king over people; the modal state justifying kingship in such societies involved the continual consent of the ruled as well as the activity of the ruler.

Installation ceremonies for African kings and chiefs often went to great lengths to reinforce this message, as in the role-reversals characteristic of many traditional South African installation rituals (Gluckman 1973).[2] These rituals would scarcely be necessary if such positions of responsibility had not been exploited for selfish ends. It, nevertheless, remained true for virtually all these regimes that the ruler could not afford to alienate his (occasionally her) support past a certain point. One result of the polygyny generally associated with African chieftainship is that there are always plenty of alternative candidates, usually with a ready-made group of supporters from their maternal kin. It was also true for almost all these societies that the standard of living of the rulers was little different from that of the ruled.

All this helps to resolve some of the difficulties at first associated with the relationship between political hierarchy and 'rationalized' regimes such as those found in modern Western societies. Political hierarchy can mean very different things in different societies, ranging from the highly conditional status of a Tiv elder to the regimes of a Hitler, a Stalin or a Pinochet. It may be suggested that the acceptance of a universal subject–object dichotomy, and so the objectification of the external world, is an integral part of the rationalizing process. Such a process of objectification naturally also objectifies people, who come to be seen as exploitable resources, just as the natural environment is seen as an exploitable resource.

This is perhaps the key to the association of political leadership with dichotomizing and rationalizing strategies. Political leadership works, because this mode of operation allows the manipulation of manpower and other resources on a scale inconceivable according to the shamanic approach. Decisions made in shamanic terms involve the reaching of agreement among all concerned through the slow processes of mutual attunement of individual modal states into a common modal state through discussion or ritual. At the same time, the potentially dehumanizing aspects of the rationalized approach are obvious enough, and they are exemplified in the development of slave-owning societies and feudalism and in the gross social inequalities of contemporary Western societies.

The emphasis on equality and human rights associated with the American and French Revolutions, and with the British parliamentary system, is no exception to this process by which government operates within a single dominant objectifying modal state. It is rather an attempt to counteract some of the worst effects of this situation by instituting rationally defined limits to what can take place within that dominant modal state. These societies have at most succeeded in institutionalizing certain limited and circumscribed defences against their own faults.

Political centralization and shamanic mechanisms

The above suggests an association between mediation and shamanic mechanisms on the one side, and hierarchy and centralized decision-making on the other. We can move on to consider why centralized power and the full-scale shamanic approach should apparently be incompatible. Centralized states may certainly include shamanic practitioners but, as we shall see later in this chapter, such specialists tend to be kept very much in a subordinate role. Why should this inverse relationship exist between political hierarchy and the dominance of shamanic mechanisms?

Suppose that political hierarchy begins to become institutionalized within a particular community where shamanic mechanisms have been dominant. We can see that there are certain tendencies built into the situation that may lead to further growth.

The modal states that favour successful leadership have a certain self-perpetuating quality. An effective leader, at any rate in a society without the modern state's elaborate technology for enforcing obedience, requires people who are willing to follow and so to contribute their part to the new joint modal state. Even when a particular leader has died, retired, or been removed, the community has the potential for accepting a successor.

As modal states develop within which leadership is seen positively, early political leaders will tend to favour cultural modal states that increase their power. Whether or not the early leaders are themselves 'shamans' in the sense defined in chapter 9, a shift from the shamanic principle of authority to a different principle is likely to take place, since other shamans are now possible rivals and challengers.

This shift away from the shamanic approach may be seen in the widely occurring idea that rulers are gods or are descended from gods (cf. Feeley-

Harnik 1985). These concepts imply that the spiritual power of the 'other realm', which in the shamanic system may be accessed by anyone with shamanic powers, is available only to the ruling lineage or to those acting under their auspices. They also imply a shift in the concept of the gods or spirits themselves, from symbols of sociocentric modal states operative within all people and in the natural world and towards forces that are specially associated with one group in the population. The move from immanent to external and transcendent deities is a further step in the same direction, and the deities now become symbols of the hierarchical power exerted by the ruler.

The shaman operates in different terms, and the procedures of shamanic ritual are concerned with keeping a balance within society that precludes more than a minimum of political leadership. Thus, there is an inbuilt opposition between leader and the shaman, or rather between the modal currents that they respectively represent. This opposition can be resolved by the defeat of the movement towards political hierarchy or by the subordination of shamans to the new political leadership.

Pierre Clastres has argued convincingly that what I have called shamanic societies continue to exist precisely because they do contain mechanisms to inhibit the growth of political power (Clastres 1977). His argument has been taken up and extended by Gilles Deleuze and Félix Guattari. Deleuze and Guattari regard the 'nomadic', unstructured and creative nature of what we have called the shamanic mechanism as itself intrinsically opposed to the rationalizing and centralizing mode of thought characteristic of the state apparatus (Deleuze and Guattari 1987: 351–473, Deleuze and Parnet 1987: 141–3, cf. Samuel 1988).

Most pre-modern human societies that we know of possessed a state apparatus, and here the opposition was resolved, at least temporarily, by the subordination of the shaman. Shamanic mechanisms and the shamanic powers were tolerated only in so far as they respected the ruler's authority and accepted the modal states that supported the ruler's power. Such a situation is quite different from that of societies such as the Nuer, Senoi and Ndembu.[3]

Shamans may survive in this subordinate position, as in the South-East Asian states discussed later in this chapter. The typical religious practitioners of these societies are not, however, shamans, since their *modus operandi* is not that of balancing the modal states through access to the 'other realm', but of reinforcing directly through ritual and other means the states that support the ruler's power. We can refer to these practitioners as *clerics*, a term that suggests their frequent association with rational and literate modes of thought.[4]

In societies where clerical mechanisms have become dominant, 'religion' generally comes to be seen as something separate from secular concerns, as it does not within the shamanic pattern. Clerical religion becomes institutionalized within the state as part of the ruler's armoury for maintaining dominance. It forms part of a wider process that may be called, following Max Weber's extensive treatment of the subject, 'rationalization'. In the language of the contemporary German sociologist Jürgen Habermas, it corresponds to the 'colonization of the life-world' (cf. Brand 1986).

While Buddhism, Islam, Christianity and the other major literate world religions may have started with a shamanic impulse, this process of clericalization and rationalization was the historical cost of their becoming religions of state in one or another centralized polity. Each of these traditions has maintained the potentiality for a revival of the shamanic process; recent charismatic and fundamentalist movements within Christianity and Islam are cases in point. Exceptionally, a whole society where one of these literate world religions has been established may maintain or recreate a social order based on shamanic rather than clerical procedures for substantial periods of time. This has happened periodically in parts of the Islamic world, as with the so-called 'maraboutic crisis' in Morocco, and in Tibet, where such patterns have never been totally dominated by hierarchical and 'clerical' processes (see below, and Samuel 1982, 1989). Tibet forms a particularly instructive case-study, since it is possible to trace the partial decline of shamanic modes of thought, and their later incorporation in a partially clericalized system, in some detail.

Shamanic and clerical coexistence: Tibet

Tibet in and before the early seventh century seems to have been a society where sociocentric modal states were symbolized internally as forces within the individual and externally as 'spirits' dwelling in the ground, in lakes and particularly in the high mountains, in a way rather similar to the Dreaming concept in Australian Aboriginal societies. The development of political centralization in the first few centuries A.D. was associated with an ideology according to which the ruling families of what is now Central Tibet were descended from various mountain-gods, such as Yarhla Shampo (Spanien 1971, Kvaerne 1981: 382). Eventually, at the start of the seventh century, one of these families became the ruler of a large and expansionist state that lasted for some two centuries before its eventual collapse. During most of its subsequent history, the Tibetan region contained both numerous small centralized polities and extensive regions without any effective centralized government. The Dalai Lama's government at Lhasa, which was institutionalized in 1642 and lasted until the

Chinese takeover in 1959, was the largest of the centralized polities from the seventeenth to the twentieth centuries, but more than half of the Tibetan population lived outside its area of control, and it was in any case not a strongly centralized regime (cf. Samuel 1989).

Along with the initial processes of political centralization in the first few centuries A.D., a dichotomy seems to have developed between the internal and external aspects of the modal-state symbolizations. In more recent times the Tibetans have had both 'deities' (*lha*) associated with the mountains and lakes of Tibet and a concept of 'spirit-essence' (*bla*, a near-homophone) within the individual. It is probable that the deities and the spirit-essence go back to an earlier unitary concept, which was both 'in' the individual and 'in' the external world (cf. Stein 1972: 226–9). Even today the deities have retained a personal protective role in relation to individuals and households, while the 'spirit-essence' retains an association with various external objects, such as trees and stones.

We may assume that a fully developed concept of an external ('transcendent' rather than 'immanent') deity, such as the Christian 'God' as generally understood, cannot correspond to a sociocentric state. The relationship between individual and deity in such cases is explicitly dichotomizing. As a source of imagery for the self, these deities emphasize themes such as autonomy, self-sacrifice and individual power that accentuate the self–other dichotomy.[5]

The Tibetans never developed to this point, for reasons that I have suggested above and discussed in detail elsewhere (Samuel 1989). Despite the 'clerical' trappings conspicuous in many Western descriptions of Tibetan religion, the underlying system was at least as reliant on shamanic as on clerical mechanisms.

Tibet had some aspects of a centralized system of government. Tibet also had books, scholars and histories, and a religious tradition, Buddhism, that appears, with its scriptures, its ethical and moral teachings, and its universalistic concerns, to be a classical clerical religion. Nevertheless, much of what was going on behind this familiar-looking structure was firmly within the shamanic universe. In particular, Tibetan societies had what was probably the most sophisticated range of techniques for manipulating states of consciousness of any human societies known to us. These techniques derived from the Tantric religion of eighth- to twelfth-century India but were adapted over the succeeding centuries to meet the requirements of their new Tibetan context.

Tantric Buddhist practice involved meditation on the so-called Tantric 'deities' (e.g. Beyer 1973, Hopkins 1984, Cozort 1986). These were not deities in a conventional external sense. The Tibetans referred to them by the same word, *lha*, as they used for the 'real' deities thought to exist within the material world and in the various heavens of the Indian and Tibetan cosmology (the term is used to translate Sanskrit *deva*). However, the Tantric deities were not so much forces external to the individual as potentialities within the individual, as within everything that exists. They fell into the category, in other words, that I have referred to as sociocentric modal states.

These potentialities (= states) could be awakened or actualized by appropriate practices. The development of these potentialities was complemented by other practices, concerned with becoming aware of and controlling the various psychic centres and flows within the body. The two sets of practices together led to the ultimate goal of Tibetan Buddhism, the attainment of the enlightened state believed to have been achieved by the historical Buddha and his successors.

The potentialities acquired as part of the 'path' were thought to convey powers of healing, defence against misfortune, prediction and divination, and these powers were highly valued by Tibetans in their own right. They provided the techniques through which the Tibetan lamas carried out a quasi-shamanic function in relation to the Tibetan lay population (Beyer 1973, Aziz 1976, Samuel 1975).

It may seem surprising to describe Tibetan Buddhism as concerned with innovation, since there is a tendency in the literature to stress the traditional and conservative aspects of Tibetan Buddhist society. While the innovative aspects are frequently neglected, they formed an important part of the functioning of Buddhism in pre-modern Tibetan societies. The process of change and innovation went back throughout the entire history of Tantra in Tibet and before it in India (Samuel 1989). Tibetan Buddhist practitioners were always in a tradition of teaching that could be traced through a named series of teachers, either right back to named Indian teachers or, especially – but by no means only – in the two most Tibetanized of the religious traditions, Bön and Nyingmapa, to a Tibetan lama who received that teaching directly in a visionary state.

Even in the case of deities that went back to well-known Indian originals, the traditions and the visual images employed by Tibetans frequently derived from later visionary revelations to Tibetan lamas. It was relatively common within all Tibetan Buddhist traditions for lamas to receive revelations from particular deities in which religious texts, musical compositions, and also particular divine forms and mandalas are transmitted to them.

Thus one of the principal forms of Avalokiteshvara, the Bodhisattva of compassion, who was one of the main deities of later Indian Buddhism, was revealed in a vision to the fifteenth-century lama T'angtong Gyelpo (Gyatso 1980, 1981). The whole cult of Avalokiteshvara, with its important political ramifications, grew up as a series of such revelations. It is these revealed or discovered texts (*terma*) that form the basis for the belief that the Dalai Lamas, the temporal rulers of much of Tibet for the last three centuries, were emanations of Avalokiteshvara (Kapstein 1980). This process of visionary revelation has continued right into modern times and still occurs today.

It seems likely that the original Tantric texts were revealed in a similar way in India in the sixth to twelfth centuries. Certainly descriptions of the journeys made by discoverers of these Tantras sound more like the record of internal spiritual experiences than of journeys in the real world. It is not always easy to be sure, because the correspondence between internal and external processes, between microcosm and macrocosm, is a fundamental Tantric datum (Bernbaum 1980, Tsuda 1978).

The *tertön* or finders of 'discovered texts' (*terma*) were the shamanic innovators *par excellence* in Tibetan culture and were found in all major traditions, though more particularly among the Nyingmapa and Bön. As with the Indian Tantras, the idiom of *terma* revelation was generally that of the discovery of an ancient manuscript, often written in ancient and symbolic writing comprehensible only to the *tertön*. While some actual physical texts probably were discovered, many *terma* doubtless derived from inner revelations in states of shamanic vision. Some were explicitly described as *gongter*, texts discovered in the depths of the *tertön*'s own consciousness (Dargyay 1978: 63–4, Gyatso 1981: 59ff, Thondup 1986).[6]

Much of the Tibetan religious literature derived from such mechanisms, including such well-known texts as the various *namt'ar* or biographies of Padmasambhava (Douglas and Bays 1978, Blondeau 1980) and Yeshe Ts'ogyel (Dowman 1984, Tarthang 1983) and the *Bardo T'ödöl* or 'Tibetan Book of the Dead'(Fremantle and Trungpa 1975). As with the Nuer or the Senoi, these various forms of revelation frequently had social and political consequences. Among the most significant examples were those *tertön* lamas who discover texts explaining how to reach previously unsettled valleys. These valleys were believed, like the *terma* texts themselves, to have been deliberately concealed until the appropriate moment. Several areas, including Sikkim, parts of Sherpa country, and Pemakö in South-East Tibet were held to have been settled in this way (Bernbaum 1980, Brauen-Dolma 1985, Martin 1985). Again, the consequences of the various Avalokiteshvara revelations for the political function of the Dalai Lama have already been mentioned.

This Tantric-shamanic idiom in Tibetan societies coexisted with a second and subordinate group of shamanic practitioners. These men and women (*lhapa* or *pawo*) divined while possessed by local non-Tantric deities (Berglie

1976, Prince Peter 1979). Some large monasteries, and the Dalai Lama's government at Lhasa, maintained spirit-mediums of this kind on a regular basis.

For the Tibetans, spirit-revelation through Tantric deities was by no means the only form of innovation. Innovations also took place as a result of adoption from other cultures, as in the case of Buddhism itself, although the question of the legitimation of such adoption sometimes involved visionary techniques. It was also undoubtedly true that innovations took place as a result of conscious decisions by persons in a position of authority. The initial introduction of Buddhism in Tibet, and the choice of Indian over Chinese versions of Buddhism, are described by Tibetan historians as decisions made by Tibetan rulers of the time, and whatever the accuracy of the traditional accounts, they bear witness to such actions being regarded as legitimate and proper.

Thus Tibetan societies represented in many ways an intermediate situation, in which, as a result of specific local conditions, in this case probably specifiable in terms of geography and technological limitations, the process of rationalization did not go as far as in the typical Asian states to be considered in the next section. Consequently, the Tibetan region developed a series of accommodations between shamanic and clerical procedures that are in certain respects *sui generis*.[7]

Shamanic encapsulation: Thailand and Burma

In the traditional Buddhist states of South-East Asia, such as Burma, Thailand, Cambodia and Laos, the processes of rationalization and centralization were by contrast much more fully developed. In these states, shamanic procedures were present, but clearly subordinate to the overall political hierarchy.

Stanley Tambiah's model of the 'galactic polity' provides an overall approach to the social structure of these states in pre-modern times (Tambiah 1976, 1985). The galactic polity consisted of a core region governed from the capital city and surrounded by smaller principalities and domains whose rulers acknowledged the central ruler's supremacy. The hierarchical structure of these polities was symbolized by elaborate cosmological schemes, often duplicated at the level of kinship by marriage links between the central ruler and women from the various local ruling families.

The central ruler did not necessarily exercise much direct control at the local level. Within these states, villagers would pay tax and tribute to the central government through the local rulers. Villagers would also have to participate in certain circumstances in military campaigns, building irrigation works or performing other duties, but they would not expect day-to-day intervention in the political affairs of the village itself.

In practice, the perennial shortage of population in relation to cultivable land that seems to have characterized these states acted as a constraint on the degree of economic depredation or other interference in the villagers' lives. In cases of excessive exploitation, a village or a local ruler could easily switch allegiance from one central ruler to another. The primary objective of war in South-East Asia, according to Tambiah, was not to occupy territory but to capture prisoners in the first place, booty in the second (Tambiah 1976: 119–20).

If we look at this situation in terms of the clerical and shamanic approaches, it can best be characterized as one of shamanic encapsulation. There is little doubt that the overall cosmological and religious schemes of these states were representative of rationalized, 'clerical' religion. Theravada Buddhism was subordinated to the political hierarchy of the state, and its shamanic aspects were minimized in relation to the thoroughly rational pursuit of 'merit', a scheme in which the ruler could figure as the greatest donor to the Buddhist Sangha and so the most meritorious of all lay patrons (Tambiah 1976).

At the village level, while Buddhism was present, shamanic religion continued to be of major importance, in the form of 'animist' rituals, spirit-possession and other characteristically shamanic features. The Buddhist clergy themselves formed part of this system, since amulets, charms and other objects 'charged' by particular monks respected for their shamanic power were highly valued and widely used. This situation continued into modern times, where it is described in the studies of, among others, Tambiah himself for North-East Thailand and Melford Spiro for neighbouring Burma (Tambiah 1970, 1984; Spiro 1967, 1971). In Thailand and Burma the political style within the villages also seem to have had as much in common with the 'big man', mediation-based approach of the shamanic pattern as with the rationalized system of bureaucratic administration (Sahlins 1963).

This kind of situation, with shamanism tolerated at the local level, where it reaches some kind of accommodation with clerical religion, but clerical religion dominant at the centre, seems to have been common in pre-modern states and has survived in modern non-Western states. Mediaeval Catholicism had a similar acceptance of shamanic elements, as does contemporary Hinduism, and Islam in those areas not overrun by the modern fundamentalist movement.[8] These shamanic elements have not necessarily declined with the growth of industrialization or Westernization. In some cases they have been incorporated into the mode of operation of modern Asian states and have, if anything, grown in importance through providing means of coping with new social demands and pressures (cf. Tambiah 1984, Obeyesekere 1977). In the process, they are perhaps becoming transformed into something substantially different from the old sociocentric shamanic mechanisms discussed in the previous three chapters. We can see something of these processes of adaptation and transformation from a third case study, that of the deity-cults of West Africa and their transformations in Afro-American societies.

Shamanism and modernity: West African and Afro-American cults

We begin with the Yoruba notion of *orisha*. The *orisha*, entities usually rendered into English as 'god' or 'spirit', retain many of the attributes of a sociocentric modal state. As Karin Barber notes in a recent study of Yoruba traditional thought, each *orisha* 'has its own temperament and generates its own atmosphere and mood' (Barber 1981: 732; cf. also Schiltz 1985). The *orisha* in Yoruba thought exist only because their devotees keep them in existence by performing their rituals. Without human support, they would dwindle to nothing. Barber suggests an analogy with the 'big man' politics of Yoruba societies and contrasts the *orisha* with the ancestor spirits of the Tallensi, where the status of lineage heads has a much more permanent and intrinsically authoritarian cast.

Possession of devotees by the *orisha* is a central part of these cults, as is communication with the *orisha* through a possessed 'medium'. The transatlantic equivalents of these West African deities, such as the *loa* of Haitian Voudou and the *orixa* and lesser spirits of the Afro-Brazilian religions such as Candomble and Umbanda are also not simply 'gods' external to the individual, but 'states' that the individual can enter into directly through the rituals of spirit-possession (Huxley 1966, Bastide 1978, Pressel 1974, Sturm 1977, Bramly 1977, Turner 1985: 119–50). Both in the West African religions and their Afro-American counterparts, the *orisha, loa* and other 'spirits', viewed as modal states, provide a kind of indigenous analysis of forces active within a community or within society as a whole.

At the same time the *orisha* appear to have a more independent and autonomous existence in Yoruba thought than do the Ndembu modes of affliction, the Senoi and Chewong concepts referred to above or the Aboriginal beings of the Dreaming. Individuals are commonly regarded as having a special link to one *orisha* or another, although their allegiance is not necessarily permanent. While there is an egalitarian and 'big man' cast to traditional southern Nigerian politics, the Yoruba have traditional chiefs and a considerable degree of institutionalized political authority. The priests of the *orisha* cults retain substantial autonomy from this system of chiefs.

In Brazil (and to a lesser degree Haiti) the situation is somewhat different. Here the cults of *orisha* and *loa* take place within a modern centralized state, and the powers of the spirits are used within a modern individualistic commercial economy (as is increasingly the case in West Africa as well). The cult-centres of these gods and spirits may provide a refuge of collective and communal values within these highly individualistic societies, but the way in which the gods and spirits are conceptualized seems to move increasingly away from the immanent powers of the small-scale societies discussed in chapters 7 to 9 and towards the external and transcendent deities characteristic of the centralized state.

The decline of shamanic language in Europe

The language of immanent gods and spirits found in the *orisha* cults of West Africa and their transatlantic equivalents is not totally unfamiliar to modern Westerners, because it was quite common at one stage in European thought. Our gradual loss of the ability to understand this kind of discourse has cut off much of the literature of our own past from us and made it difficult to understand other cultures where such a language is still spoken. Examining this process may help to clarify the nature of the transformation between the sociocentric situation and modern Western societies.

To describe the growth of an aggressive and militaristic mood, for example, as the work of Mars, or of Shango, the West African and Afro-American 'war god', is not just a piece of poetic or mythological licence. It is a description within the terms of a system that does not dichotomize consciousness and activity. As a description, it has certain advantages over anything possible within the modern English language.

In particular, such descriptions offer a possibility of control that our own standard descriptions do not present. When one has identified a particular force at work in a community as being responsible for the current state of imbalance, there are appropriate ritual counter-measures to apply, which may be able to bring the damaging force back into balance. We have already seen this kind of procedure in the case of Ndembu rites of affliction. For the Ndembu, to diagnose a problem as being caused by a spirit attacking in the 'mode' of Chihamba implies that the appropriate solution is to perform a Chihamba ritual so as to counter its effects.

This mode of thinking is only possible in a society that avoids committing itself to rigid mind–body and self–other dichotomies, and that allows for a range of forces or entities to operate within and across the space thus undivided. This still appears to have been true to a considerable degree in Greek and Roman times, although what I have described in this chapter as the 'clerical' approach, with its strong associations of self–other and mind–body dichotomies, was growing in strength. There is evidence at any rate that attitudes to the classical gods and goddesses still had much in common with the kind of thinking I have been discussing here. Venus and Mars were forces within the world because they were forces within the minds of human beings as well; the two were not distinct.[9]

The rise to dominance of Christianity in Europe did not entirely destroy this mode of discourse, which formed a major part of the literary and poetic tradition of Western Europe until the seventeenth and eighteenth centuries. We still think of such a mode of expression as 'poetic', but it requires a considerable imaginative effort to recover the thinking underlying the work of Dante, Chaucer, or of Blake, whose prophetic books are, among other things, a sustained attempt to reinstate this mode of argument (cf. Northrop Frye 1969). In modern Western societies the mind–body and self–other dichotomies have been deeply entrenched, and language that refers to processes that cut across these dichotomies has long since become difficult to take seriously.

The MMF, nevertheless, suggests that such processes form an integral part of all societies, including our own. In chapter 11 we shall consider how they operate within modern Western industrial societies and the ways in which they appear to the consciousness of human beings living in those societies.

11   Technical and transformational mechanisms

This is the last of the sequence of chapters in which we have been discussing modal-state mechanisms in human societies. In this chapter we look at the societies in which most readers of this book probably live: the modern industrial societies of North America, Western Europe and Australasia. I refer to these for convenience as 'modern Western societies'.[1]

I begin by examining some of the factors associated with the emergence of this type of society. A discussion of modal states in modern Western societies follows. This suggests that the *shamanic mechanisms* discussed in chapters 7 to 9 are a sub-group of a wider class of mechanisms. I refer to this wider class as *transformational mechanisms* and contrast them with the *technical mechanisms* more familiar within modern Western societies. I compare the distinction between technical and transformational mechanisms with similar distinctions in the work of Martin Southwold and Roy Wagner. Finally I make some comments about the nature of value-systems in different types of society.

The concomitants of rationalization

In the previous chapter we noted that the process of rationalization and the development of political hierarchy are closely associated. While we should be wary of regarding modern Western societies as some kind of evolutionary product of these developments, there is, nevertheless, a sense in which modern Western societies have taken both these developments considerably further than any previous human societies known to us. It is, therefore, worth looking at some of the other processes that have accompanied rationalization and political centralization, and that have contributed to the modal-state structure of modern Western societies.

136

Among these are the development of literacy, of a universal currency and technology. The modal states connected with literacy and with the introduction of a universal currency have what Weber would have termed an 'elective affinity' with rationalization (Weber 1958, cf. R. H. Howe 1978). Once rationalization and political leadership are entrenched in a particular society, literacy and money will naturally, when they appear, become integrated into that society, since they assist in the attainment of the goal structure already implicit in the society. As such they are doubtless among a wide range of innovations of major and minor importance that have become associated with the rationalizing impulse in various societies.

Literacy, as the Barotse (Lozi) example in chapter 10 showed, is not essential to a centralized, hierarchical society, but it undoubtedly makes it easier to operate. Here, it should be remembered that literacy as a cultural item can be utilized in a wide range of ways, and that there are many patterns other than that of the 'universal literacy' (in practice still involving significant differences in access for different sectors of the population) of modern Western societies (Goody 1968, 1977, Frake 1983).

Two very widespread concomitants of literacy may be noted here. The first is the use of literacy for administrative purposes, a pattern that goes back to the early states of Egypt, Crete, Mesopotamia, the Indus Valley and China. Literacy enables law codes to be written and enforced with a degree of uniformity through a large society impossible with purely oral transmission. Literacy also allows for the administration and recording of tribute and tax payments on a scale far beyond that manageable in its absence.

A second important point about literacy is its potential implications for the relationship between the rational and analogical aspects of thought. Much of the early use of literacy was connected with divinatory and other analogical procedures, such as the oracle-bones of ancient China and the astrological procedures of Central America and Mesopotamia. Indeed, in the case of astrology in particular, literacy was to allow the attainment of a precision and exactness previously impossible.

This precision contained the seeds of the collapse of the analogical way of thinking; the role of astrological calculation in the development of Western science is no accident. Shamanic thought operates with approximate schemes, continually adjusted to meet the demands of the present situation (cf. Bourdieu 1977: 109–13, 140–3). That adjustment is made possible by the lack of historical record and the constant small- and large-scale changes justified through direct access to the realm of the shamanic powers (= modal states). The accurate keeping of records allowed by literacy has the potential to destroy this whole way of operating. The continual adjustments now become obvious, and the possibility of modifying the categories through shamanic vision is weakened when the old categories can be appealed to directly through the written record.

Astrology, the most rationalized of divinatory procedures, is the most obviously vulnerable to such problems, but they can occur in many contexts. A related case is that of the calendar, a prime example in Bourdieu's analysis of the indeterminate, practical logic of Kabyle society (Bourdieu 1977: 130–59, 143–58). Bourdieu sees the calendar as articulated around what we could describe as fundamental alternations of modal states within Kabyle life. Literacy, as Goody notes, places all the data on the same level (Goody 1977). By making the inconsistency between reasoning within different modal states explicit, literacy encourages abstraction within a single rational scheme.

Compromises can be, and historically have many times been, reached between literacy and the shamanic perspective. The history of Tibetan societies is in part the history of one such compromise. The potential for literacy to destroy the mode of thinking on which shamanic society is based is, nevertheless, clear enough. This potential reached its full development in the growth of modern Western societies.

There is a close parallel between the role of literacy in reducing all information to the same level and the role of a universal currency in imposing a single scale of values on all exchanges. Like literacy, this has been a major factor in the destruction of the culturally defined patterns of modal states within small-scale societies. Shamanic societies are typically subsistence societies. Most goods are produced for immediate use, although their distribution may be governed by complex traditional patterns, as with the yam exchanges in Malinowski's classic Trobriands study (Malinowski 1953, Mauss 1969).

Goods not locally available are again usually obtained through regular patterns of long-distance trade in which the rates of exchange are specific to the particular exchange and often more or less permanent. Salt is an example of a commodity obtained in such a way in a number of societies, including the Himalayas and the New Guinea Highlands (Fürer-Haimendorf 1975, Salisbury 1962). Other long-distance exchange cycles are concerned primarily with political relations between groups, as again in the New Guinea Highlands or the Trobriands *kula* cycle (Strathern 1971, Malinowski 1953, Singh Uberoi 1962).

In other words, economic exchanges are specific, and each commodity has its specific place and meaning within the structure of modal states (cf. Humphrey 1985, 1987). Consequently, the reduction of all commodities, and also of human labour and of rights in land, to a common basis of measurement throws the whole structure into jeopardy. Karl Marx's discussion of commodity fetishism as part of the rationality of capitalism is the classic depiction of this particular process in its culminating stages (Marx 1958).

The cases of literacy and currency are far more complex than the above very brief account can suggest. Nevertheless, the existence of a whole range of intermediate cases of restricted use of literacy and currency does not detract from the general interpretation suggested.

The case of the development of technology, a third process connected with rationalization and the growth of political hierarchy, is rather different. Technology is in a sense part of any society. It is scarcely possible to draw any clear line between the simple tools of a hunting and gathering culture and the computers and atom bombs of modern Western societies purely in terms of tool usage itself.

The critical point is rather the attitude within which technology is used and developed. In shamanic societies, technology is circumscribed by the structure of modal states, and new technological devices are admissible only if they are first incorporated into the culture's modal state repertoire. Rationalized societies have developed general modal states that allow for unlimited technological innovation within the constraints of the currently accepted body of theory, and even beyond it. The limitations on such processes are those of economic rationality rather than of cultural 'appropriateness'. For the most part these technological solutions do not involve the introduction of new modal states (in Kuhn's terms, scientific paradigms, Kuhn 1970). The processes of modal-state innovation in modern Western societies are from other channels, some of which are considered below.

This does not prevent technological change from bringing in its train large-scale material and cultural transformations that must ultimately affect society's modal-state structure. Innovations such as electric power, motor transport, telephones or nuclear weapons are obvious examples. Here, advanced industrial societies work, again, in the reverse direction to shamanic societies, where innovations take place first at the analogical level, and only then in material terms. We turn now to look at modal-state processes in Western industrial societies in more detail.

Modal states in Western industrial societies

Modern Western societies lack the deliberate and shared patterning of modal states produced by the myths and rituals of shamanic society. Instead, there is a vast accumulation of cultural material that may be presumed to be responsible for the formation and maintenance of modal states and currents within these societies. It includes books, newspapers and magazines, films, television and advertising of all kinds. Modal states are also implicit within the practices of business, law and the social institutions of our society in general.

Shamanic societies give much attention to what can be termed a deliberate training of its members in the appropriate modal states. This is the primary point of the rites of passage that induct individuals into new social statuses and so into the appropriate modal states. It is at least a secondary function of ritual and myth in general in these societies.

In referring to a deliberate training it is not implied that there is an explicit equivalent to the MMF within which this training is conceived of, although the cosmological and religious ideas within shamanic societies often amount to an analogical restatement of such a theory. The point is, rather, that education within these societies is as much concerned with creating the states within the individual, with producing the right emotional or psychological structure in our terms, as with giving a training in rational thought.

The educational system in modern Western societies is almost exclusively concerned, as far as its formal and explicit purposes go, with the accumulation of factual information and with training in rational thought. The educational system has a 'hidden curriculum', as modern sociologists of education have insisted, that inculcates a series of modal states. Thus, the educational system in modern Western societies trains children, with varying degrees of success, to accept hierarchical authority, to be conformist in their thinking, to believe in empiricism and the absolute authority of science, and the like. At the same time, the teachers operating this system are themselves largely unaware of what they are doing.

Much the same is true of the massive body of imagery provided by the media in modern Western societies, which is of an intensity and scale that has no parallel at all in shamanic societies or indeed in any societies before the late twentieth century. The apparent blunting of our perceptions in regard to the modal states may be in part a defensive reaction against this continual onslaught. To the extent that all this material has themes in common and constructs a coherent body of modal states it does so as a result of the constraints of economic rationality.

In the following discussion I concentrate on advertising, which is a key component of this system. It should be remembered, though, that it is only part of a wider body of material, including television programmes, feature films, magazine stories and novels, popular music, styles of dance and of movement, which are influenced by similar criteria of commercial success and audience feedback.

We can see how economic rationality will tend to give coherence to the messages presented by advertising. In the first place, there is the underlying message delivered by advertising as a whole, analysed with considerable percipience in recent years by writers such as John Berger (1972), Roland Barthes (1973) and Judith Williamson (1978). Advertising works by creating dissatisfaction, by creating a need the product can fill, and it characteristically does this by creating an image of what we should be, so that we feel impelled to buy the product in order to become the image.

Advertising, however, is nothing if not responsive to society, since the essence of economic rationality is to identify and then exploit a potential niche in the market. Advertising takes the patterns already existing in society and uses them. It provides a kind of continuous feedback of the analogical structure of our society, with built-in amplification and distortion.

One can see how this happens in the kind of advertising surveys that identify a series of consumer 'types' in the market so that products can be directed towards one or another type. These both *describe* the market and also, since their whole purpose is to guide the actions of capitalist enterprise in exploiting the market, act to *construct* the categories they describe.[2]

A couple of examples from contemporary Australian society may clarify how this process works. A 'detailed research study' carried out on a thousand Sydney and Melbourne women in 1980 by the advertising agency SSC&B:Lintas discovered 'eight distinct groups of women' – the Aussie Mum, the Young Working Mum, the Young Home Mum, the Sophisticate, the Genteel Woman, the Nervous Returner, the Pre-children Woman and the Big Spender.[3] The previous year a study of Australian men on behalf of a male cosmetics firm divided Australian men into five groups – Young Jocks, Sophisticates, Losers, Account Executives and Establishment Types.[4]

These are only two out of thousands of such surveys within modern Western societies. Each category is carefully described as to age, numbers, attitudes and (the point of the exercise) purchasing habits and media consumption habits. Promising categories are then targeted by products designed and advertised in terms of that category, with the advertisements placed in media (television, radio, newspapers, magazines, billboards) appropriate to the habits of that group.

This kind of process is by now a familiar and central part of the operation of modern Western economies. It is worth examining its implications a little more closely. Australian men, for example, are presented by their society with a choice. They are not simply being offered the material accessories appropriate to Young Jocks, Sophisticates, Losers, Account Executives or Establishment Types (or close variants of these categories identified by other surveys). They are being offered the conceptual material and the imagery appropriate for building those modal states.

While other choices are, in theory, available, these alternatives are difficult for the individual to construct. They cannot be viewed daily on the advertising billboards or nightly on the television screen. The appropriate clothes, car and aftershave are not specified, so that a considerable effort of creative imagination is required. It is hardly surprising that most Australian men more or less happily accept what they are given and become Young Jocks, Sophisticates or whatever other identity from the supplied set is most appropriate for their circumstances. The set is, after all, well researched and heavily reinforced by all kinds of analogical mechanisms.

The key point here is the reciprocal nature of the relationship between industry and society. Those living in such a society have little choice but to construct their existence out of the items offered to them, and those items are offered in terms of the kinds of stereotypes used in advertising surveys. The members of modern Western societies choose their identity out of the apparently extensive but in practice quite limited range offered to them. The capacity of this system to absorb possible rebellion is also notable, as with the swiftness with which it responded to the growth of the women's movement in the 1970s and the new market this has provided.

In the surveys we can see the process going on explicitly, but it would happen even in their absence. A successful advertisement, and a successful product, is by definition one that intuitively strikes a chord in the market; that latches onto and so transforms an existing modal state. This alone would lead to the distorting feedback alluded to before. We might note that to the extent that advertisers become good at their job, and learn to produce successful advertisements, they probably do so through intuitive and analogical talents as much as through rational procedures.

There is little doubt that advertisers are becoming more sophisticated in their use of analogical material. The 1960s and 1970s have witnessed a radical transformation of advertising away from the provision of factual information and towards the use of imagery, fantasy and cultural symbolism. This is particularly so in areas such as the tobacco industry, where rational thought is a real danger, or the advertising of perfumes and cosmetics, which are directly concerned with the creation of image, but it is noticeable throughout the whole sphere of capitalist production.

The old defence of advertising as merely informing the consumer about the product once had a plausibility that it has certainly lost today. All these points have been made elsewhere, and an extensive discussion of them here would hardly be appropriate (cf. Berger 1972, Williamson 1978). However, their significance in defining the structure of contemporary society cannot be overestimated. To the extent that other spheres within modern Western societies, and perhaps above all politics, have become assimilated to the techniques and procedures of advertising, the same arguments apply to them also.

These techniques are most successful if those subjected to them are not fully conscious of what is being done. As advertising and its dangers become a public issue, the advertisers have responded by providing more and more sophisticated advertisements, commenting on and so bypassing public cynicism about advertising. Advertisements can make fun of advertising through exaggerated claims (as with the famous Smirnoff vodka series), can act as a frame within which another advertisement is placed and can implicitly dismiss other advertisements as dishonest while subtly exempting themselves.[5]

The real protection for the advertisers and the politicians, and so far it has proved a most effective one, is provided by the subject–object dichotomy itself. Members of modern Western societies have been taught to regard rational and emotional, objective and subjective as separate categories, as distinct spheres and to attach a high value to rational, objective thought. They are unwilling to think of themselves as being vulnerable to emotional manipulation; they can entertain the idea in theory but in practice remain convinced that their thought processes are not subject to any such factors.

This is why it is necessary to emphasize continually that all human thought, even the most perfectly rational, takes place within a framework, the construction of which is not, as such, a question of rationality, but of analogy. The MMF, and in particular the vocabulary of modal states and currents, is intended to make it possible for us to comprehend these processes at least to some degree within the structures of rational thought.

Rational thought operates with pictures, images, concepts built up within us, and these at any time form a *Gestalt* which is our dominant modal state at that time. An important aspect of this situation is that the dominant modal states within modern Western societies may well have little to do with what their citizens see consciously as desirable or tolerable goals. The pursuit of profit at the cost of what appears certain to be dramatic and irreversible environmental damage, and the willingness of all modern Western nations to supply arms, directly or indirectly, to whoever can afford them, are conspicuous examples.

It will be seen that the line of argument followed here differs from approaches that oppose rational and analogical thought as two essentially unconnected modes of operation of the human brain. Much of the popular discussion of left-brain and right-brain thinking has unfortunately fallen into precisely this trap. This is a serious mistake, because the real goal should surely be to use analogical thinking to understand and guide the purposes of rationality. To be able to do this, we need to see the two as intimately related, as two sides of a unitary process of thinking, and to see that process as not being located simply in our brains, but as permeating our whole bodies and going beyond them to shape the form of our relationship to each other, and to the entire universe.

Technical and transformational mechanisms

The sets of modal states found in 'shamanic' societies are representations of something found in all societies. They provide a description of what can be called the analogical structure of thought within a particular society or a particular individual. Alternatively, they can be thought of as describing the motivational structure for behaviour at the individual or societal level. Shamanic mechanisms provide a way in which these states are balanced and manipulated. As our discussion of modern Western societies has made clear, these societies also have mechanisms, such as advertising and the media in general, which operate on and transform the modal states of society.

Shamanic mechanisms are evidently only a sub-class of such mechanisms. It will be useful to have a general term to refer to mechanisms that operate on modal states. I shall refer to them as *transformational* mechanisms and contrast them with the *technical* devices or mechanisms which involve direct material action upon the environment and upon other human beings.[6]

Shamanic mechanisms are then a sub-class of transformational mechanisms. Perhaps the most important delimiting feature of shamanic mechanisms within this general class is that shamanic mechanisms assume and operate with a set of dominant modal states that are sociocentric in character (cf. chapter 8). They construct, that is, a unity between the individual and the wider social group. The self–other distinction is a basic structural pattern presumably acquired in the process of socialization by all normal human individuals, so that all societies may be assumed to have modal states based on such a self–other dichotomy. Shamanic societies, however, compensate and balance these egocentric states by emphasizing in myth and ritual other states that do not presuppose this dichotomy.[7]

There are other characteristic features of societies where the shamanic approach is central. These societies frequently employ dominant modal states which dissolve not only the self–other dichotomy, but also the *mind–body* dichotomy. These states enable the shaman to carry out the kind of therapy, at once mental and physical, individual and social, that we saw for the Ndembu in chapter 7. Such societies also typically seem to maintain relatively closed sets of modal states that are continually reinforced and kept in a state of balance through ritual and myth.

Thus, the shamanic pattern corresponds both to a particular (decentralized) distribution of power and authority, and a particular 'psychic economy', a particular structure of feeling within the individual and a particular sense of self. As always within the MMF, these are not really separate, but part of a unity. More precisely, since we are talking about a family of more or less similar approaches in different societies, each shamanic society contains its own version of the general structures of self, emotion, hierarchy and power that we have been discussing.

The 'rationalized' pattern found to some degree in the centralized states of chapter 10, and in a more developed form in the modern Western societies, contrasts strongly with this shamanic pattern. Rationalized societies have their own typical structures of self, of emotion and of distribution of power. As with shamanic societies, rationalized societies are not necessarily similar to each other at the level of explicit cultural content or social organization. What they have in common is a central mode of approach to human problems, and this mode itself may be more developed or emphasized in some rationalized societies than in others. This approach involves the employment of what I have called technical mechanisms.

The rationalized approach assumes a fixed subject–object dichotomy. There is an appropriate set of concepts for approaching any given issue or phenomenon, and understanding the issue or phenomenon is a question of applying the correct set of concepts. Correctness is conceived of as a kind of objective rightness, whereas in the shamanic approach correctness is rather a question of appropriateness of modal state or 'mood'.

A person using a rationalized mode of thinking assumes that there is an objectively correct way of understanding any given situation. It may be noted that positivism implies a rationalized mode of thinking, but that rationalized thinking is not necessarily positivistic. The 'objectively correct way of understanding the situation' might be according to the law of karma or otherwise incorporate spiritual agencies not admissible within the positivistic framework. The rationalized way of dealing with a problem is then to use rational thought within the correct concept-frame to discover the method of achieving a positive outcome.

The shamanic way would be to adjust the modal state until a generally harmonious situation is achieved. The appropriate action would then flow more or less directly out of the modal state. In other words, the rationalized approach employs rational thinking and ignores analogical thinking. The shamanic approach emphasizes analogical thinking and treats rational thinking as derivative.

There is little doubt that as a strategy for manipulating the material world, the rationalized approach has major advantages. The relatively fixed connections set up between objects and concept-frames make it possible to develop elaborate and extended concept-frames within which complex rational arguments can take place. These are the foundation for the sophisticated technical mechanisms of modern industrial societies.

Science as it developed in Western societies was a product of rationalized thinking, and it reflected a particular objectifying attitude towards nature.

By contrast, the shamanic approach is likely to treat natural phenomena primarily as indicators of diverse modal states. It has been argued that the lack of progress in Chinese science from the twelfth century onwards was largely due to the use of the *I Ching* or 'Book of Changes', a classic modal-state catalogue, as the primary tool of scientific explanation. Once a particular phenomenon had been labelled by the appropriate *I Ching* hexagram sequence, there was little scope for rational manipulation. Different phenomena, since they expressed different hexagram sequences, were essentially incommensurate (Needham 1956, Vol. 2: 298). Ironically, the substantial degree of rationalization present within Chinese society may have made matters worse, since it led to the hexagrams being treated as eternal and unchangeable rather than open to shamanic innovation.

The great advantage of shamanic mechanisms, and of transformational mechanisms in general, arise when it comes to dealing with human behaviour. The logical consequence of rationalized thinking is the attempt to prescribe human behaviour through law codes, religious injunctions and the like, while transformational mechanisms, instead, attempt to create a mood such that people behave in an appropriate manner. The discussion of modes of decision-making in rationalized societies in chapter 10 illustrates this point.

It may help to look at the two approaches in the context of the socialization of a child within a particular society. Socialization (or enculturation, which in the modal state framework is essentially an equivalent term) consists in the acquisition of a set of modal states and of the associations through which they are evoked in specific circumstances. Any society requires certain constraints to be placed upon human behaviour; the child must somehow acquire behaviour patterns that are consonant with the survival of society.

Transformational mechanisms do this by instilling in the child modal states and associations such that in a given situation the adult will *want* to do what society needs. The rationalized strategy attempts to reach the same end by providing a series of rules for behaviour and positive and negative sanctions associated with those rules.

As our discussion of modern Western societies pointed out, transformational mechanisms exist within rationalized societies, although they are likely to take different forms from those found in the shamanic society. Nevertheless, the objectification associated with the rationalized framework makes it very difficult to make sense of transformational mechanisms within modern Western societies. Analogical shifts in modal states are incomprehensible within a framework that assumes a fixed modal state by denying that there is any linkage between consciousness and perceived reality.

Transformational mechanisms, therefore, have a kind of hidden status in rationalized societies, and the rationalized approach tends to preclude the systematic use of analogical thinking. Instead, we find a confused vocabulary of hunches, flashes of inspiration and intuitions.

Some parallels: Roy Wagner and Martin Southwold

Several anthropologists have developed distinctions similar to that between technical and transformational mechanisms, and I shall discuss two of these that are both of interest in their own right and have had some influence on my own thinking. These are Roy Wagner's distinction between *conventional* and *tropic* uses of metaphor, and Martin Southwold's contrast between *instrumental* and *sapiental* action.

Roy Wagner distinguishes in his writings between two styles of using metaphor that he refers to as 'conventional' and 'tropic'. The 'conventional' usage applies the metaphor as it is already understood within the culture. The term 'tropic' derives from the literary usage of 'trope'; it refers to situations where the metaphor is applied creatively to a new situation (Wagner 1975, 1978).

Wagner employs the term 'metaphor' in a much extended sense to refer to all kinds of cultural symbolism and to include many or all of the kinds of processes discussed in chapter 6 as part of the creation of individual modal states. His distinction can be translated into the MMF by saying that conventional usage maintains the modal state, while tropic use transforms it. We can thus develop an opposition between processes (corresponding to Wagner's 'conventional' usages) that maintain and continue an established modal state (MS_i/MS_m) and processes (Wagner's 'tropic' usages) that involve creative and transformative use of the existing body of modal states, and possibly the creation of new modal states. These correspond to what I have above called *technical* and *transformational* mechanisms.

As before, it is important to recall that this is not a dichotomy between types of society. Any particular society may contain either, both or neither pattern. In general, both approaches seem to be present to some degree in all known human societies. There, nevertheless, seem to be characteristic combinations and emphases in the occurrence of these patterns, and these are what we have been discussing in chapters 7 to 11.

Wagner's formulation helps in defining the difference between technical and transformational mechanisms. When employing a technical approach, the response to a situation is primarily in terms of finding the required action within the given modal state, which can here be regarded as defined at the cultural or societal level (MS$_c$). The ways of dealing with the world are laid down in rule-books, scriptures, agreed procedures and regulations. In any situation, what must be done is to find the correct response in terms of the rules.

As the reference to books and scriptures suggests, writing is frequently a vital part of this pattern (hence the central role of the cleric). The pattern can, nevertheless, exist to some degree in preliterate societies. Max Gluckman's analysis of legal procedures in Barotse (Lozi) society, referred to in chapter 10, demonstrated the existence of a well-defined law-code among a people without writing (Gluckman 1965, 1967).

Societies that depend heavily on technical mechanisms always, though, have a well-developed political hierarchy and authority structure. There must be some authority to impose the rules, and I can think of no case where that authority is purely 'ideological'. It is always reinforced by practical sanctions, carried out by individuals or groups within the society who stand to benefit in some way from the perpetuation of the law-code or set of procedures in question.

The shamanic approach may or may not coexist with hierarchy, but it does not imply hierarchy. The shamanic response to a situation is not to find the appropriate procedure *within* a given modal state. It is to find the appropriate modal state and, if one is not already available, to develop a new one. This is in part what Wagner alludes to when he speaks of tribal peoples like the Daribi in New Guinea, and the traditional cultures of Asia and the Near East, as

> orient[ing] their actions and interpretations around ideologies that are in every respect semiotic inversions of our own. They are based on the deliberate articulation of tropic, differentiating constructions, identifying these constructions as the proper and legitimate subject of human action and assigning man's conventions to the realm of that which is innate.
> (Wagner 1978: 27)

Wagner goes on to argue that while this 'style of living and acting' may appear irresponsible to Westerners, it makes its own demands. 'Its responsibilities (which are quite formidable, in fact) are those of appropriate "spirit" or "style"' (Wagner 1978: 28).

Wagner's dichotomy between 'them' and 'us' is appealing, but if interpreted in any literal sense surely unrealistic. As I have already implied, it seems to me more realistic to see this 'style of living and acting' as a pattern present, at least potentially, in all societies, rather than as some kind of polar opposite to ourselves. As Wagner himself points out, it has its analogues in our own society, 'such as advertising, showmanship, and leadership' (1978: 28). Equally significantly, the 'clerical' or 'rationalized' pattern is important in many human societies, including the traditional states of Asia and the Near East to which Wagner alludes.

In his recent study of Buddhism in Sri Lanka, *Buddhism in Life*, Martin Southwold introduced the terms *instrumental* and *sapiental* to refer to a distinction very similar to that between technical and transformational as defined here. Southwold defines 'instrumental' as follows:

> Much...human action is predicated on the assumption that our states of subjective experience are determined by the states of our environment, the world about us...Given the assumption, in order to change our state of subjective experience (for the better) we have to change the state of the world which determines it. Action which is oriented to changing the state of the world as a means to the end of changing one's state of subjective experience is often termed 'instrumental'; I shall specialize the term in just this sense. (Southwold 1983: 184–5)

The 'sapiental' strategy, by contrast, aims to 'ameliorat[e] experience by altering the mind and the self, rather than the environing world' (1983: 188). Southwold goes on to suggest a correlation between sapientalism and the right hemisphere of the cerebral cortex, and between instrumentalism and the left hemisphere (1983: 189).

Southwold's distinction has obvious similarities to mine, despite the more individualistic and 'psychological' mode of expression that comes through in particular in his stress on 'subjective experience'. It is also worth emphasizing that, in contrast with Southwold's formulation, though not with the overall trend of his argument, transformational strategies (including shamanic mechanisms) may lead to new modes of dealing with the world in 'instrumental' terms, while 'religions' as we know them typically have as much or more to do with the technical as with the transformational.

Another aspect of Southwold's argument parallels my discussion of sociocentric states (chapter 8). Southwold suggests that 'instrumentalism' is typical of left-hemisphere thinking in being 'fundamentally egoistic – though not necessarily egotistic – and analytic, concerned with making and marking distinctions'. 'Sapientalism', as with right-hemisphere thinking in general, 'tends to be holistic and synthetic, overriding distinctions in its perception of patterns and gestalts' (1983: 189). Southwold goes on to suggest that the integrative and unitive feelings and modes of thought associated with religion have their physiological basis in the right hemisphere, while warning us that

> the two hemispheres are not independent, so that any simple identification of cultural systems as exclusive products of one hemisphere or the other is inexact, (Southwold 1983: 190)

Southwold's grounding of his two modes of thinking in the structure of the brain should perhaps be treated with caution (cf. chapter 12, below), but his reference to holistic versus analytic modes of thought corresponds to a central element in the MMF. As I observed in chapter 8, shamanic approaches emphasize what I referred to as 'sociocentric' modal states, which override and counter such dichotomies as mind–body, subjective–objective and, above all, self–other. 'Rationalized' or 'clerical' approaches, on the contrary, tend to accept these dichotomies in practice, if not in theory. They also tend to structure their modes of thinking upon other strongly dichotomizing concepts that parallel the unidimensional hierarchies accompanying clerical dominance; purity–pollution, sin–virtue, low I.Q.–high I.Q.[8]

The drive to unity and coherence

I have, for the most part, avoided using evolutionary language in my presentation of shamanic and rationalized patterns. Too little is known about the complex historical sequences leading to the shamanic and rationalized societies of today to make any generalizations about the overall trend of such sequences. Instead, I have treated each human society (and each individual) as characterized by a repertoire of modal states, itself a kind of synchronic section through the continuing flow of the modal currents. In rationalized societies, the rationalizing modal current and its associated technical mechanisms have achieved a certain degree of dominance, while in shamanic societies shamanic mechanisms dominate.

Nevertheless, the onward flow of the modal currents seems to reflect an inner dynamic towards unity and coherence, such that societies do mostly end up with either one or the other dominant. We can ask why this should be. A partial answer in the case of rationalization has already been suggested, in that the drive towards political centralization, once begun, will develop a certain inner momentum, favouring other developing modal states that strengthen hierarchical power.

It may also be that, as with the case of language, there is a limit to how many structural principles can be simultaneously active without the system becoming too complex for convenient use. It is well known that no human language uses more than a small proportion of the total range of possible phonemic distinctions. Some languages use tone, some use a wide range of consonant distinctions, others a wide range of vowel distinctions, but in no case does the total system go beyond a certain level of complexity.

Perhaps, if a society is to exploit technical strategies fully, transformational approaches have to receive less stress, at least for a while. Certainly this has been the case within Western European societies, although it would be risky to deduce that it is always necessarily the case. We may suppose, though, that any system of modal currents, in the absence of interference from other systems, will move towards a condition of greater simplicity and internal coherence.

This simplicity may also be phrased in terms of inclusiveness. The system moves towards a condition where as small a repertoire of modal states as possible is capable of dealing with as wide a range of situations as possible. The Western progress to 'universal rationality' may be taken as an example.

Here, as elsewhere, applying the MMF leads one sooner or later to ask questions about the biological constraints on the functioning of the modal states. In chapter 12 we shall look explicitly at what the MMF allows us to say about the interface between anthropology and biology.

12   Mind, body and culture

It will be clear by now that the title of this book, *Mind, body and culture*, is not an endorsement of our ordinary-language or social-scientific usages of the three terms 'mind', 'body', and 'culture'. Instead, it indicates a domain of enquiry within which these terms are questioned and alternative terms suggested. The alternative terms are the modal states of the MMF. These states are descriptions of patterns of relationships, both relationships among human beings and relationships between human beings and their natural environment. In other words, they are states of the entire human ecosystem. They are also, as I have emphasized repeatedly, unified states of mind and body.

On the whole, the mental or psychic side of this mind–body unity has been to the forefront in chapters 7 to 11. In part this reflects the nature of the ethnographic material I have used. We can recall some of the places where the body has been considered in these chapters:

(i)   the role of the body in ritual: the Ndembu rituals, as with many rites of passage, involved processes that operate directly on the body. Examples include the girl's motionless position, wrapped in a blanket at the foot of the young *mudyi* tree, through the first day of Nkang'a, her controlled demeanour during the period of seclusion and the dance through which she emerges as an adult woman, as well as the physical operation of circumcision in the case of the equivalent ritual for boys (Mukanda). We might add the consummation of the marriage, in Nkang'a, as a physiological experience given strong social meaning by its context in the ritual sequence and in Ndembu society (cf. chapter 7).

(ii) Semai-Temiar ritual also emphasized the body techniques of singing and dancing and the associated physiological experience of 'coolness' (cf. chapter 9).

(iii) the physiological basis of shamanic visionary states was referred to in passing (chapter 9). We could also consider the physiological bases of the meditational states of Tibetan Buddhism and of the possession states of the *orisha* and *loa* cults (chapter 10).

These examples could be multiplied. In chapter 6 I pointed to the importance of paralinguistic and non-linguistic aspects of communication, of gesture and movement, in the learning of modal states. The significance of physiological processes in child socialization is a staple theme of American cultural anthropology, as with Geoffrey Gorer's swaddling hypothesis for Russians (Gorer and Rickman 1949), or Gregory Bateson and Margaret Mead's analysis of Balinese child socialization in terms of sequences of exciting and frustrating the child (Bateson and Mead 1942, Bateson 1973: 85).[1]

Another area where a modal-state approach to the body may be particularly appropriate is that of illness and healing. Lévi-Strauss's classic paper on the sorcerer and his magic (1972: 167–82) prefigures this type of analysis, as does Turner's discussion of Ndembu healing ritual (cf. chapter 7). It would be worth examining the literature of medical anthropology in detail to see whether a reinterpretation in terms of modal-state trans-formations proves useful.

Such studies are also likely to throw light on the difficult and complex area of the 'interface' between biology and anthropology, which is the principal subject of this final chapter. In the following sections I look at two areas along this interface in some detail: the neurological basis of the MMF and the MMF's implications for evolutionary theories of culture.

Neither of these is an area in which I have specialist knowledge. My discussions are meant as suggestions of what the MMF might imply for theories in these areas, and not as exhaustive treatments of the issues involved.

The MMF and the structure of the brain

Here we begin with the question of specialization of function between the left and right cerebral hemispheres, and then move on to some more general issues. The distinction between modes of thought associated with 'left' and 'right' hemispheres of the brain was established by the work of Roger Sperry, Michael Gazzaniga and others (cf. Springer and Deutsch 1981), and popularized by the psychologist Robert Ornstein (1973). It has subsequently been adopted by some anthropologists (e.g. Southwold 1979, 1983, Beck 1978, Turner 1985).

There are obvious correspondences between the specialization of functions between left and right hemispheres and the two levels of operating with the modal states that were introduced in chapter 5. These two levels are (a) rational or digital activity within a state and (b) analogical movement between states. They form the basis of the technical and transformational mechanisms discussed in chapter 11. As I pointed out there, Martin Southwold equated his own very similar dichotomy between 'instrumental' and 'sapiental' kinds of thinking with the contrast between left-brain and right-brain thinking (1983). In the terms of chapter 5, the right brain corresponds to analogic communication and primary process and to manipulation of symbolic material (and so of MS_is), and the left brain to digital communication and secondary process and to rational computation within a particular MS_i.

The evidence for hemispheric specialization within the brain is strong and persuasive (cf. Springer and Deutsch 1981 for a critical summary of the research). However, it seems unlikely that specialization is 'hard-wired' within the brain. There is some evidence that lateralization is absent at birth and develops as the child grows and acquires specific learning strategies (Turner 1985: 258 citing Gardner 1975: 386).[2] There are also indications of differences in lateralization between populations (e.g. Sibatani 1980 on Japanese versus Americans) and extensive evidence of the brain's ability to compensate for damage (Springer and Deutsch 1981).

Thus, it appears plausible that the mode of operation in particular individuals is learnt on a cultural basis. In terms of the MMF, the precise pattern of cerebral lateralization would itself be a function of the MS_i or body of MS_is employed by that individual. In other words, the exact specialization of function would be a question of 'culture' as well as biology.

While this would be entirely compatible with the MMF, the two levels of operation within the MMF do not necessarily imply any specific brain structure. The MMF allows for human beings operating within modal states and moving between them. It does not suggest any specific mechanism by which this takes place. Consequently, while the specialization between hemispheres, and its apparent cultural basis, supports the MMF in a general sense, the MMF is in no way dependent on it. Instead, the MMF suggests a particular interpretation of it as a mechanism for the processing of modal states.

There is need for some caution here, because of the ease with which hemispheric specialization can be taken as implying a dichotomy between 'left-brain' and 'right-brain' activity. The MMF implies that human functioning always involves *both* types of activity (a point also made by Southwold, cf. chapter 11). This is what we would expect from the neurological evidence. Much of the evidence for hemispheric specialization comes precisely from deficits occurring when the linkage between the hemispheres has been partially broken. In general, while the evidence for localization of cerebral functions both within and outside the cerebral hemispheres is strong, it is also clear that the brain (and indeed the whole nervous system) operates in many respects as a single unit (cf. Changeux 1986).

At this stage we do not have a detailed view of how this single unit incorporates both digital and analogical processing, or how that processing relates to the sense of self. One promising suggestion comes from Alex Comfort's book *I and That* (1979). Comfort speculated that input from the world external to the individual was 'split between two analyzers, one "intuitive", gestalt and nonverbal, which is both the more primitive and the faster, and one logical-verbal as well as pattern-detecting, which is measurably the slower' (1979: 56). Sensory information about the body itself is processed mostly in the analogical mode, and the output of this 'channel' includes the body image and the experienced sense of self. Comfort went on to incorporate Karl Pribram's hologram model of brain processing (Pribram 1971, 1984) and to speculate how 'visionary states' such as those experienced in Hindu yogic practices might be incorporated within such a model (1979: 59).

The delay between the faster 'analogue-intuitive' and the slower 'logical-verbal' analysis means that the first process is able to provide logical patterns for the second to use. In the MMF's terms, the 'analogue-intuitive' analysis of internal and external sensory data would produce the continual if mostly small-scale shifts between modal states within which logical processing takes place (see chapter 6). Comfort commented on his hypothesis that while it was probably wrong in detail, 'it lies in the right universe of discourse and something like it is probably right' (1979: 57).

From the MMF's point of view, the phraseology of the model is too individual-centred. The relationship with the social manifold would need to be built in in some systematic way. Comfort's model, nevertheless, suggests how the analogical and digital aspects of human sensory processing (whether or not located in 'right' and 'left' brain) may be integrated into a single continuing process.

Turner's late essay 'Body, brain, and culture', originally published in *Zygon* in 1983, also attempted a grounding of culture in the brain, using not only hemispheric specialization but also Paul MacLean's work on the three components of the brain (Turner 1985: 249–73). Rather than explaining Ndembu ritual symbols through the sub-Freudian psychology of *The Drums of Affliction*, Turner now saw them as making connections between different sections of the brain (270–71). Other classic Turnerian themes such as liminality and play were likewise identified with particular modalities of operation of the brain.

The line of approach suggested by the work of Comfort and Turner is a promising one, and thoroughly compatible with the MMF, provided that the balance between neurological and cultural factors (between physiological mechanism and modal state) is maintained. Turner, who was clearly aware of this danger, ended by 'reassuring' readers concerned that he might be attempting a neurological reductionism

> that I am really speaking of a global population of brains inhabiting an entire world of inanimate and animate entities, a population whose members are incessantly communicating with one another through every physical and mental instrumentality. (Turner 1985: 272)

The MMF and evolution

The second area on the anthropology–biology interface that I shall consider is the relationship between evolutionary theory and the MMF. The place of 'culture' in evolutionary theory has been the subject of much controversy in recent years. A central issue has been the status of 'sociobiology', an approach developed originally by Edward O. Wilson (1975), adopted by some anthropologists and attacked with various degrees of hostility by others.

Edward O. Wilson's sociobiology, however, was only one of a whole range of evolutionary approaches to culture that developed during the 1970s and 1980s. What is striking when reading these theorists (e.g. Alexander 1982, Reynolds and Tanner 1983, Dawkins 1976) is the diversity of approaches and the lack of agreement on matters as fundamental as the level at which selection operated (gene pool, individual or social group) and how culture was to be defined. This reflects a similar diversity of opinion within evolutionary theory in general (cf. e.g. Denton 1985, Eldredge 1986, Ho 1986).

The new evolutionary approaches to culture had in common a reduction of culture to genetics that left little place for specifically anthropological modes of explanation. Most anthropologists rejected the new approaches outright (e.g. Sahlins 1976), although a minority experimented with applying the techniques to their own data (e.g. Chagnon and Irons 1982). It is clear from what I have written so far that the MMF sees 'culture' as grounded in biology but as having a much larger degree of autonomy from evolutionary processes than most of the sociobiologists and evolutionary theorists believed. In the following pages I shall discuss some general features of these evolutionary approaches and consider what the MMF might imply for them.

The definition of culture within evolutionary approaches

Here we should first distinguish between those theorists for whom culture was simply a generalized aid to genetic fitness, as for example with Richard Alexander (1982), and those who were interested in evolutionary explanations of particular cultural features. Alexander claimed that all significant aspects of human behaviour could be derived from the principle of the maximization of 'inclusive genetic fitness' (Alexander 1982: 136, 141). Whatever human beings do should be explainable as promoting the transmission of their individual genetic content to as many descendants as possible, either directly or through close relatives sharing some of the same genes.

For theorists like Alexander, culture was significant mainly as a source of fitness-maximizing behaviour, and cultural variation was of little or no interest, a superficial veneer on an assumed underlying unity. Since the MMF implies a decoupling of any close link between human behaviour and the inclusive fitness principle, it is inconsistent with positions such as Alexander's. A particular modal state may lead to greater genetic fitness for the individual adopting it, but there is nothing in the MMF to suggest that it necessarily will. In addition, any gain for genetic fitness would have to be analysed at the level of the social manifold, not of the individual.

The appeal of Alexander's approach, as of those like it, lay in its limited and parsimonious structure. Alexander's reduction of all of human and animal behaviour to the maximization of inclusive genetic fitness has a simplicity and clarity that we can admire, but before accepting such a drastic application of Occam's razor we need also to address the question of adequacy. The problems are already apparent in Alexander's convoluted and implausible explanation for the existence of altruism, a bugbear of many evolutionary theories (1982: 79–80, 134). More generally, if we want an approach that will make some sense of the great range of ethnographic material on human cultures, we need to introduce 'culture' explicitly into the framework. Other evolutionary theorists have accepted culture in a more substantial way than Alexander and have attempted to explain the existence and distribution of specific aspects of human culture in evolutionary terms. We now turn to consider some of these theories.

Anthropology in the nineteenth century was heavily reliant on theories of sociocultural evolution, as in the work of Lewis Henry Morgan and Herbert Spencer. In British anthropology, these evolutionary theories were challenged by diffusionist theories and then largely replaced by more sociological approaches, but they have remained an important component of US cultural anthropology. Thus, the idea of culture as evolving over time and as being in a general sense *adaptive* was not particularly new. What was new in the 1970s and 1980s was the attempt to describe the evolution and the adaptiveness by mathematical models similar to those used by neo-Darwinian theorists.

As Richard Dawkins has pointed out, Darwin's original theory of evolution was only made into a coherent mathematical theory when it was reinterpreted by R. A. Fisher and his colleagues in terms of Mendelian genetics. This enabled Darwinian processes of natural selection to act on

> the relative *frequency* of discrete hereditary particles, or genes, each of which was either there or not there in any particular body. Darwinism post-Fisher is called neo-Darwinism. Its digital nature is not an incidental fact that happens to be true of genetic information technology. Digitalness is probably a necessary precondition for Darwinism itself to work.
>
> (Dawkins 1988: 115)

The need for 'digitalness' posed a problem for Darwinian-type theories of culture: could a cultural equivalent to the gene be identified? Such an entity would ideally need to operate in the same digital (on–off) manner as genetic inheritance.

Dawkins himself assumed that this entity existed and called it the *meme* (1976). Edward O. Wilson and Charles J. Lumsden took a similar course with the *culturgen* (Lumsden and Wilson 1981). As Martin Stuart-Fox has recently noted, the definitions of meme and culturgen raise serious difficulties, and neither Dawkins, Lumsden and Wilson, nor any of the other theorists in this area have as yet come up with a satisfactory unit of cultural replication (Stuart-Fox 1986).

In looking for such a unit, anthropologists and biologists were guided by the tendency of US cultural anthropology in the Boasian tradition to work with 'culture-traits'. These were isolated units of culture whose distribution over culturally diverse areas had been recorded and mapped to help establish historical processes of cultural evolution and diffusion. The culture-trait approach was itself an extension of the artefact in archaeology.

Such approaches worked best with straightforward items of technology (types of arrowheads, ways of making pottery), which could be treated as isolated digital units. They worked less well with the cognitive and conceptual aspects of social life. Dawkins, Lumsden and Wilson, and others assumed that the culture-trait (under that or a new name) could be isolated, but the question of delimitation of one trait from another was given little explicit treatment (cf. Stuart-Fox 1986: 79–80).

Stuart-Fox proposed his own solution, the *menteme*, which he defined as 'the smallest unit going to make up the structure of individual mental culture', the equivalent in terms of actual neural coding of a sememe. Dawkins' meme could then be 'any interlocking group of mentemes regularly transmitted (or learned) as a simple combination' (1986: 83).

This hardly solves the problem. As Stuart-Fox admitted, mentemes are difficult to identify: the meaning of a menteme (as with genes) depends on the other mentemes it is combined with, and the same behaviour may be maintained by more than one combination of mentemes. Given all this, Stuart-Fox's confidence in the usefulness of a menteme-based approach is surprising.[3]

In practice, sociobiological and allied approaches to culture often operated in terms of simplistic trait definitions. The difficulties this caused are apparent in Vernon Reynolds' and Ralph Tanner's *The Biology of Religion*, where it was assumed that the official religions of modern nation-states (Protestant, Catholic, Muslim, Hindu, Buddhist) could be treated as alternative culture traits selected in response to the degree of predictability of the environment. They then assumed that the predictability of the environment was measurable by energy consumption and GNP *per capita*, and demonstrated some statistical correlations (Reynolds and Tanner 1983).

Reynolds' and Tanner's assumptions that Moroccan, Saudi Arabian and Indonesian Islam, or Italian, Polish and Irish Catholicism, could be treated as uniform entities, that nation-states were sensible units of comparison, and that GNP and energy consumption were meaningful measures of the predictability of the environment are enough to cause serious doubts. The real irony of their book is that the statistical correlations resulted almost entirely from the association between Christianity (particularly Protestantism) and modern industrial society. Protestantism predated industrial capitalism and almost certainly contributed to its development (cf. Weber 1958); it can hardly be explained as a consequence of the greater 'predictability' brought about by capitalism.

An issue closely related to the delimitation of the unit of culture is its location. As we saw in chapters 3 and 4, the question of whether culture should be located at the individual (Type I) or group (Type II) level was already a topic of disagreement in US cultural anthropology. While it is clear that co-operative behaviour of various kinds is at the centre of cultural adaptation, the need to identify a satisfactory analogue to the gene drove many theorists to treat such behaviour as an attribute of the individual (as, for example, do Dawkins and Stuart-Fox).

Within the MMF, the only appropriate unit for cultural replication is the modal state itself, and the only appropriate level of evolutionary analysis is that of the social manifold. An approach in terms of modal states was foreshadowed by Sperber's epidemiology of cultural representations (cf. chapter 3). It has been anticipated in more explicitly evolutionary terms by David Rindos, who has suggested that cultural evolution be approached in terms of cultural symbols (Rindos 1985). We have already seen (chapters

3, 6 and 7) that the equivalent unit to the symbol in the MMF is the modal state itself.

Rindos' argument contains some useful points, for example the distinction between two types of cultural selection, which he refers to as CS_1 and CS_2. CS_1 is the direct selective advantage for individuals associated with a specific cultural trait (i.e. symbol), and CS_2 is the selective advantage given to that trait by the total symbolic and cultural system. While I doubt that CS_1 and CS_2 can be meaningfully separated in any actual human situation, the formulation does at least point to the interrelatedness of cultural traits within a total system.

Rindos' emphasis on the random nature of cultural variation is also of interest, although it was attacked in most of the comments following his article (cf. Rindos 1985: 77–83). Cultural variation corresponds to the production of new modal states in the MMF. I argued in chapter 9 that shamanic vision in societies such as the Nuer and Semai-Temiar may function precisely as a source of innovation outside the normal processes of rational thought (cf. chapter 9). Whether such mechanisms are truly random is another matter, and in fact Rindos' randomness is of a different kind to that found in the shamanic mechanism. For Rindos, human purpose and human consciousness are simply not part of the theoretical framework (they are 'useless for problem solving ... idealistic and inherently unverifiable', 1985: 84).

The denial of the relevance of human consciousness here goes back at least to behaviourism in psychology and is part of the enduring influence of nineteenth-century science with its Cartesian mind–matter dualism. We have already seen versions of it in the works of Alexander and of Reynolds and Tanner.

I suspect that this kind of materialistic bravado will seem very *passé* within a couple of decades. The MMF's approach is quite different, since it treats mind and body as a unity. Where Rindos excludes the conscious, purposive behaviour of individuals, the MMF incorporates it as part of the modal state. This implies that the modal state can be treated, at least conceptually, as a unit of analysis without further reference to conscious purpose.

Consequently, the use of the MMF does not exclude in principle a neo-Darwinian analysis of the rise and decline of modal states. There are some serious problems involved in such an analysis, and it may be that in practice these will be sufficient to limit its applicability severely, at least for the present. I shall consider three of these: how to delimit modal states, how to determine their frequency and intensity within the social manifold and how to deal with their interaction in defining the total environment for selection.

The first problem, that of delimiting modal states, is not insuperable. I suggested in chapter 6 that it was not a major problem for anthropological analysis, since analysts can choose sets of modal states appropriate for the problem they are considering. Nevertheless, we are some way from an adequate mathematical language to describe modal states, even assuming that such a language is possible in principle.[4] A rigorous application of neo-Darwinian theory would ideally be based on some such language, rather than on the *ad hoc* and impressionistic identification of traits along the lines taken by, for example, Reynolds and Tanner.

The second problem, that of determining the intensity and distribution of modal states, is equally challenging. Here we need to remember that an individual has a repertoire of different modal states.[5] Consequently we cannot identify the population and distribution of states within the social manifold with the population and distribution of individuals.

The third problem is implied by Rindos himself, in his two modes of cultural selection (CS_1 and CS_2). Modal states interact with each other to define the total environment within which selection takes place. This is where Reynolds and Tanner came to grief; even assuming that 'industrialism' and 'Protestant Christianity' can be treated as labels for modal states, the analysis of their relationship has to be systemic, not causal.

If a serious attempt is made to take this interaction into account, the complexity of the resulting hypotheses is likely to be mathematically unmanageable. It should be remembered that the interaction of modal states includes the ability of human beings to create drastic alterations in their physical, material and social environments, which then affect the viability of particular modal states within those environments.

These are general problems with evolutionary approaches to culture. The MMF does not make them worse, but it does make their existence clearer than the frameworks used by most evolutionary theorists so far.

The real question is whether these approaches in their present form advance our understanding of human society in any positive way. It seems to me that this still has to be demonstrated. The choice between theoretical frameworks, as the MMF implies, has an intrinsic value-component. It is not simply to do with scientific truth but also with whether particular frameworks help us to achieve a more just, humane, and humanly satisfying society. In the concluding section of the book we turn to address these issues directly.

Conclusion

It will be apparent that I have tried to do a number of different things in this book. Primarily I have tried to demonstrate that anthropological theory can be made into a consistent and scientifically plausible whole, and that we can design that whole so as to meet the various demands that we might want to make of a general social theory. Such 'designing' is not a question of subordinating science to politics. As Terry Eagleton has commented in relation to literary theory, the politics has been there from the beginning anyway (Eagleton 1983: 194). It is rather a question of working towards a theory that makes sense both as science and as social practice.

These demands for what a social theory should do arise out of a conception of the place of theory in society. In this book I have argued that ideas (including social theories) are active participants within the general social process, rather than simple statements of disembodied 'objective' truth. The relationship between anthropology and biology (more specifically sociobiology and evolutionary biology), considered in the last few pages, may be an area where such considerations are particularly important at present. Ultimately, though, all theories (as modal states) are actors within a total situation, not simply objective commentaries upon the situation.

Chapters 1 to 6 of this book introduced a new theoretical framework, the MMF. The arguments in chapters 7 to 11 represented, in effect, reformulations of aspects of the work of Emile Durkheim, Max Weber, Victor Turner, Clifford Geertz and other social scientists as theories within the MMF. I believe that these reformulations preserve the central insights of these writers, while eliminating some of the more unsatisfactory features of their work; those, for example, pointed out by Dan Sperber and Maurice Bloch (cf. chapter 3).

Durkheim, Weber and their followers had something important to say, and rather than rejecting their work we should find ways of incorporating its positive aspects within a wider and more satisfactory framework. This, at any rate, is the spirit in which the 'sociocentric' modal states, the distinction between 'shamanic' and 'rationalized' strategies, and so on, are meant to be taken.[6]

The real point, though, is to design the wider and more satisfactory framework. Here the MMF in its present form is not intended to be more than a starting point. It has several advantages over previous theoretical frameworks in anthropology:

(i) it makes epistemological sense of cultural and conceptual relativism within a coherent overall theoretical framework;
(ii) it presents a coherent and viable relationship between concepts at the individual and group levels;
(iii) it gives a plausible account of observed differences between various kinds of societies, including what I have called 'shamanic' societies, traditional states and modern industrial societies;

(iv) it provides the basis for a sensible and consistent interface between anthropology and other natural and social science disciplines.

As I have implied, a social theory should satisfy humanistic as well as narrowly scientific demands. In this connection the MMF

(v) offers a realistic place for human freedom and creativity, and
(vi) helps to specify the points at which effective action against oppressive social systems may be possible.

The MMF is unlikely to be the only approach that will do all of these things. Nevertheless, it seems likely that any theoretical framework that can do them all will satisfy certain criteria, and no previous theoretical framework in anthropology known to me meets these criteria. In particular, the theory must avoid assuming either an individual–group dichotomy or a body–mind dichotomy in its fundamental categories. The MMF is probably the simplest and crudest of a family of such Type III theories. As presented in this book it is scarcely more than a sketch, requiring much further research and elaboration. This work will involve disciplines of which I have only limited knowledge. However, the MMF even in its present form provides a starting point from which to elaborate and look for further, more adequate frameworks.

As I noted in chapter 2, there are more or less consistent philosophical positions from which such a new framework is unnecessary. The most obvious of these is the materialistic reduction, either in the old-fashioned positivist form or in some of its new 'realist' variants. These frameworks hold that 'reality' is in one way or another directly accessible to properly conducted scientific research, and that this research yields a picture close to the current common-sense presuppositions of our culture. If other cultures see things differently, their views, being unscientific, are by definition less correct. If quantum theory or general relativity appear to assume views of the universe inconsistent with our common-sense presuppositions, then such assumptions are regarded (as in the famous Copenhagen interpretation of quantum theory) as mere mathematical devices without any intrinsic relation to the 'real' world.

The MMF will have little to say to those who are committed to such positions, and an appeal to the possibly disastrous human consequences of these views is unlikely to have any effect. It seems likely that these positions will gradually become obsolete as a consequence both of the development of new and more satisfactory scientific frameworks, and of the transformations in human consciousness as humans adapt to a genuinely multicultural planet (cf. chapter 1).

Another alternative position discussed in chapter 2 is what may be called the 'hermeneutic' alternative, that anthropology should be seen purely as an interpretive discipline and that anthropologists should avoid the construction of any general theoretical framework. As I suggested in chapter 2, this refusal to treat anthropology as a science runs the risk of excluding anthropology, and such insights as it has gained into human life, from the body of knowledge according to which our society operates. The motives for doing so may be worthy, but this is not an alternative that I find satisfactory.

I emphasize again that theory choice cannot be divorced from its social and political correlates. This does not mean that we should choose a theoretical framework on purely social or political grounds. Some frameworks are grossly inadequate at the level of accounting for our observations, having made all allowances for the theory-laden nature of those observations.

In the present state of our knowledge there are, nevertheless, several theoretical frameworks in most areas of science that do a more or less adequate job in accounting for some data, and none that satisfactorily encompass all possible data. This is likely always to be the case, though the specific frameworks at issue will change. We, therefore, have no choice but to apply other criteria in choosing between them.

The value-criterion is essentially equivalent to the choice of which kinds of data we feel it is most important to understand. It is both permissible and proper to dismiss those frameworks that regard mind and human consciousness as irrelevant to the understanding of human society on the grounds that any framework that leaves such factors out is inadequate in social terms.

I have suggested in this book that the positivistic, materialistic approaches are grossly inadequate even at accounting for observations. However, I do not believe that it is possible to establish that any theory is the 'best' available except in a limited and provisional sense. 'Best', in the terms of this book, can only mean 'best out of what we have available at present for the particular purposes and demands that we have in mind'.

I think that it is increasingly important that we should be fully conscious of this situation. Such a demand can be seen, as I suggested in chapter 1, as part of a more general cultural movement; 'post-modernist', if the reader likes. Other labels can be supplied at will. There are signs in many areas of our society of more awareness of such issues, perhaps because their urgency is not confined to the realm of theory. Violent and unmediated collisions in world-views are too dangerous in the present state of our planet. We have to find ways of coexisting and of *building* coexistence into the way in which we see the world. If there is a central message behind the MMF, it is this.

It is for individual readers to decide both whether they think the issue is an important one and whether they think that the MMF, or the general idea of a Type III reading, is of any use in dealing with it. I have no special claims for my own framework, except that it exists and it works, up to a point. It is an example of the kind of ideas that might be useful. It is an attempt to *use* theory rather than be trapped by it; to show that designing a theory can serve to point out what Deleuze and Guattari have called the lines of flight, the escape-routes, from imprisonment by outmoded and irrelevant concepts (Guattari 1984, Deleuze and Guattari 1987).

What this implies is that each of us accept that we are ultimately theorizing for ourselves. To take the MMF as another form of authoritative knowledge would defeat its whole purpose. Use the framework as an example by all means, use bits of it, cannibalize it, reconstruct it, make it into what you need for your own work, your own politics and your own lives. It is not meant to be a perfect or conclusive statement.

Nobody today is in a position to make any such final statement. Different readers and groups of readers will surely find that the MMF in its present form leaves out matters of vital importance to them but they will also find in it things they can remake into their own and use for their own purposes. This book is meant to help its readers to design their *own* anthropology.

Notes

1. New paradigms and modal states

1. The 'cultural materialism' of Marvin Harris and his followers (e.g. Harris 1969) represents an alternative reductionism, but one that has, it seems to me, failed through the inadequacy of its explanatory language. Similar comments might be made about the reductionist versions of Marxist social science.
2. Cf. Jonathan Friedman's analysis of post-modernism in terms of the 'cultural logics of the global system' (1988). Friedman treats the crisis of modernity as characteristic of the 'declining centres of the world system' (457). I see it as present throughout the whole system and as resulting from the greatly increased connections between all parts of that system.
3. E.g. *Milton*, plate 15; *Four Zoas*, Night the Sixth.

2. A natural science of society

1. Though this is what Bergland, astonishingly, does. The book is typical of the coexistence of great experimental sophistication and very little theoretical self-awareness in the writings of many scientists.
2. There have been some recent attempts to combine the frameworks, including books by the philosopher Patricia Churchland (1986) and the biologist J. Z. Young (1987).
3. I leave aside the question of the precise sense in which 'value-freedom' has been interpreted by Weber and by the Weberian tradition since Weber. Weber's position made more sense in his time than in the 1980s, where an allegedly 'value-free' but in fact naively value-laden style of sociology has become dominant in large parts of the academic world.
4. There is some variation in how the terms positivism and empiricism are used by different authorities. E.g. empiricism may be a theory about the status of observations ('facts'), positivism may be about the discovery of laws. I am treating positivism as a general label for the dominant scientific epistemology of the nineteenth century.
5. I am indebted to Jane Azevedo for her lengthy discussion of 'mirror' and 'map'

metaphors (Azevedo 1986). She cites Ziman 1978 as a primary source for the 'map' metaphor. For an earlier usage, cf. Korzybski's famous maxim, 'the map is not the territory'. Another recent proponent of this metaphor is Hooker 1987.

6. Though not necessarily in other societies, which often have elements of much greater epistemological sophistication even at the 'common-sense' level. Cf. Wagner 1978 on New Guinea or the general Tibetan awareness of *stong pa nyid*, Skt. *śūnyatā* = 'emptiness'.

7. This discussion is adapted from that in Samuel 1985a.

8. A phrase I take from Munevar 1981 : 50. Munevar's book is a stimulating argument for a 'relativistic' conception of science. See also Munevar 1984.

9. Azevedo 1986 also argues for this position.

10. Of course anthropologists in practice have been involved in 'real world' decisions, even without any coherent theory. This has generally been confined to areas where their ethnographic role has been seen as relevant, however, as in Australian Aboriginal or Native American affairs. The present argument is concerned with the contribution of anthropology to our society's understanding and regulation of itself in a more general sense.

11. I am not suggesting that 'translation' is necessarily a simple matter, especially between very different cultures.

3. Starting points I

1. As later chapters of this book suggest, I find Turner's work, less polished and more exploratory in nature as it often was, more productive than Geertz's. Among ideas that I have found particularly stimulating are Turner's suggestions concerning the bipolar nature of ritual symbolism, his concept of the 'root paradigm' and his attempt to develop a theory of cultural creativity through his opposition between 'structure' and 'anti-structure'. None of these ideas is entirely satisfactory as Turner presents it, but each points to a basic and largely neglected problem-area and suggests how it may be approached. All three formulations influenced the theoretical framework of this book.

2. Along with Turner's style of symbolic analysis, Sperber also included Lévi-Straussian structuralism and Freudian interpretation among the modes of symbolic analysis he criticized.

3. Turner's background was in the 'Manchester school' of British anthropology, and he had throughout his work an awareness, typical of this tradition, of how symbols and conceptions were manipulated within small-scale political processes (cf. in particular Turner 1957, 1974). Geertz was already warning in his articles of the mid-1960s against any over-easy assumptions of cultural homogeneity (e.g. 'Person, time, and conduct in Bali', reprinted in Geertz 1973).

4. If we adopt a less confining model than Kuhn's, the contrast with the 'closed' Zande model is even stronger.

5. I use the term 'paradigm' here for convenience, but will introduce a different terminology later in the argument ('modal state').

6. 'Rational' is a term used in many ways. The context defines what I mean by it in this work. In chapters 5 to 11 it will be seen that this is not the only kind (or aspect) of thought within the MMF.

7. Cf. their usage by Durkheim himself in *Elementary Forms of the Religious Life*: 'Moreover, without symbols, social sentiments could have only a precarious

existence. Though very strong as long as men are together and influence each other reciprocally, they exist only in the form of recollections after the assembly has ended, and when left to themselves, these become feebler and feebler...But if the movements by which these sentiments are expressed are connected with something that endures, the sentiments themselves become more durable' (1976: 231).

8. The MMF suggests an implicit answer. If we can specify our goals, then at least in principle we can decide whether or not a particular modal state (or scientific framework) assists us in achieving these goals.

9. The heavy criticism levelled against Louis Dumont's *Homo Hierarchicus* (1970) is a case in point here (cf. Madan et al. 1971, Meillassoux 1973). Dumont's book undoubtedly has its problems, but his critics show a remarkable unwillingness to appreciate the point he is making.

4. Starting points II

1. They first began to re-emerge in British anthropology in the late 1970s, in the work of e.g. Peter Wilson (1980), who had studied cultural anthropology at Yale, and Charles Woolfson (1982), who was influenced by the evolutionary aspects of Marxist theory.

2. The production of a genuinely new intellectual synthesis, such as Marx's, is a work of creative imagination, not of mere rational computation, and creative imagination is an attribute of the shamans and artists, not the practitioners of what Kuhn would call 'normal science'. This point is amplified later in my argument.

3. Although a few writers, e.g. Fortes 1959, anticipated this interest in several respects. Ironically perhaps, one of Hallowell's main references is to the 1938 Huxley lecture by Marcel Mauss which was to form the centrepiece of the Carrithers, Collins and Lukes volume (Hallowell 1955: 78, cf. Carrithers, Collins and Lukes 1985).

5. Interpreting the flow

1. Bateson's account has occasionally been accused of being excessively cognitive. His defence of Claude Lévi-Strauss (and implicitly of himself) against such a charge is worth quoting: 'They [Anglo-Saxon anthropologists] say he emphasizes too much the intellect and ignores the "feelings". The truth is that he assumes that the heart has precise algorithms' (Bateson 1973: 112).

2. Conceptually, even a natural scientist is imposing a structure on a field which includes the scientist as well as the subject of study. In fields such as theoretical physics, of course, this has had to be recognized explicitly.

3. I am not suggesting that Bateson was unaware of the possibility of such situations. On the contrary, they are typical of his own analyses of schizophrenia, on which Watzlawick et al. build in their book. Where I differ from both Bateson and Watzlawick et al., perhaps, is in assuming that such situations are typical, rather than exceptional, in human interaction.

4. Even so, as far as I know, the Hindu Brahmin community in Kashmir has not been particularly involved in recent conflicts in the area.

5. Geertz makes some suggestions about how such communities may operate in

relation to contemporary Morocco in Geertz 1985 and in Geertz, Geertz and Rosen 1979.

6. A similar point has been made by Bocock (Bocock 1980).

7. Obeyesekere 1981 has been influential on the forming of my ideas in this area, but my distinction between individual and shared symbolism does not correspond exactly to that which he makes between public and private symbolism. Symbolism may be shared by many members of a culture but not be an overt part of public culture.

8. In terms of Kuhn's work, this is equivalent to the contrast between 'normal science', carried out within a particular paradigm, and the 'scientific revolution', where there is a change of paradigm. In ordinary life, we change 'paradigms' all the time, for example whenever we change our social role; we employ different 'paradigms' with our family, with our friends or at work.

6. The multimodal framework

1. I do not mean to imply a rigid dichotomy between material situation and cultural flow, since the impact of a particular situation depends very much on the cultural resources (modal states) available with which to respond to it. The modal states themselves are explicitly states of *both* body *and* mind. The distinction is introduced here purely for purposes of clarity of exposition.

2. There is no reason to assume that *all* modal states are equally constraining or that all individuals (given their current repertoires) are equally capable of creating new states in response to a particular situation. Simple observation would suggest that neither is the case and that the human ability to do this generally falls off rapidly after childhood. This fall-off presumably has neurological correlates, in terms of the establishments of patterns of connections within the brain. At the same time, some individuals retain greater ability in this area, and, as we shall see in later chapters, some cultures deliberately cultivate and employ this creativity.

3. This assumption of the 'givenness' of the stream of experience is clearly a simplification in relation to the current state of theoretical physics.

4. The modal state corresponds less to a program than to a subroutine or component part of a program. I have developed this analogy somewhat further elsewhere (Samuel 1985b).

5. Cf. Turner's concept of 'root paradigm' in Turner 1974. Also note Kapferer 1979 (borrowing from George Herbert Mead's work on the self) and Heald 1982.

6. Donald Winnicott's work on 'transitional objects' and on the role of play in general is relevant to this discussion (Winnicott 1971).

7. See especially the introduction to Turner 1975. Turner in his earlier writings tends to take human psychology as a transcultural given; this is not assumed here.

8. Cf. his 'Colour classification' paper, 1970: 59–92.

9. This line of argument offers possibilities for drawing connections between elements of psychoanalytic theory and the MMF. It will be noticed that it is not necessary to assume that these early states are pan-human or uninfluenced by culture.

10. Michael Allen has recently argued for a similar position (1985).

7. The Ndembu modal state repertoire

1. 'Life-crisis rituals' correspond to what anthropologists more generally refer to as *rites de passage* or 'rites of passage'. Turner avoids this term in part because Ndembu 'rituals of affliction' also share the basic structure of the *rite de passage* as outlined by van Gennep.
2. There is also the related case of the 'spirit' through whom the Ndembu diviner is able to divine (see following note).
3. It is here that the Ndembu (as described by Turner) come closest to the vocabulary of spirits and spirit-possession reported for other parts of Africa (cf. Turner 1968: 31, 32–3).
4. Von Brandenstein 1970, 1972, 1974, 1977; Ridington and Ridington 1975. Native American schemes of this kind are often, as here, explicitly concerned with the acquisition of moral concepts. For another example, cf. the Navajo scheme of directional 'winds' or *nilch'i*, McNeley 1981. Like other indigenous concepts discussed in this chapter, these are powers operative both within the world and within the individual.

8. Sociocentric modal states

1. Strictly speaking, individual–society and self–other are different dichotomies. They are obviously closely related. I treat the individual–society dichotomy as a rational formulation of the self–other dichotomy which would seem to be logically and ontogenetically prior. Consequently, I generally refer to individual–society when referring to social theory, and to self–other when referring to modal states.
2. Cf. the reaction to Sheldrake's theory, some of which is reproduced in Sheldrake 1987: 213–39.
3. Hence the prevalence of such messy and poorly theorized concepts as 'somatization'.
4. There is a parallel here to some of the recent attempts to rethink psychoanalytical categories in non-hierarchical and non-patriarchal terms. Cf. Deleuze and Guattari 1984, Salleh 1984, Gross 1986.
5. Such states may be associated with chemical distributions within the brain that give them a certain emotional 'premium'; it feels good to be in a non-egoic state. Cf. Schuman 1980, and Davidson and Davidson 1980 in general.
6. For some recent comments on Semai non-violence cf. Robarchek and Dentan 1987, Knauft 1987, Betzig et al. 1988.
7. Cf. Roseman 1984. Cf. also Howell's comment in relation to the Chewong that humans are subject to disease and death, unlike the spirit-beings, because humans have 'hot' blood and 'hot' eyes while blood and eyes of the spirit-beings are cool (1981).
8. The following interpretation relies mostly on the work of W. G. H. Stanner (1959–63, 1979), T. G. H. Strehlow (1947, 1971) and Robert Tonkinson (1974, 1978).
9. I would agree with Bloch, and with later commentators on Balinese society such as Leopold Howe 1981, that the non-linear, detemporalized sense of time is only part of the Balinese scene. Here Geertz followed Bateson, and for that matter Sapir and Whorf, in implying that Balinese lived entirely and permanently in a detemporalized and non-egoic state, which seems to me

implausible. Stanner incidentally does not make this assumption in relation to the Aboriginal 'Dreaming' (1979).

9. Shamanic mechanisms

1. These states may well differ from each other more than do 'ordinary' modal states, precisely because of their relatively free-floating nature. What is important, after all, is that the shaman devises some way of doing the job which the culture requires. On the psychobiology of such states, cf. Schuman 1980, Heinze 1985.
2. Cf. Bateson's concept of 'Learning III', which he links *inter alia* to Zen Buddhism and psychotherapy (Bateson 1973: 272–9).
3. I omit reference to the Chewong here because – while analogous procedures among the Chewong appear to exist – I have not yet come across any detailed description of them.

10. The growth of the clerical approach

1. At least this is the impression given by Turner, who describes the positions of chief and headman as having great prestige value but little political authority. The various Ndembu titles of chiefs and headmen seem to have been mostly a carry-over from the Lunda empire to which the Ndembu once belonged. The Ndembu may, therefore, be another example of the growth of the shamanic approach in the wake of the collapse of a partially centralized state.
2. By contrast, the installation rituals of our own societies, where not purely residual, tend to emphasize the rulers' relationship to a hierarchically conceived deity as much as or more than to the people over whom they are being invested with authority.
3. The Ndembu chiefs (see note 1) derive historically from the Lunda state which the Ndembu once formed part of, but according to Turner's account the chiefly titles today are concerned with prestige rather than any real power.
4. This gives the characteristic Indo-European distinction between ruler and priest (cleric), discussed at length by Georges Dumézil and treated as fundamental to Indian society by Louis Dumont, cf. Dumont 1970, Littleton 1973, Allen 1987.
5. There have always been understandings even of the Christian deity, especially in the mystical tradition, which stress loss of ego through union with God. In most Christian societies, however, they have been untypical and they have frequently been regarded as heretical.
6. Many discussions of *terma*, including some by more rationally inclined Tibetan scholars, have centred around the assumption of fraud. However, *terma*-type phenomena are widespread not only within Tibet but in many other cultures (cf. the prophetic books of the Old Testament, the Book of Revelation, the Koran, the Book of Mormon and many more recent examples). It would seem likely that in many or most of these cases we are dealing with revelations received in shamanic visionary states rather than with deliberate fraud.
7. Though cf. the similarities with some Islamic societies noted in Samuel 1982.
8. A notable early anthropological attempt to theorize this situation was Robert Redfield's and Milton Singer's work on 'great traditions' and 'little traditions' (Redfield and Singer 1954, Singer 1980).

9. This is related to the point made by Julian Jaynes (1976), although the model of the early Greek mind in Jaynes's work seems to me to be too simple.

11. Technical and transformational mechanisms

1. Obviously the patterns described also apply in varying degrees to other modern industrial societies such as those of the Far East, Latin America and Eastern Europe.
2. Anthropologists may recall Clifford Geertz's point about religion being both a 'model of' and a 'model for' society (cf. Geertz 1973: 93).
3. *Australian*, 1–2 March 1980, Weekend Magazine, p. 1.
4. *National Times*, week ending 8 December 1979, p. 9.
5. There are some particularly striking examples in Williamson 1978.
6. Cf. Victor Turner's definition of ritual as 'a *transformative* performance' (e.g. 1985: 251).
7. This is a restatement and extension of Emile Durkheim's point about the real object of religion being the maintenance of the social group (1968). The contradiction which has sometimes been seen between Durkheim's analyses of social structure and his later studies of 'primitive classification' vanishes in the MMF. It arose because the first group of studies was, to some degree, assimilable to a positivistic conception of social science, while the second was not.
8. The distinction which Peter Wilson makes (in the context of Black English-speaking Caribbean society) between 'respectability' and 'reputation' seems to me to capture something essential about the contrast between the linear and absolute value systems derived from technical mechanisms and the more polymorphous and multiple modes of valuation characteristic of small-scale egalitarian societies (Wilson 1973: 227–9).

12. Mind, body and culture

1. For a mainly British collection of studies on the body in anthropology, see Blacking 1977.
2. Springer and Deutsch, however, regarded it as 'premature to draw conclusions regarding change in asymmetry with age' (1981: 138–41).
3. Ironically, Stuart-Fox's model of mental functioning is based on the work of P. N. Johnson-Laird (1983, cf. Stuart-Fox 1986: 74–8, 82) who takes a much less atomistic approach. Johnson-Laird gives a central place to *mental models* which bear some resemblance to the mental aspects of the MS_i.
4. Elsewhere I have used the analogy of a computer system in which each modal state at the individual level (MS_i) corresponds to having a certain number of the 'subroutines' that operate different parts and aspects of the human organism switched on and certain others switched off (Samuel 1985b). This is a crude and mechanistic analogy, and it is certainly too simple. It may, nevertheless, help as a starting point, as well as pointing towards the kind of mathematical models which might be appropriate to any attempt to operationalize the concept of a modal state.
5. A point made, in other words, by C. J. M. R. Gullick in his comment on Rindos (cf. Rindos 1985: 81), and prefigured by Wallace and Goodenough (cf. chapter 4).
6. The same is true of the references to psychoanalytic theory in chapter 5.

References

Agassi, Joseph. 1975. 'Institutional individualism'. *British Journal of Sociology* 26, 144–55.

Alexander, Richard D. 1982. *Darwinism and Human Affairs*. University of Washington Press, Seattle.

Allen, Michael. 1985. 'The "hidden power" of male ritual: the North Vanuatu evidence'. Paper presented to the International Association for the History of Religions Conference, Sydney, August 1985.

Allen, N. J. 1987. 'The ideology of the Indo-Europeans: Dumézil's theory and the idea of a fourth function'. *International Journal of Moral and Social Studies* 2(1), 23–39.

Ardener, Edwin. 1978. 'Some outstanding problems in the analysis of events'. *Yearbook of Symbolic Anthropology* 1, 103–23.

Arens, W. 1983. 'Evans-Pritchard and the prophets: comments on an ethnographic enigma', *Anthropos* 78, 1–16.

Aris, Michael and Aung San Suu Kyi, eds. 1980. *Tibetan Studies in Honour of Hugh Richardson*. Aris and Phillips, Warminster.

Asad, Talal. 1979. 'Anthropology and the analysis of ideology'. *Man* (n.s.) 14, 607–27.

  1983. 'Anthropological conceptions of religion: reflections on Geertz'. *Man* (n.s.) 18, 237–59.

Austin-Broos, Diane J. (Austin) 1979. 'Symbols and culture: some philosophical assumptions in the work of Clifford Geertz'. *Social Analysis* 3, 45–87.

  (Austin) 1981. 'Born again...and again and again: communitas and social change among Jamaican Pentecostalists'. *Journal of Anthropological Research* 37, 226–46.

  1987a. 'Clifford Geertz: culture, sociology and historicism.' In Austin-Broos 1987b, 141–59.

  ed. 1987b. *Creating Culture: Profiles in the Study of Culture*. Allen and Unwin, Sydney.

Azevedo, Jane. 1986. 'Towards a meta-theory of sociology'. B.A. Honours Thesis, Department of Philosophy, University of Newcastle, N.S.W.

Aziz, Barbara N. 1976. 'Reincarnation reconsidered – or the reincarnate lama as shaman'. In Hitchcock and Jones 1976, 343–60.

References

Aziz, Barbara N. and Matthew Kapstein, eds. 1985. *Soundings in Tibetan Civilization.* Manohar, Delhi.

Barber, Karen. 1981. 'How man makes god in West Africa: Yoruba attitudes towards the òrìṣà'. *Africa* 51(3), 724–45.

Barthes, Roland. 1973. *Mythologies.* Paladin, Frogmore.

Basilov, V. N. 1981. 'Some results of the study of the vestiges of shamanism in Central Asia'. Paper at the International Congress of Anthropological and Ethnological Sciences, Intercongress, Holland.

Bastide, Roger. 1978. *The African Religions of Brazil.* Johns Hopkins.

Bateson, Gregory. 1970. 'An old temple and a new myth'. In *Traditional Balinese Culture,* ed. Jane Belo, Columbia University Press, New York, 111–36.

1973. *Steps to an Ecology of Mind.* Paladin, Frogmore.

1979. *Mind and Nature: A Necessary Unity.* Wildwood House, London.

Bateson, Gregory and Mary Catherine Bateson. 1987. *Angels Fear: Towards an Epistemology of the Sacred.* Macmillan, New York.

Bateson, Gregory and Margaret Mead. 1942. *Balinese Character: A Photographic Analysis.* New York Academy of Sciences, New York.

Beck, Brenda E. F. 1978. 'The metaphor as a mediator between semantic and analogic modes of thought'. *Current Anthropology* 19, 83–97.

Becker, A. and A. Yengoyan, eds. 1979. *The Imagination of Reality.* Ablex, New York.

Benjamin, Geoffrey. 1979. 'Indigenous religious systems of the Malay Peninsula'. In Becker and Yengoyan 1979, 9–27.

Berger, John. 1972. *Ways of Seeing.* Penguin and BBC, Harmondsworth.

Bergland, Richard. 1985. *The Fabric of Mind.* Penguin, Ringwood, Vic.

Berglie, Per-Arne. 1976. 'Preliminary remarks on some Tibetan "spirit mediums" in Nepal'. *Kailash* 4, 85–108.

Bernbaum, Edwin. 1980. *The Way to Shambhala.* Anchor (Doubleday), Garden City, N.Y.

Berndt, Roland M. 1951. *Kunapipi: A Study of an Australian Aboriginal Religious Cult.* F. W. Cheshire, Melbourne.

Berndt, Roland M. and Catherine H. Berndt. 1970. *Man, Land and Myth in North Australia: The Gunwinggu people.* Ure Smith, Sydney.

Betzig, Laura et al. 1988. 'On reconsidering violence in simple human societies'. *Current Anthropology* 29, 624–36.

Beyer, Stephan. 1973. *The Cult of Tara: Magic and Ritual in Tibet.* University of California Press, Berkeley.

Black, Mary B. 1973. 'Belief systems'. In *Handbook of Social and Cultural Anthropology* ed. John J. Honigmann. Rand McNally, Chicago, 509–77.

Blacking, John, ed. 1977. *The Anthropology of the Body.* Academic Press, London.

Bloch, Maurice. 1974. 'Symbols, songs, dance and features of articulation: is religion an extreme form of traditional authority?' *Archives Européennes de Sociologie* 15(1), 55–81.

1976. 'The past and the present in the present'. *Man* (n.s.) 12(2), 278–92.

Blondeau, Anne-Marie. 1980. 'Analysis of the biographies of Padmasambhava according to Tibetan tradition: classification of sources'. In Aris and Aung 1980, 46–51.

Blount, Ben G. 1974. *Language, Culture and Society: A Book of Readings.* Winthrop, Cambridge, Mass.

Bocock, Robert et al., eds. 1980. *Introduction to Sociology.* Fontana, London.

Bohannan, Paul. 1957. *Justice and Judgement among the Tiv.* Oxford University Press.

References

Bohm, David. 1976. 'Imagination, fancy, insight, and reason in the process of thought'. In *Evolution of Consciousness*, ed. Shirley Sugerman. Wesleyan University Press, Middletown, Conn., 52–68.

1981. *Wholeness and the Implicate Order*. Routledge and Kegan Paul, London.

Boon, James. 1982. *Other Tribes, Other Scribes: Symbolic Anthropology in the Comparative Study of Cultures, Histories, Religions and Texts*. Cambridge University Press, New York.

Bono, Edward de. 1970. *The Mechanism of Mind*. Cape, London.

Bourdieu, Pierre. 1977. *Outline of a Theory of Practice*. Cambridge University Press, Cambridge.

Bramly, Serge. 1977. *Macumba: The Teachings of Maria-José, Mother of the Gods*. St Martin's Press, New York.

Brand, Arie. 1986. 'The "colonization of the lifeworld" and the disappearance of politics – Arendt and Habermas'. *Thesis Eleven* 13, 39–53.

1987. 'Weber: man, the prime mover'. In Austin-Broos 1987b, 50–72.

Brandenstein, C. G. von. 1970. 'The meaning of sections and section names'. *Oceania* 41(1), 39–49.

1972. 'The Phoenix "totemism"'. *Anthropos* 67(3–4), 586–94.

1974. 'Die Weltordnung der Frühzeit nach den vier Wesensarten (Neuentdeckungen auf dem Gebiet des Totemismus)'. *Zeitschrift für Religions- und Geistesgeschichte* 26, 211–21.

1977. 'Aboriginal ecological order in the south-west of Australia – meaning and examples'. *Oceania* 47(3), 169–86.

Brauen-Dolma, Martin. 1985. 'Millenarianism in Tibetan religion'. In Aziz and Kapstein 1985, 245–56.

Brown, C. W. 1988. 'A new interdisciplinary impulse and the anthropology of the 1990s'. *International Social Science Journal* 116, 211–20.

Burridge, Kenelm. 1971. *New Heaven, New Earth*. Basil Blackwell, Oxford.

Carrithers, Michael, Steven Collins and Steven Lukes, eds. 1985. *The Category of the Person: Anthropology, Philosophy, History*. Cambridge University Press, Cambridge.

Chagnon, Napoleon A. and W. Irons, eds. 1982. *Evolutionary Biology and Human Social Behavior: An Anthropological Perspective*. Duxbury Press, North Scituate, Mass.

Changeux, Jean-Pierre. 1986. *Neuronal Man: The Biology of Mind*. Oxford University Press, New York.

Churchland, Patricia S. 1986. *Neurophilosophy: Toward a Unified Science of the Mind-Brain*. MIT Press, Cambridge, Mass.

Clastres, Pierre. 1977. *Society Against the State*. Urizen, New York.

Clifford, James and George E. Marcus, eds. 1986. *Writing Culture. The Poetics and the Politics of Anthropology*. University of California Press, Berkeley.

Colby, Benjamin N. and Lore M. Colby. 1981. *The Daykeeper: The Life and Discourse of an Ixil Diviner*. Harvard University Press, Cambridge, Mass.

Comfort, Alex. 1979. *I and That: Notes on the Biology of Religion*. Crown, New York.

1981. 'The implications of an implicate: notes on David Bohm's *Wholeness and the Implicate Order*'. *Journal of Social and Biological Structures* 4, 363–74.

Cozort, Daniel. 1986. *Highest Yoga Tantra: An Introduction to the Esoteric Buddhism of Tibet*. Snow Lion, Ithaca, New York.

Crapanzano, Vincent. 1980. *Tuhami: Portrait of a Moroccan*. University of Chicago Press, Chicago.

References

Cunningham, Adrian and Deborah Tickner. 1981. 'Psychoanalysis and indigenous psychology'. In Heelas and Lock 1981, 225–45.
Dargyay, Eva M. 1978. *The Rise of Esoteric Buddhism in Tibet.* Samuel Weiser, New York.
Davidson, Julian M. and Richard J. Davidson, eds. 1980. *The Psychobiology of Consciousness.* Plenum, New York.
Dawkins, Richard. 1976. *The Selfish Gene.* Oxford University Press, Oxford.
1988. *The Blind Watchmaker.* Penguin Books, Harmondsworth.
Deleuze, Gilles and Félix Guattari. 1984. *Anti-Oedipus.* Athlone Press, London.
1987. *A Thousand Plateaus.* University of Minnesota Press, Minneapolis.
Deleuze, Gilles and Claire Parnet. 1987. *Dialogues.* Athlone Press, London.
Dentan, Robert K. 1968. *The Semai.* Holt, Rinehart and Winston, New York.
Denton, Michael. 1985. *Evolution: A Theory in Crisis.* Burnett Books/Hutchinson, London.
Domhoff, G. W. *The Mystique of Dreams: A Search for Utopia through Senoi Dream Theory.* University of California Press, Berkeley, Calif.
Douglas, Kenneth and Gwendolyn Bays. 1978. *The Life and Liberation of Padmasambhava.* Dharma Publishing, Emeryville, Calif. (two vols.)
Dowman, Keith. 1984. *Sky Dancer: The Secret Life and Songs of the Lady Yeshe Tsogyel.* Routledge and Kegan Paul, London.
Dumont, Louis. 1970. *Homo Hierarchicus. An Essay on the Caste System.* University of Chicago Press, Chicago.
Durkheim, Emile. 1976. *Elementary Forms of the Religious Life.* Allen and Unwin, London.
Eagleton, Terry. 1983. *Literary Theory.* Basil Blackwell, Oxford.
Edwards, Adrian C. 1983. 'Seeing, believing, doing: the Tiv understanding of power'. *Anthropos* 78, 459–80.
1984. 'On the non-existence of an ancestor cult among the Tiv'. *Anthropos* 79, 77–112.
Eldredge, Nils. 1986. 'Progress in evolution?' *New Scientist,* 5 June 1986, 54–7.
Erwin-Tripp, Susan M. 1972. 'On sociolinguistic rules: alternation and co-occurrence'. In Gumperz and Hymes 1972, 213–50.
1974. 'Sociolinguistics'. In Blount 1974, 268–334.
Evans-Pritchard, E. E. 1940. *The Nuer.* Clarendon Press, Oxford.
1956. *Nuer Religion.* Clarendon Press, Oxford.
1972. *Witchcraft, Oracles and Magic among the Azande.* Clarendon Press, Oxford.
Factor, Donald, ed. 1985. *Unfolding Meaning: A Weekend of Dialogue with David Bohm.* Foundation House, Mickelton and Loveland.
Faraday, Ann and John Wren-Lewis. 1984. 'The selling of the Senoi'. *Lucidity Letter* 3(1), 1–3.
Feeley-Harnik, Gillian. 1985. 'Issues in divine kingship'. *Annual Review of Anthropology* 14, 273–313.
Fortes, Meyer, 1959. *Oedipus and Job in West African Religion.* Cambridge University Press, Cambridge.
Foucault, Michel. 1984. 'Preface' in Deleuze and Guattari 1984, xi-xiv.
Frake, Charles O. 1983. 'Review article: did literacy cause the great cognitive divide?' *American Ethnologist* 10, 367–71.
Fremantle, Francesca and Chogyam Trungpa. 1975. *The Tibetan Book of the Dead.* Shambhala, Berkeley, Calif.

Friedman, Jonathan. 1988. 'Cultural logics of the global system: a sketch'. *Theory, Culture and Society* 5, 447–60.

Frye, Northrop. 1969. *Fearful Symmetry: A Study of William Blake*. Princeton University Press, Princeton, N.J.

Fürer-Haimendorf, Christoph von. 1975. *Himalayan Traders: Life in Highland Nepal*. John Murray, London.

Gardner, Howard. 1975. *The Shattered Mind*. Vintage, New York.

Geertz, Clifford. 1973. *The Interpretation of Cultures: Selected Essays*. Basic Books, New York.

  1985. *Local Knowledge: Further Essays in Interpretive Anthropology*. Basic Books, New York.

Geertz, Clifford, Hildred Geertz and Lawrence Rosen. 1979. *Meaning and Order in Moroccan Society: Three Essays in Cultural Analysis*. Cambridge University Press, New York.

Gellner, Ernest. 1978. 'Notes towards a theory of ideology'. *L'Homme* 18(3–4), 69–82.

Giddens, Anthony. 1984. *The Constitution of Society: Outline of the Theory of Structuration*. Polity Press, Cambridge.

Gluckman, Max. 1963. *Order and Rebellion in Tribal Africa: Collected Essays with an Autobiographical Note*. Cohen and West, London.

  1965. *The Ideas in Barotse Jurisprudence*. Yale University Press, New Haven.

  1967. *The Judicial Process among the Barotse of Northern Rhodesia*. 2nd edn, Manchester University Press.

  1973. *Custom and Conflict in Africa*. Blackwell, Oxford.

Goffman, Erving. 1959. *The Presentation of Self in Everyday Life*. Harper and Row, New York.

  1961. *Asylums*. Doubleday, Garden City, New York.

  1974. *Frame Analysis: An Essay on the Organization of Experience*. Harper and Row, New York.

  1981. *Forms of Talk*. Blackwell, Oxford.

Goodenough, Ward H. 1963. *Cooperation in Change*. Russell Sage, New York.

  1978. 'Multiculturalism as the normal human experience'. In *Applied Anthropology in America*, ed. E. M. Eddy and W. L. Partridge. Columbia University Press, New York, 79–86.

  1981. *Culture, Language, and Society*. Benjamin/Cummings, Menlo Park, Calif. (2nd edn.)

Goody, Jack. 1968. 'Introduction'. In *Literacy in Traditional Societies*, ed. J. Goody. Cambridge University Press.

  1977. *The Domestication of the Savage Mind*. Cambridge University Press.

Gorer, Geoffrey and J. Rickman. 1949. *The People of Great Russia*. Cresset Press, London.

Gross, Elizabeth. 1986. 'Philosophy, subjectivity and the body: Kristeva and Irigaray'. In Pateman and Gross 1986, 125–43.

Grottanelli, Cristiano. 1983. 'Tricksters, scapegoats, champions, saviours'. *History of Religions* 23, 117–39.

Guattari, Félix. 1984. *Molecular Revolution: Psychiatry and Politics*. Penguin, Harmondsworth.

Gulliver, P. H. 1963. *Social Control in an African Society. A Study of the Arusha, Agricultural Masai of Northern Tanganyika*. Routledge and Kegan Paul, London.

References

Gumperz, John J. and Dell H. Hymes, eds. 1972. *Directions in Sociolinguistics: The Ethnography of Communication*. Holt, Rinehart and Winston, New York.

Gyatso, Janet. 1980. 'The teachings of Thang-stong rGyal-po.' In Aris and Aung 1980, 111–19.

1981. 'The literary transmission of the traditions of Thang-stong rGyal-po'. Ph.D. dissertation, University of California, Berkeley.

Halifax, Joan. 1980. *Shamanic Voices*. Penguin, Harmondsworth.

Hallowell, A. Irving. 1955. *Culture and Experience*. University of Pennsylvania Press.

Hamayon, Roberte. 1978. 'Les héros de service'. *L'Homme* 18 (3–4), 17–45.

Harris, Marvin. 1969. *The Rise of Anthropological Theory*. Routledge and Kegan Paul, London.

Heald, Suzette. 1982. 'The making of men: the relevance of vernacular psychology to the interpretation of a Gisu ritual'. *Africa* 52(1), 15–35.

Heelas, Paul and Andrew Lock, eds. 1981. *Indigenous Psychologies: The Anthropology of the Self*. Academic Press, London.

Heinze, Ruth-Inge, ed. 1985. *Proceedings of the Second International Conference on the Study of Shamanism*. Center for South and Southeast Asia Studies, University of California, Berkeley, Calif.

Hiley, B. J. and F. David Peat. 1987. *Quantum Implications: Essays in Honour of David Bohm*. Routledge and Kegan Paul, London.

Hitchcock, John T. and Rex L. Jones, eds. 1976. *Spirit Possession in the Nepal Himalayas*. Aris and Phillips, Warminster.

Ho, Mae-Wan et al. 1986. 'A new paradigm for evolution?' *New Scientist* 27 February 1986, 41–3.

Hollis, Martin and Steven Lukes, eds. 1982. *Rationality and Relativism*. MIT Press, Cambridge, Mass.

Hooker, Cliff. 1987. *A Realistic Theory of Science*. State University of New York Press, Albany, New York.

Hopkins, Jeffrey. 1984. *The Tantric Distinction: Introduction to Tibetan Buddhism*. Wisdom, London.

Horton, Robin. 1967. 'African traditional thought and Western science'. *Africa* 37, 1–2.

1982. 'Tradition and modernity revisited'. In Hollis and Lukes 1982, 201–60.

Howe, Leopold E. A. 1981. 'The social determination of knowledge: Maurice Bloch and Balinese time'. *Man* 16(2), 220–34.

Howe, Richard H. 1978. 'Max Weber's elective affinities: sociology within the bounds of pure reason'. *American Journal of Sociology* 84, 366–85.

Howell, Signe. 1981. 'Rules not words'. In Heelas and Lock 1981, 133–44.

Humphrey, Caroline. 1985. 'Barter and economic disintegration'. *Man* 20, 48–72.

1987. 'Fairness and fertility: moral ideas in the barter of the Lhomi of North-East Nepal'. Seminar paper, Department of Anthropology, University of Cambridge.

Huxley, Francis. 1966. *The Invisibles*. Hart-Davis, London.

Hymes, Dell H. 1974a. 'The ethnography of speaking'. In Blount 1974, 189–223.

1974b. 'Sociolinguistics and the ethnography of speaking'. In Blount 1974, 335–69.

Jaynes, Julian. 1976. *The Origins of Consciousness in the Breakdown of the Bicameral Mind*. Houghton Mifflin, Boston.

Johnson-Laird, P. N. 1983. *Mental Models*. Cambridge University Press, Cambridge.

References

Kapferer, Bruce. 1979. 'Mind, self and other in demonic illness: the negation and reconstruction of self'. *American Ethnologist* 6, 110–33.

Kapstein, Matthew. 1980. 'Remarks on the Maṇi bka'-'bum and the cult of Avalokiteśvara in Tibet'. Paper presented to the 2nd Annual Conference of the North American Tibetological Society, Berkeley, California, August 1980.

Keesing, Roger. 1986. 'Conventional metaphors and anthropological metaphysics: the problematic of cultural translation'. *Journal of Anthropological Research* 41, 201–17.

1987. 'Anthropology as an interpretive quest'. *Current Anthropology* 28, 161–76.

Keil, Charles. 1979. *Tiv Song*. University of Chicago Press.

Knauft, Bruce M. 1987. 'Reconsidering violence in simple human societies'. *Current Anthropology* 28, 457–82.

Koestler, Arthur. 1964. *The Act of Creation*. Dell, New York.

Koepping, Klaus-Peter. 1985. 'Absurdity and hidden truth: cunning intelligence and grotesque body images as manifestations of the trickster'. *History of Religions* 24, 191–214.

Kristeva, Julia. 1984. *Revolution in Poetic Language*. Columbia University Press, New York.

Kronenfeld, David and Henry W. Decker. 1979. 'Structuralism'. *Annual Review of Anthropology* 8, 503–41.

Kuhn, Thomas. 1970. *The Structure of Scientific Revolutions*. University of Chicago Press. (2nd edn.)

Kuper, Adam, ed. 1977. *The Social Anthropology of Radcliffe-Brown*. Routledge and Kegan Paul, London.

Kvaerne, Per. 1981. 'Royauté divine. Au Tibet'. In *Dictionnaire des mythologies et des religions des sociétés traditionnelles et du monde antique*, ed. Yves Bonnefoy vol. 2. Flammarion, Paris. 381–4.

Lakoff, G. and M. Johnson. 1980. *Metaphors We Live By*. University of Chicago Press, Chicago.

Laufer, Berthold. 1914. 'Bird divination among the Tibetans, with a study of the phonology of the ninth century'. *T'oung Pao* 15, 1–110.

Lévi-Strauss, Claude. 1969. *The Raw and the Cooked: Introduction to a Science of Mythology*, vol. 1. Harper and Row, New York.

1972. *Structural Anthropology*. Penguin, Harmondsworth.

1973. *Totemism*. Penguin, Harmondsworth.

Lewis, Gilbert. 1980. *The Day of Shining Red: An Essay on Understanding Ritual*. Cambridge University Press.

Lewis, Ioan M. 1971. *Ecstatic Religion*. Penguin, Harmondsworth.

1986. *Religion in Context: Cults and Charisma*. Cambridge University Press.

Littleton, C. Scott. 1973. *The New Comparative Mythology: An Anthropological Assessment of the Theories of Georges Dumézil*. University of California Press, Berkeley, Calif.

Loye, David et al. 1986. 'New paradigm thinking in the social sciences and business'. *ReVision* 9(1), 65–72.

Lumsden, C. J. and Edward O. Wilson. 1981. *Genes, Mind and Culture*. Harvard University Press, Cambridge, Mass.

McLeod, M. 1972. 'Oracles and accusations among the Azande'. In *Zande Themes*, ed. A. Singer and B. V. Street. Blackwell, Oxford, 158–78.

McNeley, J. K. 1981. *Holy Wind in Navajo Philosophy*. University of Arizona Press, Tucson, Ariz.

References

Madan, T. N. 1972, 'Religious ideology in a plural society: the Muslims and Hindus of Kashmir'. *Contributions to Indian Sociology* (n.s.) 6, 106–41.
Madan, T. N. et al. 1971. 'On the nature of caste in India: a review symposium on Louis Dumont's *Homo Hierarchicus'*. *Contributions to Indian Sociology* (n.s.) 5, 3–78.
Mair, Lucy. 1962. *Primitive Government*. Penguin, Harmondsworth.
Malinowski, Bronislaw. 1953. *Argonauts of the Western Pacific*. Routledge and Kegan Paul, London.
Marcus, George E. and Michael M. J. Fisher. 1986. *Anthropology as Cultural Critique: An Experimental Moment in the Human Sciences*. University of Chicago Press, Chicago and London.
Marsella, Anthony J., George DeVos and Francis L. K. Hsu, eds. 1985. *Culture and Self: Asian and Western Perspectives*. Tavistock, New York and London.
Martin, Dan. 1985. 'Pearls from bones – relics, chortens, tertöns, and the signs of saintly death in Tibet'. Unpublished MS.
Marx, Karl. 1958. *Capital*. Vol. 1. Progress Publishers, Moscow.
Maturana, Humberto R. and Francisco J. Varela. 1980. *Autopoiesis and Cognition: The Realization of the Living*. Reidel, Dordrecht, Boston and London.
   1988. *The Tree of Knowledge: The Biological Roots of Human Understanding*. Shambhala (New Science Library), Boston and London.
Mauss, Marcel. 1969. *The Gift: Forms and Functions of Exchange in Archaic Societies*. Cohen and West, London.
   1979. 'Body techniques'. In M. Mauss, *Sociology and Psychology: Essays*. Routledge and Kegan Paul, London, 95–123.
Meillassoux, Claude. 1973. 'Are there castes in India?' *Economy and Society* 2, 89–111.
Mulkay, Michael. 1979. *Science and the Sociology of Knowledge*. Allen and Unwin, London.
Munevar, Gonzalo. 1981. *Radical Knowledge*. Hackett, Indianapolis.
   1984. 'Towards a future epistemology of science'. *Explorations in Knowledge* 1, 1–17.
Needham, Joseph. 1956. *Science and Civilization in China*. Vol. 2. Cambridge University Press.
Noone, H. D. (Pat). n.d. Notes accompanying the gramophone record *Temiar Dream Music of Malaya* (Ethnic Folkways FE4460).
Noone, Richard with Dennis Holman. 1972. *In Search of the Dream People*. William Morrow, New York.
Obeyesekere, Gananath. 1977. 'Social change and the deities: rise of the Kataragama cult in modern Sri Lanka'. *Man* 12, 377–96.
   1981. *Medusa's Hair*. Chicago University Press, Chicago.
Oesch, Hans. 1973. 'Musikalische Kontinuität bei Naturvölkern'. In *Studien zur Tradition in der Musik: Kurt von Fischer zum 60. Geburtstag*, ed. H. H. Eggebrecht and M. Lütolf, Munich, 227–46.
   1974. 'Musikalische Gattungen bei Naturvölkern'. In *Festschrift für Arno Volk*, ed. C. Dahlhaus and H. Oesch, Cologne, 7–30.
O'Neill, J., ed. 1973. *Modes of Individualism and Collectivism*. Heinemann, London.
Ornstein, Robert E. 1973. *The Psychology of Consciousness*. W. H. Freeman, San Francisco.
Ortner, Sherry B. 1984. 'Theory in anthropology since the Sixties'. *Comparative Studies in Society and History* 26, 126–66.

References

Pateman, Carole and Elizabeth Gross, eds. 1986. *Feminist Challenges: Social and Political Theory*. Allen and Unwin, Sydney.

Perry, Nick. 1977. 'A comparative analysis of "paradigm" proliferation'. *British Journal of Sociology* 28, 38–50.

Peter, Prince. 1979. 'Tibetan oracles'. *Tibet Journal* 4, 51–6.

Popper, Karl L. 1973. *Objective Knowledge: An Evolutionary Approach*. Clarendon Press, Oxford.

Pressel, Esther. 1974. 'Umbanda trance and possession in Sao Paolo, Brazil'. In *Trance, Healing, and Hallucination: Three Field Studies in Religious Experience*, ed. Felicitas D. Goodman et al. Wiley, New York, 113–225.

Pribram, Karl H. 1971. *Languages of the Brain*. Prentice-Hall, Englewood Cliffs, N.J.
    1984. 'The holographic hypothesis of brain function: a meeting of minds'. In *Ancient Wisdom and Modern Science*, ed. Stanislav Grof, State University of New York Press, Albany, New York, 167–79.

Prigogine, Ilya. 1980. *From Being to Becoming: Time and Complexity in the Physical Sciences*. W. H. Freeman, San Francisco.

Radin, Paul. 1955. *The Trickster: A Study in American Indian Mythology*. Routledge and Kegan Paul, London.

Rappaport, Roy A. 1967. *Pigs for the Ancestors: Ritual in the Ecology of a New Guinea People*. Yale University Press, New Haven.
    1979. *Ecology, Meaning, and Religion*. North Atlantic Books, Richmond, Calif.

Redfield, Robert and Milton Singer. 1954. 'The cultural role of cities'. *Economic Development and Cultural Change* 3(1), 53–77.

Reichel-Dolmatoff, G. 1976. 'Cosmology as ecological analysis: a view from the rain forest'. *Man* (n.s.) 11(3), 307–18.

Reynolds, Vernon and Ralph E. S. Tanner. 1983. *The Biology of Religion*. Longman, London.

Ridington, Robin and Tonia Ridington. 1975. 'The inner eye of shamanism and totemism'. In Tedlock and Tedlock 1975.

Rindos, David. 1985. 'Darwinian selection, symbolic variation, and the evolution of culture'. *Current Anthropology* 26, 65–88.

Robarchek, Clayton A. 1977. 'Frustration, aggression and the non-violent Semai'. *American Ethnologist* 4, 762–79.
    1979. 'Learning to fear: a case study of emotional conditioning'. *American Ethnologist* 6, 555–67.

Robarchek, Clayton A. and Robert K. Dentan. 1987. '"Blood drunkenness" and the bloodthirsty Semai: unmaking another anthropological myth'. *American Anthropologist* 89, 356–65.

Roberts, John M. and Brian Sutton-Smith. 1962. 'Child training and game involvement'. *Ethnology* 1, 166–85.

Roseman, Marina. 1984. 'The social structuring of sound'. *Ethnomusicology* 28, 411–45.

Royce, Joseph. 1980. 'Play in violent and non-violent cultures'. *Anthropos* 75, 799–822.

Sahlins, Marshall. 1963. 'Poor man, rich man, big-man, chief: political types in Polynesia and Melanesia'. *Comparative Studies in Society and History* 5, 285–303.
    1976. *The Use and Abuse of Biology: An Anthropological Critique of Sociobiology*. University of Michigan Press, Ann Arbor.

Said, Edward. 1979. *Orientalism*. Random House, New York.

References

Salisbury, Richard F. 1962. *From Stone to Steel*. Cambridge University Press.
Salleh, Ariel. 1984. 'Contribution to the critique of political epistemology'. *Thesis Eleven* 8, 23–43.
Samuel, Geoffrey. 1975. 'The crystal rosary: insight and method in an anthropological study of Tibetan religion'. Ph.D. dissertation, University of Cambridge.
    1982. 'Tibet as a stateless society and some Islamic parallels'. *Journal of Asian Studies* 41(2), 215–29.
    1984. 'Shamanic and rational religion in fifteenth-century Tibet'. Paper for the Bicentenary Csoma de Körös Symposium, Visegrad, Hungary, September 1984.
    1985a. 'Science, anthropology and Margaret Mead: a Galilean dialogue'. *Search* 16(9–12), 251–8.
    1985b. 'The computer as metaphor: explorations in anthropological theory'. Paper presented to the Australian Anthropological Society Conference, Darwin, August 1985.
    1985c. 'The early history of Buddhism in Tibet: an anthropological perspective'. In Aziz and Kapstein 1985, 383–96.
    1988. 'Gesar of Ling: shamanic power and popular religion'. Paper for the Australian Anthropological Society Conference, Newcastle, August 1988.
    1989. 'Shamanic and clerical Buddhism in Tibet'. Typescript.
Schapera, Isaac. 1967. *Government and Politics in Tribal Societies*. Schocken Books, New York.
Scheflen, Albert with Alice Scheflen. 1972. *Body Language and Social Order*. Prentice-Hall, Englewood Cliffs, N.J.
Schiltz, Marc. 1985. 'Yoruba thunder deities and sovereignty: *Ara* versus *Ṣango*'. *Anthropos* 80, 67–84.
Scholte, Bob. 1984. 'Comment on Paul Shankman's "The thick and the thin: on the interpretive theoretical program of Clifford Geertz"'. *Current Anthropology* 25, 540–2.
    1986. 'The charmed circle of Geertz's hermeneutics: a neo-Marxist critique'. *Critique of Anthropology* 6(1), 5–15.
Schrödinger, Erwin. 1954. *Space–Time Structure*. Cambridge University Press.
Schuman, Marjorie. 1980. 'The psychophysiological model of meditation and altered states of consciousness: a critical review'. In Davidson and Davidson 1980, 333–78.
Sheldrake, Rupert. 1987. *A New Science of Life: The Hypothesis of Formative Causation*. New edition with appendix of comments, controversies and discussions provoked by the 1st edn, Paladin, London.
Sibatani, A. 1980. 'Inscrutable epigenetics of the Japanese brain'. *Journal of Social and Biological Structures* 3, 255–66.
Singer, Milton. 1980. *When a Great Tradition Modernizes*. University of Chicago Press.
Singh Uberoi, J. P. 1962. *The Politics of the Kula Ring*. Manchester University Press.
Southwold, Martin. 1979. 'Religious belief'. *Man* (n.s.) 14, 628–44.
    1983. *Buddhism in Life: The Anthropological Study of Religion and the Sinhalese Practice of Buddhism*. Manchester University Press, Manchester.
Spanien, Ariane. [= Ariane Macdonald.] 1971. 'Une lecture des P.T. 1286, 1287, 1038, 1047 et 1290. Essai sur la formation et l'emploi des mythes politiques dans la religion royale de Sroṅ-bcan sgam-po,' in *Etudes tibétaines dédiées à la mémoire de Marcelle Lalou*, ed. A. Macdonald, Librairie d'Amérique et d'Orient, Adrien Maisonneuve, Paris, 190–391.

References

Sperber, Dan. 1975. *Rethinking Symbolism*. Cambridge University Press.
    1980. 'Is symbolic thought prerational?' In *Symbol as Sense*, ed. Mary Foster and Stanley Brandes. Academic Press, New York.
    1982. 'Apparently irrational beliefs'. In Hollis and Lukes 1982.
    1985a. 'Anthropology and psychology: towards an epidemiology of representations'. *Man* (n.s.) 20(1), 73–89.
    1985b. *On Anthropological Knowledge: Three Essays*. Cambridge University Press.
Spiro, Melford E. 1967. *Burmese Supernaturalism: A Study in the Explanation and Reduction of Suffering*. Prentice-Hall, Englewood Cliffs, N.J.
    1971. *Buddhism and Society: A Great Tradition and its Burmese Vicissitudes*. Allen and Unwin, London.
Springer, Sally P. and Georg Deutsch. 1981. *Left Brain, Right Brain*. Freeman, San Francisco.
Stablein, William G. 1976. 'Mahakala the neo-shaman: master of the ritual'. In Hitchcock and Jones 1976, 361–75.
Stanner, W. E. H. 1936–7. 'Murinbata kinship and totemism'. *Oceania* 7, 186–216.
    1959–63. *On Aboriginal Religion*. University of Sydney Press, Sydney. (Oceania Monograph no. 11.)
    1979. 'The dreaming'. In W. E. H. Stanner, *White Man Got No Dreaming: Essays 1938–73*. Australian National University Press, Canberra.
Stein, Rolf A. 1972. *Tibetan Civilization*. Faber and Faber, London.
Stewart, Kilton. 1969. 'Dream theory in Malaya'. In Tart 1969, 159–67.
Strathern, Andrew. 1971. *The Rope of Moka*. Cambridge University Press.
Strathern, Marilyn. 1987. 'An awkward relationship: the case of feminism and anthropology'. *Signs* 12(2).
Strehlow, T. G. H. 1947. *Aranda Traditions*. Melbourne University Press.
    1971. *Songs of Central Australia*. Angus and Robertson, Sydney.
Stuart-Fox, Martin. 1986. 'The unit of replication in socio-cultural evolution'. *Journal of Social and Biological Structures* 9(1) 67–90.
Sturm, Fred G. 1977. 'Afro-Brazilian cults'. In *African Religions: A symposium*, ed. Newell S. Booth. NOK, New York.
Tambiah, S. J. 1970. *Buddhism and the Spirit Cults in North-East Thailand*. Cambridge University Press. (Cambridge Studies in Social Anthropology, 2.)
    1976. *World Conqueror and World Renouncer: A Study of Buddhism and Polity against a Historical Background*. Cambridge University Press. (Cambridge Studies in Social Anthropology, 15.)
    1984. *The Buddhist Saints of the Forest and the Cult of Amulets: A Study in Charisma, Hagiography, Sectarianism and Millenial Buddhism*. Cambridge University Press.
    1985. *Culture, Thought, and Social Action: An Anthropological Perspective*. Harvard University Press, Cambridge, Mass.
Tart, Charles T. ed. 1969. *Altered States of Consciousness: A Book of Readings*. Wiley, New York.
Tarthang Tulku. 1983. *Mother of Knowledge: The Enlightenment of Ye-shes mTsho-rgyal*. Dharma Publishing, Berkeley, Calif.
Taussig, Michael. 1981. Seminar paper given to the Anthropology Department, University of Sydney, November 1981.
Tedlock, Dennis and Barbara Tedlock. 1975. *Teachings from the American Earth: Indian Religion and Philosophy*. Liveright, New York.
Thondup Rinpoche, Tulku. 1986. *Hidden Teachings of Tibet: An Explanation of the Terma Tradition of the Nyingma School of Buddhism*. Wisdom, London.

References

Tonkinson, Robert. 1974. *The Jigalong Mob: Aboriginal Victors of the Desert Crusade.* Cummings, Menlo Park, Calif.
   1978. *The Mardudjara Aborigines: Living the Dream in Australia's Desert.* Holt, Rinehart and Winston, New York.
Tsuda, Shinichi. 1978. 'A critical Tantrism'. *Memoirs of the Toyo Bunko* 36, 167–231.
Turnbull, Colin M. 1962. *The Forest People.* Simon and Schuster, New York.
   1965. *Wayward Servants.* Natural History Press, New York.
   1983. *The Mbuti Pygmies: Change and Adaptation.* Holt, Rinehart and Winston, New York.
Turner, Edith T. 1987. *The Spirit and the Drum: A Memoir of Africa.* University of Arizona Press, Tucson, Ariz.
Turner, Victor W. 1957. *Schism and Continuity in an African Religion: A Study of Ndembu Village Life.* Manchester University Press.
   1962. 'Three symbols of *passage* in Ndembu circumcision ritual'. In *Essays on the Ritual of Social Relations*, ed. Max Gluckman, 124–81. Manchester University Press.
   1968. *The Drums of Affliction.* Clarendon Press, Oxford.
   1969. *The Ritual Process.* Routledge and Kegan Paul, London.
   1970. *The Forest of Symbols.* Cornell University Press, Ithaca.
   1974. *Dramas, Fields, and Metaphors.* Cornell University Press, Ithaca.
   1975. *Revelation and Divination in Ndembu Ritual.* Cornell University Press, Ithaca.
   1979. *Process, Performance and Pilgrimage: A Study in Comparative Symbology.* Concept, New Delhi.
   1982. *From Ritual to Theatre: The Human Seriousness of Play.* PAJ Publications, New York.
   1985. *On the Edge of the Bush: Anthropology as Experience.* University of Arizona Press, Tucson, Ariz.
Wagner, Roy. 1975. *The Invention of Culture.* Prentice-Hall, Englewood Cliffs, N.J.
   1978. *Lethal Speech: Daribi Myth as Symbolic Obviation.* Cornell University Press, Ithaca and London.
Wallace, Anthony F. C. 1956a. 'Mazeway resynthesis: a biocultural theory of religious inspiration'. *Transactions of the New York Academy of Sciences* 18, 626–38.
   1956b. 'Revitalization movements'. *American Anthropologist* 58, 264–81.
   1966a. *Culture and Personality.* Random House, New York.
   1966b. *Religion: An Anthropological View.* Random House, New York.
Watzlawick, Paul, Janet Beavin and Don D. Jackson. 1968. *Pragmatics of Human Communication.* W. W. Norton, New York.
Weber, Max. 1958. *The Protestant Ethic and the Spirit of Capitalism.* Scribner's, New York.
Whorf, Benjamin Lee. 1956. *Language, Thought and Reality: Selected Writings.* Wiley, New York.
Williamson, Judith. 1978. *Decoding Advertisements: Ideology and Meaning in Advertising.* Marion Boyars, London.
Willis, Paul. 1978. *Learning to Labour.* Saxon House, Farnborough.
Wilson, Edward O. 1975. *Sociobiology: The New Synthesis.* Harvard University Press, Cambridge, Mass.
Wilson, Peter J. 1973. *Crab Antics: The Social Anthropology of English-speaking Negro Societies of the Caribbean.* Yale University Press, New Haven and London.
   1980. *Man, the Promising Primate: The Conditions of Human Evolution.* Yale University Press, New Haven.

References

Winnicott, Donald W. 1971. *Playing and Reality*. Basic Books. New York.
Woolfson, Charles. 1982. *The Labour Theory of Culture: A Re-Examination of Engels' Theories of Human Origins*. Routledge and Kegan Paul, London.
Worsley, Peter. 1970. *The Trumpet Shall Sound: A Study of "Cargo" Cults in Melanesia*. Paladin, Frogmore.
Young, J. Z. 1987. *Philosophy and the Brain*. Oxford University Press, Oxford and New York.
Ziman, J. 1978. *Reliable Knowledge: An Exploration of the Grounds for Belief in Science*. Cambridge University Press.

Index

N.B. Terms introduced or used in a specialized sense in this book are given in **bold type** as is the place in the book where they are explained.

Index